First published in the United States in 2000 by

Thunder Bay Press

An imprint of the Advantage Publishers Group

5880 Oberlin Drive, Suite 400

San Diego, CA 92121-4794

htttp://www.advantagebooksonline.com

First published in Great Britain in 2000 by Hamlyn, an imprint of Octopus Publishing Group Ltd, 2-4 Heron Quays, London E14 4JP

ISBN 1-57145-239-7

Encyclopedia of the dog / general editor, Caroline Taggart.– NorthAmerican ed.
    p. cm.
   ISBN 1-57145-239-7
   1. Dogs. I. Taggart, Caroline

SF426 .E563 2000

636.7'1–dc21

              99-088057

Printed in China.

Publisher Alison Goff
Executive Editor Jane McIntosh
Editor Nicola Hodgson
Copy Editor and Proofreader Juliet Bending
Veterinary Consultant (Part Five)
    Aaron Hunt BVSc, MRCVS
Creative Director Keith Martin
Senior Designer Leigh Jones
Designer Jo Tapper
Illustrator Kate Nardoni at MTG
Picture Researcher Jo Carlill
Production Controller Lee Sargent

North American Edition
Managing Editor JoAnn Padgett
Associate Editor Elizabeth McNulty

Encyclopedia of the
DOG

General Editor: Caroline Taggart

THUNDER BAY
P·R·E·S·S

Contents

INTRODUCTION

ENCYCLOPEDIA OF THE DOG was first published in 1981, with contributions from the foremost authorities in their specialized fields. This new edition has been revised and updated to reflect the increasing popularity of breeds that were unfamiliar 20 years ago, recent revisions to the Kennel Club standards, advances in veterinary science, and a growing sense of awareness that dog-owning is a long-term responsibility.

As before, the encyclopedia presents a comprehensive picture of all aspects of the dog—its evolution; physiology and instinctive behavior; basic care; illnesses, first aid, and veterinary treatment; dog shows, field, and obedience trials; and the variety of useful functions the dog performs in modern life.

The dog has been "man's best friend" for thousands of years—indeed, although dogs were originally domesticated as hunters and guards, archaeological evidence suggests that they have been kept as companions for at least 12,000 years. They have also come to be versatile workers, herders of flocks, warriors, and the basis of numerous forms of sport. They have been selectively bred to fight bulls, haul sleds, and hunt badgers. They have been indispensable to shepherds, customs officers, and the police and, in the 20th century, have become the eyes and ears of many disabled people.

Many of the early functions of the dog are recognized in the breed groups used by Kennel Clubs—today's gundogs, terriers, and working dogs still show the characteristics for which they were originally bred, even though many are now kept only as companions and show dogs. The selective breeding that produced such a wide range of abilities means that Kennel Clubs the world over now recognize over 300 distinct breeds, each of which is described by a "standard" that defines the appearance and character of an ideal specimen. Many of these breeds are rare and hardly known outside their country of origin. About 120 of the most popular are described in Part Two of this book.

For each breed the entry gives an abbreviated form of the standard, for reference purposes or as a guide for those interested in showing their dog. The entries are also intended to help potential dog owners who are undecided about the most appropriate breed for their particular circumstances. Not every dog is suited to every home—it is cruel to keep a large, active dog in a small apartment with inadequate exercise, and foolish to expect a fragile toy breed to cope with the rough-and-tumble games of small children. The Humane Society of the United States estimates the number of dogs destroyed annually in the U.S. to be above three million. For any civilized nation, this is a shameful statistic. Owning a happy and healthy dog is one of the most rewarding pleasures in life, but no dog will be happy and healthy unless it is properly cared for. I hope that the information given in this book will help all dog-owners, both present and future, to choose their pet wisely, to train it and look after it sensibly and to enjoy its companionship and devotion to the full.

Part One

The Development of the Dog

The evolution of the dog as a species and the manner in which it became both servant and friend of humankind took place over millions of years, in response to environmental changes and the growth of our civilization.

THEORIES OF EVOLUTION

Below: The Siberian Husky exhibits similarities to the modern dog's possible ancestor – the wolf.

FOSSIL EVOLUTION SUGGESTS that about 40 million years ago, during the late Eocene and early Oligocene periods, there flourished a small carnivorous mammal called *Miacis*. This creature, an offshoot of the stock which gave rise to all carnivores, is similar to the ancestors from which bears, racoons, weasels, civets, hyenas, cats, and dogs are descended. During the mid-Oligocene period, *Miacis* gave rise to *Cynodictis* which, during the late Miocene epoch, over 10 million years ago, in turn gave rise to *Cynodesmus* and *Tomoritus*, forerunners of present-day canids. The evolution of the canid line then continued through the Pliocene and Pleistocene epochs, up to about 10,000 years ago, culminating in the appearance of wolves, foxes, jackals, and coyotes as they are today. While the evolution of the domestic dog is very recent in fossil terms, the seeds of the association that exists between dogs and humans may have been sown as humans emerged in their present form, about a million years ago.

During the many years which it took the dog to evolve from a wild animal into one which lived in the closest relationship with humans, its physical characteristics adapted in many ways to meet changing needs. But the selective breeding of dogs by humans probably developed only between 20,000 and 10,000 years ago.

The earliest fossil finds of domestic dogs date from about 12,000 years ago. One find from this period was in the Palegawra cave in Iraq, and another in northern Israel. Other finds dating from about 8,000 to 10,500 years ago have been made in such widespread sites as Idaho, Turkey, Staw Cave in Yorkshire, Maglemosian deposits in Denmark, and similar settlements in Switzerland.

In spite of a growing body of archeological evidence, it is not possible to say with certainty from which wild ancestor domestic dogs evolved. Many scientists have made the attempt, but no one has yet been able to support their theories with any real weight of scientific evidence. Charles Darwin suggested that two species—the wolf (*Canis lupus*) and the golden jackal (*Canis aureus*)—might have given rise to the domestic dog, with some degree of cross-breeding. The great 20th-century zoologist Konrad Lorenz at one time supported this idea, and considered that certain breeds, such as the Chow Chow and Husky, displayed a high degree of wolf ancestry, while other breeds displayed mainly jackal ancestry. Lorenz subsequently altered his opinion

on behavioral grounds and came to consider the wolf to be the ancestor of all domestic dogs.

R.I. Pocock, writing in 1935, suggested that four types of wolf contained the genetic information necessary to develop all modern breeds of dog. The fact that the modern dog is able to produce fertile offspring when mated to wolves adds weight to the belief that we need look no further for its ancestor. The four types cited by Pocock were the Northern gray wolf (*Canis lupus*), the pale-footed Asian wolf (*Canis lupus pallipes*), the small desert wolf of Arabia (*Canis lupus arabs*), and the woolly-coated wolf of Tibet and northern India (*Canis lupus laniger*). The more recent research of Richard and Alice Fiennes

The African wild dog, like its cousin the wolf, lives in packs with a strict hierarchy. The need for one individual to be dominant is still evident in the behavior of the domestic dog.

has tended to confirm Pocock's view.

It is also possible that domestication from certain breeds of wolf might have taken place in various geographical sites at around the same time, for example in North America, China, and Africa as well as in the Middle East. This could also help to explain some of the variations seen among today's breeds of dogs. It may be that the desire to find an ancestor for our favorite companion other than the frequently despised wolf is, in fact, based on nothing more than a lack of understanding of the nature of wolves.

THE FIRST DOMESTICATED DOGS

JUST AS THE EXACT ANCESTRY of the domestic dog is uncertain, so too is the nature of the relationship between humans and dogs at the start of domestication. There are several theories for this, and it is possible to describe hypothetical scenarios to illustrate them.

A first theory is that dogs were originally used by humans to help with hunting. At close quarters, humans were physically no match for many of the animals with which they had to compete for food, and no match for them as hunters either. However, by throwing sticks and stones from a distance they were able to drive other animals from their kills, and thereby to enjoy the benefits of their skills and hunting prowess. Often the animals from which humans scavenged food would be wolves which, deprived of their hard-won dinner, might remain close until the humans had satisfied their hunger. Perhaps by means of training orphaned wolf cubs humans might have begun to employ wolves' hunting skills more directly.

From that beginning a much closer relationship might have developed. Wolves and humans had in common with one another a social system based on the family, as adult wolves retain contact with their offspring long after the cubs are fully grown and able to live independent lives. This social system made a degree of organization necessary. Leaders emerged, and the rest of the family responded to this leader. Sharing a common social organization gave humans and wolves the ability to recognize in one another abilities which could be used to their mutual advantage, and also meant that wolves would respond to a human's leadership.

A second possible theory behind the original domestication of the wolf is that humans may at first have hunted wolves for food. This is not by itself very likely because the wolf would have been a relatively scarce species compared with various herbivores such as deer. However, the killing of adult wolves would sometimes have left helpless young, which in times of plenty might have been taken back as playthings for young children—much as today's children might bring up the young of wild species such as fox and badger.

A third theory for the domestication of the dog is that dogs were, right from the start, pets or companions rather than working animals. It is easy to see how children might have reared wolf cubs as pets. It is perhaps more difficult to see why humans should apparently have given up some of their hard-won food in order to support another species. Yet recent support for this theory was provided by a fossil find in Israel of the skeleton of a puppy with the hand of a man's skeleton resting upon it. This configuration was highly suggestive of a companionable relationship between humans and dogs 12,000 years ago. Thus perhaps the working uses of the dog followed from an understanding

A stone relief from the palace of Ashurbanipal (Assyria, c. 645 BC) shows a snarling mastiff held back by a soldier.

Left: An Ancient Egyptian sculpture, dating from the 18th Dynasty of the New Kingdom (about 3,500 years ago), showing a chase hound taking part in a rich man's sport.

Below: A 15th-century treatise on hunting by Gaston Phebus, Comte de Foix, portrays hunting dogs similar in appearance to today's hounds. Many breeds have developed from this type.

developed between young children and pet dogs that grew up with them in or close to their homes.

A fourth theory is that early domestic dogs were used for guarding rather than for hunting. Their superior senses of sound and smell may have alerted humans to unnoticed danger threatening their campsite, whether from wild animals or other humans. Perhaps this is why barking is a common behavior in the domestic dog, but not in the wolf. This guarding could then have been extended to use with flocks of sheep and cattle,

since humans soon began to domesticate both of these as well.

A fifth theory is that perhaps humans did not actively domesticate the dog, but that a relationship developed for mutual advantage. The way humans and wolves probably existed side by side, since they were hunters of similar prey, has already been described. Perhaps the initiative was not taken entirely by humans; wolves too may have learned to exploit food humans had discarded, as well as hunting the rats and other species that may have lived on grain stored by humans. Tamer

individuals that were thought useful in keeping down vermin may have been tolerated and then befriended by humans. The friendship would then have developed from this initial mutual understanding, leading to the dog as the worker and companion of today.

It is unlikely that the exact process of domestication will ever be fully known. Probably the relationship built up through a combination of reasons, and it may have started in slightly different ways in different geographical areas. As time went on, the wolf offspring must have come to live and grow in the closest possible association with humans. They learned to respond to moods and to obey commands, while humans too might have learned from the inherent hunting skills of these partially domesticated wild creatures.

THE DEVELOPMENT OF BREEDS AND BREEDING

AFTER THE ARCHEOLOGICAL remains testifying to the close association which existed between dogs and humans, the next evidence of such a relationship comes from Paleolithic cave paintings in the Pyrenees, which show bowmen and dogs cooperating in a hunt. These dogs are invariably lightly built and long-legged, with pointed muzzles and prick ears—very similar to the wolves which then inhabited southern Europe, but possibly possessing some differences which demonstrate that humans were already beginning to select the dogs which best suited their purpose and that the favored type differed slightly from wild stock.

The discovery in 1928 of the so-called Windmill Hill dog in excavations at a Neolithic settlement near Avebury, Wiltshire, showed that the process of domestication and the effects of selective breeding were already well advanced in Britain, as elsewhere in Europe, about 5,000 years ago. At this time humans were ceasing to be nomadic hunters; they were beginning to make permanent settlements and to farm the land. The development of this new way of life placed new demands on dogs which lived with them. No longer were they used exclusively as hunters, to track, hold, and kill animals for the benefit of humans. Now dogs had to learn not to kill the cattle which humans kept, but to protect them from attacks by their own wild relatives. Humans now had possessions to be guarded, a home, a stock of food, farm animals; and they expected their dogs to help them protect this new lifestyle. In return, humans gave their dogs the means of a meager existence, to be supplemented as best they might by independent hunting trips.

As humans became more prosperous they were able to afford the luxury of keeping dogs which did not hunt, protect their flocks, or guard their homes. They began to keep dogs simply because their appearance or their temperament was pleasing. Humans had become a race of dog breeders and learned henceforth to produce dogs able to accomplish a wide variety of tasks. This was seen in the periods of some of the great civilizations.

At the height of the great Babylonian empire about 5,000 years ago, huge mastiff-like dogs were represented in art. They were massive creatures with heavy wrinkled heads and curled tails. The sheer size of these dogs, probably used as guards or in war, is in sharp contrast both with the small, long-legged, short-backed, and small-headed Windmill Hill dog of roughly the same period, and with the hunting dogs bred by the Assyrians some 2,000 years later. These

"Driving the Tandem Cart," a watercolor painted in 1905 by Henry William Standing.

This illustrates that the Dalmatian was still in use as a carriage dog in the early 1900s.

A portrait of a young lady and her lapdog, by Abraham Lamberts Jacobsz van den Tempel (1622–1672).

Below: An Assiniboin hunter with his two wolf-like pack dogs, photographed by Edward S. Curtis in 1926. This sort of relationship is thought to be the basis for the domestication of the dog.

breeding, is used in the investigation of crime, and they have gone into space to test the ability of mammals to survive in that alien world. Dogs are bred to guide blind people, and they can bring comfort and help to those whose mental or emotional condition makes it difficult for them to relate to their fellow human beings. In very many ways dogs continue to contribute to the quality of our lives.

fleet-footed Assyrian hounds are very similar to those found in Egypt and most often associated with that country, but they are quite unlike the short-legged, long-backed dog found on the Beni-Hassam carvings, also from Egypt and dating from about 4,000 years ago.

It can therefore be conclusively demonstrated that, several thousand years ago, dogs had diversified into a number of very different breeds which exhibited none of the more obvious characteristics of their wild ancestors. Despite this marked degree of physical adaptability, the extent of mental adaptation which dogs had to achieve was much more impressive.

From this stage the way was open for humans to employ their growing skill at, and interest in, breeding animals, using the scope offered by the genetic pool available in the dog's wild ancestors to develop types of dog which suited particular purposes. As civilization advanced, humans learned to appreciate appearance for its own sake. They also had the leisure to indulge in sporting activities. No longer therefore were dogs bred purely for utilitarian purposes. Some were bred for the novelty or beauty of their appearance or to provide companionship in the home, and so the toy dogs slowly began to evolve. Others were encouraged to chase game, or to fight, either one another or other animals. Both

of these specialities were developments of existing valuable traits, but the desire for sport produced types of hounds and terriers which had not previously existed. Then humans, ever aggressive animals, realized that they could utilize the dog's loyalty and its desire to protect them to breed large and ferocious creatures for use in conjunction with armies, to harass their enemies as well as to protect their own army encampments and supplies. From this source developed many of the massive guard dogs.

Then, too, a dog's incredible degree of adaptiveness and desire to please its master encouraged humans to use the animal for many purposes which arose from a developing civilization. Such development has continued to this day, when many of the traditional uses to which dogs have been put have declined while some, thankfully, have become illegal. There is now no need for Comforters to attract the lice and fleas which would otherwise infest their owners. The necessity for Turnspits to turn meat cooking over an open fire has disappeared. The use of dogs as carriage animals is replaced by mechanical transport, and civilized human beings no longer enjoy seeing dogs fight among themselves or against bears or bulls. Nevertheless, our society has introduced other needs which dogs willingly seek to satisfy. Their acute sense of smell, developed by selective

Part Two

The Breeds

INTRODUCTION

Above: Skye Terrier   *Below: Golden Retriever*

THIS SECTION IS DERIVED from official standards of the Kennel Club (KC) in Great Britain, the American Kennel Club (AKC), the Fédération Cynologique Internationale (FCI) in Europe, and the Australian National Kennel Council (ANKC). The Kennel Club now recognizes over 180 breeds and the most popular are described here, along with a number of recent arrivals from Europe and a few that are more familiar in other parts of the world.

The groupings given in this section are those used by the Kennel Club of Great Britain: Hounds, Gundogs, Terriers, Utility, Working, Pastoral, and Toys. The Pastoral group came into being in January 1999 and contains a number of breeds previously classified as either Utility or Working. The American Kennel Club categories are roughly similar, except that what the Kennel Club classes as Utility and Pastoral are called Non-sporting and Herding, respectively. The Fédération Cynologique Internationale operates a very different and more complex system and, where there is no direct comparison between the FCI and other classifications, the appropriate group is given for each entry.

When new breeds are introduced to the UK from abroad, they are normally placed on the Imported Breed Register and given an Interim standard, usually based on the standard of the country of origin, but agreed between the individual Breed Club (formed by owners, breeders, and other enthusiasts of the breed) and the Kennel Club. This Interim standard will be monitored over a period of years to check that it produces satisfactory dogs. It may prove acceptable or it may have to be modified before the breed is transferred to a list of Rare Breeds and finally to the full Breed Register. Rare Breeds and those on the Imported Breed Register have their own classes at Championship and Open Shows, and are allowed to win Kennel Club Challenge Certificates only once they reach the Breed Register.

The AKC operates a broadly similar system, listing newcomers in a Miscellaneous Group until they are deemed to have attained full breed status. Again, "Miscellaneous" breeds are limited to Miscellaneous Classes at shows and are not eligible for championship points. Country of origin, date of introduction, and the indefinable qualities which decree whether or not a breed will become popular have led to a few differences between the Breed Registers of the KC and AKC. At the time of writing, among those breeds to have Interim standards from the KC are the Shar Pei, which has full AKC recognition, and the Neapolitan Mastiff, which is not recognized by the AKC at all. The AKC Miscellaneous Class includes the Italian

Right: Boxer puppy   *Below: Basenji*

Spinone and the Löwchen, both of which have been recognized by the Kennel Club in recent years.

Perhaps the most controversial of all is the Jack Russell Terrier, which has an Interim standard in the UK and is in the AKC Miscellaneous Class. Part of its difficulty lies in the fact that—in the UK, at least—it is not an import but a familiar if ill-defined home-grown product. It has been a recognized "type" throughout the 20th century, but the great variation from one individual to another made it difficult to establish a standard. Pressure from a large number of Jack Russell enthusiasts seems to have overcome this hurdle, and it may not be long before this popular and busy little terrier makes its appearance in the show rings.

The official groupings within every kennel club are based on the dog's original purpose, most of which are self-explanatory. Gundogs were bred to assist in shooting; hounds gave chase in other forms of hunting and coursing; terriers (from the Latin *terra*, "earth") dug down into the ground in pursuit of prey that burrowed underground. These three are grouped together as the Sporting breeds. Of the Nonsporting groups, toys are small dogs bred purely as companions; pastoral breeds looked after sheep, cattle, or other livestock; and working dogs helped humans in a variety of ways, including pulling sledges and guarding property. The final Nonsporting group, Utility (called simply "Nonsporting" by the AKC and ANKC), contains a number of breeds whose original function is now obsolete, such as the Dalmatian (bred as a carriage dog), the Bulldog (a fighting dog), and the Schipperke (a dog from Holland bred to guard barges).

Interestingly, the grouping of the three Sporting groups varies very little from one kennel club to another throughout the world, but there are many variations in the Nonsporting groups. The Boston Terrier, for example, developed as

a pit-fighting dog in the USA, is a Nonsporting breed in its country of origin and in Australia, and a Utility in the UK, whereas its small size makes it a Companion in the FCI. The Kennel Club and the ANKC classify the Japanese Akita as Utility, because again it was originally a fighting dog, whereas the AKC calls it Working, perhaps because it now makes a useful guard. The FCI has a separate classification for Nordic Sledge Dogs, into which this falls because it is a spitz type (loosely resembling a husky, with the characteristic tightly curled tail), although it has not been a sledge dog for several hundred years. The Kennel Club usually expresses the desired size of a breed in terms of height at the withers or shoulders, though sometimes weight rather than height is the criterion. Occasionally both height and weight are spec-

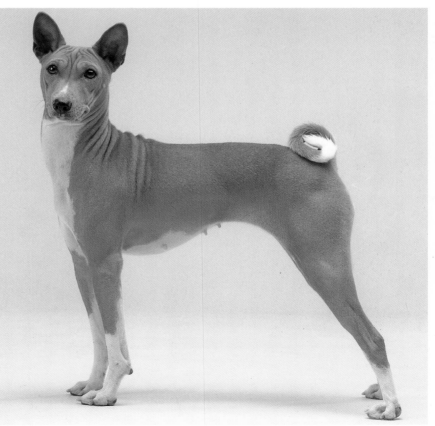

ified, and on rare occasions no size at all. Sometimes but by no means always the standard differs for dogs and bitches. The figures given below follow these conventions, with the standard for other countries specified only where it differs substantially from that of the KC.

Hounds

Breeds listed under this heading belong to the Hound group under KC, AKC, and ANKC classifications, unless otherwise stated.

AFGHAN HOUND

THIS COURSING HOUND comes from the mountains and plains of Afghanistan, developing from two distinct types which are now almost entirely intermingled. There is some evidence that Afghan hounds had moved eastward along the trade routes and had originated in the hounds of the eastern Mediterranean. They were first imported into Britain in 1894, but failed to make much of an impression until, in 1907, a dog named Zondin appeared at shows and attracted the attention of royalty. Afghan hounds were imported into North America in 1926.

Characteristics

A dignified hound, but capable of playing the fool. It needs a lot of exercise and its profuse coat demands frequent grooming. Given proper care it is one of the most striking of breeds and for this reason enjoys the mixed blessing of great popularity. The movement of the Afghan should be smooth and springy with considerable style. The dog gives the impression of strength and dignity combined with speed and power. The head is long and lean, the body strong and deep, with very muscled forequarters and powerful hind-quarters.

Group
Sighthounds (FCI).
Size
Height: Dogs 27–29 in. (68–74 cm), bitches 2 in. (5 cm) smaller. In AKC, dogs 27 in. (68.5 cm), bitches 25 in. (63.5 cm), both plus or minus 1 in. (2.5 cm).
Weight: In AKC, dogs about 60 lb. (27.2 kg), bitches 50 lb. (22.6 kg).
Coat
Color: All colors acceptable.
Texture: Long and fine and allowed to develop naturally.

BASENJI

THIS BREED ORIGINATED in Zaire. It is unique as a dog which doesn't bark, though it is an accomplished yodeller, and, as a Spitz breed from Africa, still very close to its wild ancestors. Familiar as a guard, hunter, and companion in Western Africa for centuries, it was unknown in the Western world until two were brought to Britain in 1895; unfortunately both died shortly afterward. It was not until 1937 in Britain and 1941 in America that imports were more successful and breeding stock became established. The Basenji's popularity has waned in recent years, with fewer than a hundred dogs being registered in the UK in 1997.

Characteristics

The breed is remarkable for its great cleanliness, produced not only by its short coat but by its personal habits. Basenjis are lightly built, finely boned, aristocratic animals, tall, poised, alert, and intelligent. The wrinkled head, with pricked ears, is carried proudly on a well-arched neck.

Group
Nordic Sledge Dogs (FCI).
Size
Height: Dogs 17 in. (43 cm), bitches 16 in. (40 cm).
Weight: Dogs 24 lb. (11 kg), bitches 21 lb. (9.5 kg). In FCI, dogs 23½ lb. (10.6 kg), bitches 20 lb. (9 kg).
Coat
Color: May be predominantly black, red, or black and tan, all with white feet, chest, and tail tip.
Texture: Short, sleek and close, very fine.

Afghan Hound

Basset Hound

BASSET HOUND

BASSET HOUNDS ORIGINATED with the old French hounds, which were crossed with Bloodhounds to produce the dog which Shakespeare compared with Thessalian bulls. Bassets were developed in Britain from a litter imported in 1872 from Comte de Tournour by Lord Onslow. They are slow-moving, ponderous, deep-voiced pack hounds used for hunting the hare. Bassets bred for work and those bred for the show ring may nowadays be very different animals.

Characteristics

A short-legged hound of considerable substance, capable of moving smoothly. The head is big, domed, and heavy, owing a lot in appearance to the Bloodhound; the ears are long and pendulous. The body, from prominent breastbone to the long, strong tail, is of considerable length, and comrpises a well-rounded chest, a broad, level back, and arched loins.

BEAGLE

THIS ENGLISH BREED is the smallest of the pack hounds and is used for hunting the hare with followers on foot. By the time Thomas Bewick was writing his *History of Quadrupeds* in 1790, he was able to speak of these hounds as having been known for over 300 years. In those days there were two sizes of Beagle, with the name "vaches" being reserved for the larger variety. Eventually the smaller sort ceased to be used, but in America attempts have been made to recreate the pocket Beagle.

Characteristics

Certainly one of the most popular hounds and one which makes a cheerful companion. The Beagle is compactly built and should convey the impression of great stamina and activity. The standard asks for a short body, powerful loins, clean shoulders, and very muscular hindquarters. The tail is of moderate length, and is carried proudly, but not over the back.

Group
Scenthounds (FCI).
Size
Height: 13–15 in. (33–38 cm).
Coat
Color: Generally black, white and tan or lemon and white, but any recognized hound color is acceptable.
Texture: Smooth, short, and close without being too fine. The American standard requires a hard coat and loose skin.

Group
Scenthounds (FCI).
Size
Height: Not greater than 16 in. (40 cm) or less than 13 in. (33 cm). In AKC, there are two Beagle varieties: under 13 in. (33 cm); under 13–15 in. (33–38 cm).
Coat
Color: Any recognized hound colors, except liver.
Texture: Short and dense.

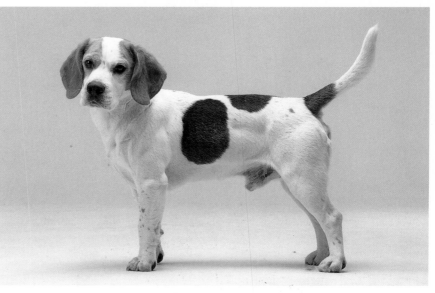

Beagle

BLACK AND TAN COONHOUND

THIS IS THE ONLY RECOGNIZED breed of half a dozen Coonhounds, popular in the United States, which include the very impressive Redbone Coonhound, the surprisingly named English Coonhound, and the more American-flavored Bluetick, Treeing Walker, and Plott. These hounds hunt by night as the racoon is a nocturnal animal. The Black and Tan Coonhound was admitted to the AKC registry in 1945.

Characteristics

Slightly resembling a lightly built Bloodhound, this is essentially a working dog, capable of withstanding the rigors of winter and the heat of summer. The general impression should be one of power, agility, and alertness.The expression should be alert, friendly, eager, and aggressive. The dog should impress with its easy, powerful, rhythmic movement.

Group
Scenthounds (FCI). Not recognized by KC or ANKC.
Size
Height: Dogs 25–27 in. (63–68 cm), bitches 23–25 in. (58–63 cm).
Weight: In AKC dogs 65–80 lb. (29.5–36 kg), bitches 50–65 lb. (22.5–29.5 kg).
Coat
Color: Coal black, rich tan markings.
Texture: Short and dense.

BLOODHOUND

THE ENGLISH PHYSICIAN and scholar Dr. John Caius, in 1553, was able to describe the Bloodhound very much in terms which are applicable today and was one of the first to make the mistake of attributing the source of the breed's name to its ability to follow a blood trail. In fact the word is used in the same sense as in "blood stock," as a reference to aristocratic breeding. Even so, the Bloodhound's reputation as a formidable tracking dog had obviously already been established and has survived to this day. The breed is one of many English hounds originally derived from French stock.

Characteristics

The Bloodhound is a powerful animal, larger than most hound breeds. It is characterized by a thin, loose skin which hangs in deep folds, especially about the head, and imparts that lugubrious expression for which it is so often caricatured. In temperament the Bloodhound should not be quarrelsome with other dogs, as its nature tends to be reserved.

Bloodhound

Group
Scenthounds (FCI).
Size
Height: Dogs 25–27 in. (63–69 cm), bitches 23–25 in. (58–63 cm); in FCI 26 in. (66 cm) for dogs.
Weight: Dogs average 90 lb. (41 kg), bitches 80 lb. (36 kg), but may reach 110 lb. (50 kg) for dogs and 100 lb. (45 kg) for bitches. Greater heights and weights preferred, provided character and quality are maintained.
Coat
Color: Black and tan, red and tan, or red, called fawny in America. Darker colors may be interspersed with lighter or badger-colored hairs.
Texture: Smooth, short, and glossy.

BORZOI

UNTIL COMPARATIVELY RECENTLY, when the Borzoi's name was changed from Russian Wolfhound, its origins could be easily and correctly assumed. Before the Revolution every Russian nobleman maintained a pack of these hounds, which were used in pairs for coursing wolves. It is amusing to note that early dog writers complained that the breed had become so effete that it was no longer able to pull down a wolf without assistance.

Characteristics

A very graceful, aristocratic, long-legged dog possessing courage, muscular power, and great speed. The head is long and lean, the neck slightly arched and powerful, the back comparatively short, rising in a graceful curve at the loins, more marked in dogs than in bitches. Although the Borzoi has a hearty appetite, even an

DACHSHUND

adult dog should be fed two or three modest meals a day rather than one large one, to avoid the risk of gastric torsion which is increased after bolting a large quantity of food (see page 149).

Group
Sighthounds (FCI).
Size
Height: Dogs from 29 in. (73 cm) upward, bitches from 27 in. (68 cm). The minimum for AKC dogs is 28 in. (71 cm), for bitches 26 in. (66 cm). In FCI, dogs 29¾ in. (75 cm), bitches 28 in. (71 cm).
Weight: In AKC, dogs 34–47.6kg (75–105lb), bitches 27.2–40.8kg (60–90lb).
Coat
Color: Any.
Texture: Long and silky, flat, wavy or rather curly, never woolly.

Borzoi

DACHSHUNDS REPRESENT a small and distinctive subgroup within the hound group and have a group of their own in the FCI system. They are differentiated from other hounds by their small size, the work for which they were intended and to some extent by the quarry they used to hunt. "Dachshund" simply means "badger dog," but must not be taken to mean that these diminutive hounds, whose history dates back to the 15th century, were used exclusively for that quarry. Larger hounds, weighing 30 lb. (13.6 kg) or 35 lb. (15.8 kg), were used for badger, while smaller ones were kept for stoat and weasel. It was not until 1915 that the Dachshund was differentiated by its different coats. Since then the breed has achieved considerable popularity as a pet and show dog, and so, inevitably perhaps, outside Europe it has become a very different animal from the one so carefully bred in Germany as a working hound.

There are three varieties of Dachshund, classed according to coat—Long-haired, Smooth-haired, and Wire-haired. Each of these occurs in a "standard" and a miniature form.

Characteristics

First and foremost a sporting dog, but equally adaptable as a house pet, a dachshund will enjoy a surprising amount of exercise for such a small dog. The general appearance is long and low, but with a compact and well-muscled body and a bold defiant head carriage. The head is long, the eyes of medium size, the neck long, muscular and clean, with no dewlap. The forelegs are very short, the lower arms slightly crooked. The body is long and muscular, the chest very oval, and the breastbone prominent. The hindquarters are full and broad, the tail high set, strong, and tapering.

Group
Dachshunds (FCI).
Size
Weight: Ideal weight 20–26 lb. (9–12 kg). Ideal weight for miniatures is 10 lb. (4.5 kg) and the maximum 11 lb. (5 kg).
Coat
Long-haired
Color: Black and tan, dark brown with lighter shadings, dark red, light red, dappled, tiger marked, or brindle.
Texture: Soft and straight or slightly waved, of shining color.
Smooth-haired
Color: Any color, other than white.
Texture: Short, dense, and smooth, but strong.
Wire-haired
Color: All colors are allowed, but any white should be confined to a small patch on the chest.
Texture: :Short, thick, hard, and rough; any sort of soft hair is faulty, as is long, curly or wavy hair.

DEERHOUND

A BREED WHICH DEMONSTRATES in the most eloquent manner that some breeds have no need of improvement or to be altered in order to follow the latest fashion. Deerhounds of today are just as they have always been when, having been produced out of the hounds used by Pictish hunters, they were used to bring deer to bay and were the prized possessions and constant companions of their masters. A good brace of Deerhounds was almost above price, credited with sufficient value to purchase the reprieve of an earl condemned to death. When the Battle of Culloden (1745) put a virtual end to the clan system, the Highland chieftains assumed exclusive ownership, so that the breed declined. It was rescued from ignominy by Lord Colonsay in around 1825. Nowadays the breed is in every way comparable to the hounds which graced Scotland in those earlier days, and which were so remarkable both for their courage in the field and for their courteous dignity in the home. All that has changed is the name of the breed, which was formerly the Scottish Deerhound.

Elkhound

Characteristics

The general conformation is similar to that of a Greyhound, but of larger size and bone and with a shaggier coat. Strong, powerful with great stamina and an easy, long-striding run, the Deerhound gives an impression of surprising gentleness in such a large dog. Good-natured and eager to please, it is easy to train and makes an affectionate and loyal pet. Its only demand is for plenty of exercise.

Characteristics

The Elkhound is a hardy sporting dog, of typically Nordic appearance and with a bold and virile nature. Its disposition is friendly and intelligent, with great energy and independence of character and with no sign of nervousness. In general appearance the Elkhound is compactly built with a short body, thick, abundant coat, pricked ears, and a tail curled tightly over the back. The head is broad in the skull, and the eyes are as dark as possible, with a fearless and friendly expression.

Group
Sighthounds (FCI).
Size
Height: Dogs not less than 30 in. (76 cm), but 30–32 in. (76–81 cm); bitches not less than 28 in. (71 cm).
Weight: Dogs about 100 lb. (45.5 kg), bitches about 80 lb. (36.5 kg). In AKC, dogs 85–110 lb. (38.5–50 kg), bitches 75–95 lb. (34–43 kg).
Coat
Color: Dark blue-gray, or darker or lighter grays or brindles, yellow and sandy red or red-fawn.
Texture: Harsh and wiry on body, neck and shoulders and about 7.6-10cm (3-4in) long. Thick, close-lying, ragged and harsh or crisp to the touch.

ELKHOUND

THE ELKHOUND, WHICH IS known in both North America and Australia as the Norwegian Elkhound, is a Scandinavian Spitz breed, which has arrived at its present distinctive appearance as a result of selection based on its ability to hunt the elk, bringing the animal to bay while summoning the hunters with its shrill barking. Careful selection for very many years has made the Elkhound a versatile hunting dog for a variety of quarry, and it has not changed as a result of its popularity as a show dog and companion.

Group
Nordic Sledge Dogs (FCI).
Size
Height: Dogs 20½ in. (52 cm), bitches 19½ in. (49 cm).
Weight: Approximately 50 lb. (23 kg) for dogs; 43 lb. (20 kg) bitches. In AKC, dogs should be 55 lb. (24.9 kg) and bitches 48 lb. (21.7 kg).
Coat
Color: Gray of various shades with black tips on the long outer coat, and a lighter color on the chest, stomach, legs, and the underside of the tail.
Texture: Thick, abundant, and weather-resistant with a longish, coarse top coat and a light-colored, soft, woolly undercoat.

GREYHOUND

THERE CAN BE NO DOUBT that Greyhounds are of very ancient origin. As early as 1016 Canute's law forbade "mean persons" from keeping Greyhounds and, in 1408, Dame Juliana Berners used an older description of the breed in her *Book of St Albans*:

The Condyscyons of A grehound and of his propyrteys. Thy grehounds most be heddyd lyke a snake y neckyd lyke a drake. foted lyke a Kat. Syded lyke a Bream. Chyned lyke a Beam. Then ys grehounde well y schapte.

Various attempts have been made to explain the origin of the name which refers not to color, but is possibly derived from the Latin *gradus*, meaning "rank." Others look to the old British word *grach*, meaning "dog," or even *Grais*, meaning "Grecian."

Characteristics

The Greyhound possesses remarkable stamina and its long-reaching movement enables it to move at great speed; over a measured sprint it is probably the fastest of all dogs. The head is long and elegant, the eyes bright and intelligent, the neck long and muscular. The chest is deep and capacious with the flanks well cut-up, the legs are strong, well boned and powerfully muscled. It is a naturally clean dog, requiring minimal grooming, and makes a loyal and affectionate pet.

Group
Sighthounds (FCI).
Size
Height: Dogs 28–30 in. (71–76 cm), bitches 27–28 in. (68–71 cm).
Coat
Color: Black, white, red, blue, fawn, fallow, or brindle. Any of these colors may be broken with white.
Texture: Fine and close.

IRISH WOLFHOUND

QUINTUS AURELIUS, the Roman Consul, recorded in AD 391 that a gift of seven wolfhounds had filled "all Rome with wonder." The breed was obviously already well established, but over the centuries the extinction of the wolf in Britain led to the breed's decline, so that, by the mid-19th century, Stonehenge, a usually reliable authority, was able to record that it was extinct. However, in the 1860s, Captain George Graham, a Scot living in Dursley in Gloucestershire, set himself the task of recreating these massive hounds from the few remaining specimens he was able to gather together. So well did he succeed in this venture that the breed is now found in healthy numbers.

Characteristics

The Irish Wolfhound's most obvious characteristics are its great size, its commanding appearance, and the impression of considerable strength it conveys. The head is long, the skull not too broad, the ears small and Greyhound-like in carriage. The neck is rather long, and very strong and muscular. The chest is very deep, the back rather long with arched loins, and the belly well drawn-up. The forequarters are muscular, the hindquarters long and strong as in the Greyhound, with large, round feet. This giant breed is not fully mature until the age of three years, so care must be given not to overexercise it throughout that time. Particular attention should also be given to its diet, to ensure that its bones grow strong and healthy. Although adult Wolfhounds enjoy a good run off the lead, they do not require a vast amount of exercise—but they do need a lot of space. Their good nature, intelligence and loyalty are legendary and they are very good with children.

Irish Wolfhound

Group
Sighthounds (FCI).
Size
Height: A minimum of 31 in. (79 cm) for dogs, 28 in. (71 cm) for bitches. In AKC, the minimum is 32 in. (81 cm) for dogs, 30 in. (76 cm) for bitches. The Kennel Club standard specifies that great size is to be aimed at, with a view to establishing a breed where the dogs measure 32–34 in. (81–86 cm).
Weight: 120 lb. (54.5 kg) as a minimum for dogs, 90 lb. (40.9 kg) for bitches. In AKC 105 lb. (47.6 kg).
Coat
Color: Gray, brindle, red, black, white, fawn, or wheaten.
Texture: Rough and hard on the body, wiry and long over the eyes and under the jaw.

OTTERHOUND

ALTHOUGH OTTER HUNTING in England dates back to the early 12th century, it was not until the reign of Edward II (1307–27) that a description of hounds which fits the modern breed was set down. For over 800 years otter hunting provided sport for the few packs which existed in Britain, by no means all of which were composed of pure-bred Otterhounds, but it was only relatively recently that Otterhounds were declared responsible for the otter's sudden decline. When, in 1977, otter hunting was declared illegal in England and Wales, there was a danger that the comparatively few remaining pure-bred Otterhounds might be lost. However, enthusiastic support for the breed encouraged the Kennel Club to accept registrations so that hounds could be shown, as they had been in the USA since 1907. Although they are not numerous, Otterhounds seem to be safely established once more.

Characteristics

The Otterhound is a large, rough-coated, squarely built hound, with an exceptionally good nose and deep musical voice. The head is large and narrow, the chest deep, with ribs carried well back, the topline is level and the tail long and sickle-shaped. The legs are heavy-boned, forelegs straight, hindlegs well muscled. The feet are large, broad, compact, and webbed. Movement is smooth and effortless, with the feet only just coming off the ground, and the dog's strength and stamina have proved capable of carrying him for many miles. A big dog with a great love of water, the Otterhound makes a good-tempered but energetic companion.

Group
Scenthounds (FCI).
Size
Height: According to the KC, the ideal height for dogs is 27 in. (67 cm), for bitches 24 in. (60 cm). The AKC allows a range—dogs 24–27 in. (61–68.5 cm), bitches 22–26 in. (56–66 cm). In FCI, dogs should be 23½–25½ in. (60-65 cm), bitches proportionately smaller.
Weight: In AKC, dogs 75-115 lb.) 34-52 kg), bitches 65-100 lb. (29.4-45.3 kg). In FCI, 66-77 lb. (29.9-34.9 kg).
Coat
Color: Any recognized hound color or combination of colors, except liver and white or a white body with separate black and tan patches.
Texture: The rough outer coat is hard and 3–6 in. (7.5–15 cm) long; the weather-resistant inner coat is short and woolly.

RHODESIAN RIDGE-BACK

THE EUROPEAN FARMERS who settled in South Africa in the 16th and 17th centuries brought with them a collection of dogs from which they developed a hound suitable for the conditions and game encountered there, and which was also willing to act as a guard. They did this by crossing their dogs with a native hunting dog which had a ridge on its back. The dog had to be tough, versatile, easy to look after, and fit well into the family. The breed, developed by the Boer farmers, was introduced into Rhodesia in 1877 by the Reverend Helm who used it for hunting lions—whence comes its other name of African Lion Hound.

Otterhounds

WHIPPET

Left: Rhodesian Ridgeback

THE WHIPPET IS NOT, in spite of obvious and undeniable similarities, a miniature Greyhound. It is the working man's sighthound, intended for coursing small ground game and for racing against its fellows. The breed came into existence in the early 19th century when punitive laws which prevented working people from keeping sporting dogs had been relaxed, at least to the extent that small ground game and vermin could legitimately be hunted. In its early days the breed was known as a snap-dog, a term that is often explained by the Whippet's ability to snap up rabbits, alhough it is possible that *snap*, an English dialect word meaning "food," also refers to its ability as a provider. The Whippet's speed over a furlong (about 200 metres) also made exciting racing; as a sport, Whippet racing pre-dates the more commercially organized Greyhound races and still flourishes in England.

Characteristics

A Whippet should be able to convey an instant impression of balanced muscular power and strength allied to elegance; it is a dog built for speed and should therefore possess great freedom of action. The skull is long and lean, the expression bright and alert, and the ears fine and rose-shaped. The neck is long, muscular, and slightly arched, set into oblique shoulders. The chest is very deep, and the back is broad and firm, showing a definite arch over the loin. The forelegs are straight and the hindquarters strong. The tail is long and tapering. The Whippet makes an ideal, easy-to-care-for family pet.

Group
Sighthounds (FCI).
Size
Height: Dogs 18½–20 in. (47–51 cm), bitches 17½–18½ in. (44-47 cm). In AKC, dogs 19–22 in. (48.2–56cm), bitches 18–21 in. (45.7–53.3 cm).
Coat
Color: Any color or mixture of colors.
Texture: Fine, short, as close as possible.

Whippet

Characteristics

The distinguishing feature of the breed is the ridge on the back formed by hair growing against the nap of the rest of the coat. The Ridgeback is a strong, muscular, and active dog, symmetrical in outline and capable of great endurance with a fair amount of speed; its movement is similar to that of a Foxhound. The head is of fair length, flat and broad between the ears, which are set high and carried close to the head. The eyes are bright and colored to harmonize with the color of the dog. Forelegs are straight and heavily boned, shoulders sloping, clean, and muscular. The chest is deep and capacious, the back powerful with strong, muscular, and slightly arched loins. The tail is carried with a slight upward curve.

Group
Scenthounds (FCI).
Size
Height: Dogs 25–27 in. (63–67 cm), bitches 24–26 in. (61–66 cm).
Weight: In AKC, dogs 75 lb. (34 kg), bitches 65 lb. (29 kg).
Coat
Color: Light to red wheaten, a uniform color all over.
Texture: Short and dense with a sleek, glossy appearance.

Gundogs

Breeds listed under this heading belong to the Gundog group under KC and ANKC classification, and to the Sporting Dog group in the AKC, unless otherwise stated.

BRITTANY

IN AD 150, OPPIAN wrote of the uncivilized people of Britain and their dogs. He used *Bretagne* to refer to Britain, whereas later the word was used to refer to Brittany in France. Certainly the Welsh Springer Spaniel and the Brittany (until recently known as the Brittany Spaniel) have much in common and may share a common heritage, though by the 18th century Dutch and French painters were depicting dogs which unquestionably are the forerunners of the modern breed of pointing spaniel. The breed shares many of the characteristics of the setter in its manner of work and is in fact the only pointing spaniel. Some puppies are born without tails, others normally have their tails docked short. Although a comparative newcomer to the show ring outside Continental Europe, the Brittany is more familiar at British field trials, where it has achieved considerable success.

Characteristics

In appearance the breed has some resemblance to a very lightly built Springer: a compact, closely knit dog of medium size, with the agility and stamina to cover a lot of ground. The stern is of medium length, rounded and slightly wedge-shaped. The ears are dark and leafy, lying flat and close to the head. The neck is of medium length. The body is square in outline, the shoulders sloping and muscular, the back short and straight, the chest deep with plenty of heart room. Hindquarters are broad, strong, and muscular. An active, intelligent, and affectionate dog, the Brittany is eager to please and easy to care for.

Group
Pointing Dogs (FCI).
Size
Height: Dogs 19–20 in. (48–50 cm), bitches 18–19 in. (47–49 cm).
Coat
Color: Orange and white, liver and white, black and white, tricolor or roan of any of these colors.
Texture: Dense, flat or wavy without excessive feathering.

ENGLISH SETTER

ALTHOUGH IT IS LIKELY that the setters originally sprang from spaniel stock imported into Britain, there is evidence that by the late 16th century the two groups of bird dogs were distinctly differentiated. The English Setter, with its long head, curly coat, and well-developed ability to find and point game, showed evidence of crosses with Pointers, the large Water Spaniel and the Springer Spaniel. The modern breed was largely developed from a strain kept pure for over 35 years by its breeder, Reverend A. Harrison. In 1825, Edward Laverack obtained stock from him, from which, by inbreeding, he produced the foundation stock for the modern breed in both Britain and North America.

Characteristics

The English Setter is an intensely friendly and quiet-natured dog with a keen game sense. It is of medium height, clean in outline, and elegant both in appearance and movement. The head is long and rather lean. The eyes should be bright, mild, intelligent, and of a dark hazel color. The ears are of moderate length, set low and hanging close to the cheek; the tips are velvet, the upper parts clothed in fine, silky hair. The neck is long, muscular, and lean, the forequarters well set back, the chest deep in brisket, and the body of moderate length. The feathering on the tail is long, soft, and silky.

Brittany

English Setter

GERMAN WIRE-HAIRED POINTER

THIS DOG WAS DEVELOPED by selectively crossing several indigenous gundog breeds—the wire-haired Pointing Griffon, the Stichelhaar, the Puderpointer, and the German Shorthair, which, apart from the coat, it very closely resembles. The breed has been quite slow to gain recognition outside its native Germany, but now has a growing band of enthusiastic followers who appreciate its outstanding abilities as a brave and hardy all-purpose gundog, able both to point and to retrieve either on land or in water.

Characteristics
Essentially a dog of the Pointer type, of sturdy build, lively manner and with an intelligent, determined expression. In disposition the breed has been described as energetic, rather aloof, but not unfriendly. The head is moderately long with a broad skull, the ears are rounded and hang close to the sides of the head. The body is a little longer than it is high, the back short, straight, and strong, the back line perceptibly sloping from withers to croup. The chest is deep and capacious. The forelegs are straight, the hindlegs strong and muscular.

Group
Pointing Dogs (FCI).
Size
Height: Dogs 25½–27 in. (65–68 cm), bitches 24–25½ in. (61–65 cm). In AKC, dogs 25 in. (63.5 cm), bitches 24 in. (61 cm).
Weight: Dogs 60–66 lb. (27.2–29.9 kg), bitches 56–62 lb. (25.4–28 kg).
Coat
Color: May be either black and white, lemon and white, liver and white, or tri-color; flecks rather than heavy patching are preferred.
Texture: Slightly wavy, long and silky, the breeches and forelegs well feathered.

GERMAN SHORT-HAIRED POINTER (KURZHAAR)

THERE ARE FEW RECORDS of this breed before the Klub Kurzhaar stud book was started in the 1870s, but as with so many working breeds it had long been established among those who appreciated its working qualities. It probably has its origins in the dogs introduced by home-coming crusaders, intermingled with indigenous bird dogs and the Spanish Pointer, with style and elegance being largely dependent on the blood of the English Pointer. Nowadays the breed has a deservedly high reputation as a general-purpose gundog.

Characteristics
An aristocratic, well-balanced, symmetrical animal displaying power, endurance, and agility. Its expression should show enthusiasm for work without any sign of a nervous or flighty disposition. The head is clean-cut, the shoulders sloping, the chest deep, and the back short and powerful. Strong quarters provide propulsion for well-coordinated, economical movement. An extremely good-natured and reliable dog, with the bonus for a dog that loves the outdoors of being easy to keep clean.

Group
Pointing Dogs (FCI).
Size
Height: Dogs 23–25 in. (58–64 cm), bitches 21–23 in. (53–59 cm). In FCI, dogs 24–26 in. (62–66 cm), bitches not less than 23–25 in. (58–63 cm).
Weight: In AKC, dogs 55– 70 lb. (25–32 kg), bitches 45–60 lb. (20.4–27.2 kg).
Coat
Color: Solid liver or any combination of liver and white; black or any combination of black and white.
Texture: The skin is close and tight, the hair short and thick.

Group
Pointing Dogs (FCI).
Size
Height: Dogs 24–27 in. (60–67 cm), bitches 22–24 in. (56–62 cm).
Weight: Dogs 55–75 lb. (25–34 kg), bitches 45–64 lb. (20.5–29 kg).
Coat
Color: Liver and white, liver roan, or black and white.
Texture: Weather-resistant and to some extent water-repellent. Outer coat straight, harsh, wiry, lying flat, 1–2 in. (2.5–5 cm) in length; the undercoat is dense in winter, thinner in summer.

GORDON SETTER

Hungarian Visla

S EARLY AS 1620, a writer named Markham was able to remark that the "black and fallow setting dog" was the "hardest to endure labour." But it was not until the end of the 18th century, when the fourth Duke of Gordon's kennel of setters had made the breed famous, that the Gordon Castle Setters began to achieve fame outside Scotland and were described as being "easy to break and naturally back well. They are not fast dogs, but they have good staying powers and can keep on steadily from morning until night. Their noses are first-class and they seldom make a false point." The Gordon Setter has never achieved the popularity of the Irish or English Setters and so, perhaps, has avoided some of the worst effects of popular demand. As a result it remains an honest, basically sensible gundog.

Characteristics

The breed is stylish, built on galloping lines, having a thoroughbred appearance consistent with its build, which is comparable to that of a weight-carrying hunter. The back is strong, fairly short and level,

Group
Pointing Dogs (FCI).
Size
Height: Dogs 26 in. (66 cm), bitches 24½ in. (62 cm). In AKC, dogs 24– 27 in. (61–68.5 cm), bitches 23–25 in. (58.4–63.5 cm).
Weight: Dogs 65 lb. (29.5 kg), bitches 56 lb. (25.5 kg). AKC dogs 55–80 lb. (25– 36 kg), bitches 45–70 lb. (20–32 kg).
Coat
Color: Deep shining coal-black without any rustiness; rich tan markings.
Texture: Should be soft and shining, straight or slightly waved, but not curly. Long hair on ears, under the stomach and on the chest, on the back of the legs and under the tail.

the tail shortish, and the head fairly long, clearly lined and with an intelligent expression. The head is deep rather than broad, with a slightly rounded skull. Eyes are of a fair size, dark brown and bright; ears are medium-sized and rather thin, set low and hanging close to the head. The coat requires a fair amount of grooming, but the gleaming results make the effort worthwhile.

HUNGARIAN VIZSLA

HIS BREED IS SOMETIMES called the Hungarian Pointer, which gives some obvious clues to its origins and use. Drawings dating from the Magyar invasions a thousand years ago show Vizsla-like dogs being used in conjunction with falcons, and manuscripts of the 14th century make it clear that the Vizsla's role in falconry was well defined and that care was taken to ensure the purity of the breed. The First World War threatened the Vizsla's future, but the breed was brought back almost from the point of extinction to become a first-class dual-purpose gundog and to embark on a very successful show career in both Britain and America. The more common breed is short-haired; there is also a Hungarian Wire-haired Vizsla, which has been given an Interim standard by the Kennel Club. It is similar in every respect except for the texture of the coat.

Characteristics

The breed is robust yet lightly built, showing power and drive in the field, but with a tractable and affectionate nature in the home. The head is lean and muscular, moderately wide between the ears; the ears are thin and silky with rounded leathers hanging close to the cheeks. The eyes are of medium size. The neck is strong, smooth and muscular, moderately long and arched. The back is short, the withers high, and the top line slightly rounded with a moderately broad and deep chest. The tail is normally docked and set just below the level of the back. The gait is far-reaching, light-footed,

Group
Pointing Dogs (FCI).
Size
Height: Dogs, 22½–25 in. (57–64 cm), bitches 21–23½ in. (53–60 cm).
Weight: 48½–66 lb. (20–30 kg).
Coat
Color: Solid, rusty gold.
Texture: Short, smooth, dense, and close-lying, without evidence of a woolly undercoat. In the Wire-hair, the coat should be lustreless, short on the head and forelimbs, longer on the body and muzzle, with a slight beard.

IRISH SETTER

RELAND IS THE HOME of two breeds of setter: the Red and White, and the Red. The former has never achieved popular recognition and now survives only in the kennels of a few enthusiasts. The Red Setter, however, has achieved a degree of popularity which may not always have been to its benefit as it has

led to its being carelessly bred. In the early 19th century the Earl of Enniskillen's kennel contained nothing but solid-colored dogs which Stonehenge records as being of a "blood red, or rich chestnut or mahogany color," and it is from the kennels of such breeders that the modern uniformly colored breed has emerged.

Characteristics

The Irish Setter must be racy, with a flowing gait and a kindly expression. The head is long and lean, the skull oval from ear to ear, with a long muzzle. The eyes are dark hazel or dark brown; the ears, of moderate size and fine texture, are set on low and hang close to the head. The body is generally slim with a deep chest, a large rib-cage giving the dog plenty of room to breathe, and powerful hindquarters. The beautifully feathered tail is a feature. This is a very affectionate but restless and bouncy breed that will give ample rewards for firm training and plenty of exercise.

ITALIAN SPINONE

RECOGNIZED BY THE Kennel Club only as recently as 1994, this is never the less a long-established Continental "hunt, point, and retrieve" hound. Its blood is probably a mixture of native Italian hounds and the French Griffons. The Spinone is already proving popular in the UK as a readily trained and easily cared-for house dog and as a hardy worker.

Characteristics

A solid, muscular dog, with a free and relaxed gait. Fearless and adaptable as a gundog, it nevertheless makes a faithful and affectionate pet. The head is long with a flat skull, large open eyes, long pendulous ears, and powerful jaws. The short, strong neck merges into powerful shoulders. The length of the body equals the height at the withers, with a slightly sloping topline and deep, broad chest. The thick tail is usually docked to half its natural length.

Group
Pointing Dogs (FCI).
Size
Height: None specified by KC, but the norm is comparable to the AKC standard of 27 in. (68.5 cm) for dogs and 28 in. (63.5 cm) for bitches.
Weight: In AKC, dogs 70 lb. (31.7 kg), bitches 60 lb. (27.2 kg).
Coat
Color: Rich chestnut with no trace whatever of black.
Texture: Of moderate length, flat, and as free as possible from curl or wave on body; long and silky on ears, brisket, legs, and tail.

Group
Miscellaneous (AKC). Pointing Dogs (FCI).
Size
Height: Dogs 23½– 27½ in. (60–70 cm), bitches 23–25½ in. (59–65 cm).
Weight: Dogs 70–82 lb. (34–39 kg), bitches 62–71 lb. (29–34 kg).
Coat
Color: Entirely or predominantly white. May be marked or speckled in orange or brown.
Texture: Tough, thick, and close-fitting, with prominent eyebrows. The coat is mainly wiry, with the moustache and beard of softer hair.

POINTER

POINTERS HAVE BEEN USED in Britain since the mid-17th century to indicate by pointing just where game was hidden; for example, to locate the forms of hares for coursing. Early in the 18th century, when guns came into use, the Pointer began to function as a gundog. The breed's distinctive appearance owes something to the Foxhound, its elegance to the Greyhound, and its attitude to game-birds may derive from the same stock from which spaniels are descended. This perhaps accounts for the insistence by some authorities that the breed originated in Spain.

Characteristics

The Pointer is bred for work in the field and should look and act the part, giving an impression of compact power and agile grace allied to intelligence and alertness. The head is aristocratic with an unusual dish-shaped muzzle, the ears pendulous, the eyes rounded and dark. The body is of moderate length, the chest deep, and the tuck-up pronounced. Forelegs are straight, and the hindquarters muscular and powerful with great propelling leverage. The tail is not docked. The gait is smooth and powerful with the head carried high. The Pointer is a friendly and sociable dog requiring lots of exercise and needing frequent brushing to clean off the mud it will inevitably attract.

Group
Pointing Dogs (FCI).
Size
Height: In KC and FCI, dogs 25–27 in. (63–69 cm), bitches 24–26 in. (61–66 cm). AKC dogs 25–28 in. (63.5–71 cm), AKC bitches 23–26 in. (58.4–66 cm).
Weight: AKC dogs 55– 75 lb. (24.9–34 kg), bitches 45–65 lb. (20.4–29.4 kg).
Coat
Color: Liver, lemon, black, orange, solid or combined with white.
Texture: Short, dense, smooth with a sheen.

RETRIEVER, CURLY-COATED

THE CURLY-COATED RETRIEVER was established as a distinct breed by 1860 when it was first exhibited at Birmingham City Show. The breed had been produced as a gundog superbly adapted to working in water, on a basis of the Old English Water Spaniel, with the judicious introduction of Irish and English Water Spaniels, St John's Newfoundland, and Poodle.

Characteristics

A smart, upstanding dog which shows activity, endurance, and intelligence. The head is long and well proportioned, with black or brown eyes, and rather small, low-set ears lying close to the head. The neck is moderately long, the shoulders very deep and muscular. The chest is also deep and the hindquarters strong and muscular. The tail is moderately short, carried straight and covered with curls. This is an elegant, independent-minded animal, friendly enough but essentially an outdoor, working dog.

Group
Retrievers, Flushing Dogs and Waterdogs (FCI).
Size
Height: Dogs 27 in. (67.5 cm), bitches 25 in. (62.5 cm).
Coat
Color: Black or liver.
Texture: The main characteristic of the breed—one mass of crisp, small curls all over.

Pointer

RETRIEVER, FLAT-COATED

THE BREED IS A SUBTLE mixture of the St John's Newfoundland (a smaller version of the Newfoundland) with setters, sheepdogs, and spaniels, and is a first-class retriever of waterfowl. It was first shown in Britain in 1859 under a classification which included curly coats, wavy- or smooth-coated retrievers, but had to wait until 1873 when Mr E. Shirley, founder of the Kennel Club, took an interest in it and stabilized type. The breed was then overtaken in popularity by other gundog breeds, but in recent years has justly come back into favor. It now appears in the ring in healthy numbers and is re-establishing its reputation in the field.

Flat-coated Retriever

Characteristics

A bright, active dog of medium size with an intelligent expression, showing power and raciness. The head is long and nicely moulded, the skull flat and moderately broad, the jaw long and strong. The eyes are dark brown or hazel, of medium size, the ears small and fitting close to the side of the head. The neck is long, the chest deep and fairly broad, the forelegs straight and well feathered, the back short. Hindquarters are muscular and the tail is short, straight, and well set-on, carried gaily and wagged with enthusiasm. A friendly dog that loves humans.

Group
Retrievers, Flushing Dogs and Waterdogs (FCI).
Size
Height: Dogs 23–24 in. (59–61.5 cm), bitches22–23 in. 9 56.5–59 cm).
Weight: Dogs 60–80 lb. (27–36 kg), bitches 55–70 lb. (25–32 kg).
Coat
Color: Black or liver.
Texture: Dense, of fine quality and texture, and as flat as possible.

RETRIEVER, GOLDEN

IT HAS BEEN SUGGESTED that the Golden Retriever has its origins in a troupe of Russian circus dogs which Lord Tweedsmouth saw and bought in Britain. It is perhaps a pity that there is no factual evidence to support such a story. What really happened was that in 1865 he bought, from a cobbler in Brighton, a yellow wavy-coated retriever bred by Lord Chichester. This he mated to a Tweedwater Spaniel, a breed local to his home in the English/Scottish Borders, and then bred on to further crosses with Tweedwater Spaniels, black retrievers, an Irish Setter and a Bloodhound, so that by 1913 the Kennel Club was able to recognize the result as a separate breed. They were first known as Retrievers (Golden or Yellow) but, in 1920, the name was changed to Retrievers (Golden). From inception to recognition as a breed had taken a mere 45 years, simply because breeders were selecting stock for their reputation as gundogs. Nowadays the breed also does good service as a guide dog for the blind.

Characteristics

The Golden Retriever is symmetrical, active, and powerful, a good level mover, sound and well put together. The head is broad, the expression kindly, the eyes dark, the muzzle squarish and the jaw strong. The body has strong shoulders, a deep chest, and muscular hindquarters. It is one of the most popular breeds, though this has led to overbreeding and the occasional fault in physique or temperament; but, if you select your puppy from good, sound stock, you will be rewarded with an affectionate pet.

Group
Retrievers, Flushing Dogs and Waterdogs (FCI).
Size
Height: Dogs 22–24 in. (56–61 cm), bitches 20–22 in. (51–56 cm). In AKC, dogs 23–24 in. (58.4–61 cm), bitches 21½–22½ in. (54.5–57 cm).
Coat
Color: Any shade of gold or cream, but neither red nor mahogany.
Texture: Flat or wavy with good feathering and a dense, water-resistant undercoat.

RETRIEVER, LABRADOR

IN 1822, REPORTS OF "small water dogs . . . admirably trained as retrievers in fowling and . . . otherwise useful" indicated that there existed in New-foundland a breed of gundog which British sportsmen were quick to recognize as first-class. Colonel Hawker, a noted sportsman of the time, described them as "by far the best for any kind of shooting," while the Earl of Malmesbury noted that they had a "close coat which turns the water off like oil and a tail like an otter." The Earl's knowledge of gundogs far surpassed his grasp of geography, because he referred to the dogs that came from Newfoundland as Labradors. When new stock from Newfoundland became hard to come by, attempts were made to introduce the blood of other gundogs, but the strong characteristics of the original breed proved to be dominant and survived. Labradors have frequently won the Kennel Club Best in Show award at Cruft's.

Yellow Labrador puppy

Characteristics

The general appearance is that of a strongly built, short-coupled, very active dog, with a broad skull, broad and deep through the chest and ribs, and broad and strong over the loins and hindquarters. The dog must move neither too wide nor too close in front or behind, but must stand and move true all round on legs and feet. The tail is a distinctive feature and should be very thick at the base, gradually tapering toward the tip and giving that peculiar rounded appearance which has been described as the "otter" tail. This is one of the most popular breeds in the world—in 1997, it accounted for one-third of all Gundog registrations in the UK, over twice as many as the Golden Retriever or the Cocker Spaniel. Because of this enormous popularity, some faults have crept in and you should be careful not to choose a puppy that seems nervous or has a tendency to snap. But if your dog comes from sound stock, it will prove a gentle, biddable, and affectionate pet. The only risk is that it will run to fat if it does not receive adequate exercise.

Group
Retrievers, Flushing Dogs and Waterdogs (FCI).
Size
Height: Dogs 22–22½ in. (56–57 cm), bitches 21½–22 in. (54–56 cm). In AKC, dogs 22½–24½ in. (57–62 cm), bitches 21½–23½ in. (54.5–60 cm).
Coat
Color: Color is generally black or yellow but other whole colors are permitted. The AKC also mentions chocolate.
Texture: The coat is short, dense, and without wave, with a weather-resistant undercoat; it should be fairly hard.

Yellow, chocolate, and black Labradors

SPANIEL, AMERICAN COCKER

A DISTINCTIVE, GLAMOROUS gundog, which was developed in America from Cocker Spaniels imported from England. It has now achieved a considerable degree of popularity on both sides of the Atlantic, both as a companion and as a show dog.

Characteristics

The smallest member of the gundog group, the American Cocker is sturdy and compact with a cleanly chiselled and refined head, rounded skull, and pronounced stop. The eyes are round, full and look directly forward, the ears long and lobular with fine leather and plenty of feathering. The neck is long and muscular, the body short and compact, the back strong, the chest deep, and the hindquarters wide and well muscled. The tail is well set-on and conventionally docked short. A well-put-together American Cocker never appears long or low. It moves effortlessly and is eager to work. As a pet it is lively, friendly and obedient, enjoying plenty of exercise. The coat, which is perhaps the most glamorous in the gundog group, requires frequent grooming and occasional trimming to maintain its superb quality. The long ears and the feet should be checked regularly for matted hair or signs of infection.

Group
Retrievers, Flushing Dogs and Waterdogs (FCI).
Size
Height: Dogs 14¼–15¼ in. (36.25–38.75 cm), bitches 13¼–14¼ in. (33.75– 36.25 cm).
Coat
Color: Black, with or without tan markings; or parti-colored, roan, or tricolor. The AKC standard also allows any solid color other than black.
Texture: Silky, flat or slightly wavy, and profuse.

SPANIEL, CLUMBER

THE CLUMBER IS A VERY different animal from other spaniels—heavier, longer, and lower to the ground—indicating that we should look elsewhere when considering its origins. The body shape suggests some Basset Hound blood, while the heavy head is suggestive of the old Alpine Spaniel. The breed seems to have been produced from imported spaniels kept by the Duke of Newcastle at his Clumber Park Estate in Nottinghamshire. As is so often the case when one kennel concentrates its attention on producing dogs for a particular purpose, a distinctive type soon emerged and was quickly appreciated by other sportsmen. By 1859, Clumber Spaniels were being shown and had achieved considerable popularity as gundogs particularly well adapted to country with abundant game. In more recent years the breed has declined in popularity but is maintained in small numbers by a few dedicated and enthusiastic breeders.

Characteristics

The Clumber is nothing if not distinctive: it is a dog with a thoughtful expression, very solidly built but active, and moves with a characteristic rolling gait. The head is large, square, and massive, with heavy brows. The muzzle is heavy with pendulous skin over the jaw. The eyes are dark amber, the ears large and vine-leaf-shaped, well covered with straight hair. The neck is fairly long, thick, and powerful. The shoulders are sloping and muscular, the chest is deep, and the legs are straight, thick, and strong. The body is long and heavy, close to the ground; the back is straight, broad, and long. The hindquarters are very powerful and extremely well developed. The tail is low set and carried level with the back. Less openly affectionate and more independent than other spaniels, the Clumber never the less makes an intelligent and good-natured companion.

Group
Retrievers, Flushing Dogs and Waterdogs (FCI).
Size
Weight: Dogs 80 lb. (36 kg), bitches 65 lb. (29.5 kg). In AKC, dogs 55–65 lb. (24.9–29.4 kg), bitches 35–50 lb. (15.8–22.6 kg).
Coat
Color: Plain white with lemon markings, orange permissible.
Texture: Abundant, close, silky, and straight. The legs are well feathered.

Clumber Spaniel

SPANIEL, COCKER

Cocker Spaniel

THE BREED'S NAME provides clues to both its early function and its origins. Like other spaniels, the Cocker (known in North America as the English Cocker) is a descendant of the dogs which, in Spain, were used to drive birds into nets. It is referred to in the prologue to Chaucer's *Wife of Bath's Tale* showing that, even by the 14th century, "Spaynels" had attained some degree of popularity in England. However, at this time the distinctions between spaniels of different types had not been drawn, though by 1780, when Thomas Bewick wrote his *History of Quadrupeds*, he was able to say "the Springer or Cocker is lively, active and pleasant, and an unwearied pursuer of its game and very expert in raising woodcocks and snipes from their haunts in woods and marshes." Then the breed was called the cocking-spaniel. The dog used to flush out woodcock, and thus it came by its present name.

Characteristics

The general appearance of the Cocker is of a merry sporting dog, well balanced and compact. The head is well developed and cleanly chiselled, neither too fine nor too coarse. The eyes should be full but not prominent, the rims tight, with an expression of intelligence and gentleness; the ears are long and set low, well clothed with long, silky, straight hair. The neck is of moderate length and clean in throat, the shoulders sloping and fine, the chest well developed, and the brisket deep. The legs are well boned, straight, and feathered. The body should be immensely strong and compact for the size and weight of the dog. The hindquarters should be wide, well rounded, and very muscular, with feathering above the hock. The tail is customarily docked, but not too short—the concern is that its constant cheerful action should not interfere with its work. The immense popularity of this breed has led to some problems of temperament, so be especially careful to select a puppy from reliable stock. A good Cocker makes a loving and gentle pet, but requires firm early training, plenty of exercise, and regular grooming with particular attention to the ears and feet.

Group
Retrievers, Flushing Dogs and Waterdogs (FCI).
Size
Height: Dogs approximately 15½–16 in. (39–41 cm), bitches approximately 15–15½ in. (38–39 cm).
Weight: Approximately 28–32 lb. (12.75–14.5 kg) for both sexes.
Coat
Color: Various.
Texture: Flat, silky in texture, never wiry or wavy, with sufficient feather; not too profuse and never curly.

SPANIEL, ENGLISH SPRINGER

THOMAS BEWICK, WRITING during the 18th century, did not differentiate between Springer and Cocker Spaniels, though there was in the early 17th century a tendency to refer to the larger spaniels, which were used to startle game so that they sprang into the air, as Starter or Springer Spaniels. With the advent of quick-firing guns which increased their popularity, these early Springers were divided into the lighter Welsh Springers and the heavier English ones. The latter, for a while, included a variety, which was developed by a Duke of Norfolk, known as Norfolk Spaniels, but they became uniformly known as English Springers in 1902.

Characteristics

The modern Springer is a symmetrical, compact, strong, upstanding, merry, and active dog, built for both endurance and

SPANIEL, FIELD

Field Spaniel

activity. It is the longest-legged and the raciest of the British land spaniels. The body is solid and muscular with a deep chest and slight arch up to the loins. The tail is set low and, when allowed to grow, is well feathered and has a lively action. It is, however, normally docked. The Springer Spaniel moves with a distinctive, easy stride that gives it an air of relaxed confidence. It has boundless energy but will reward firm training and plenty of exercise by becoming a friendly and obedient companion.

THIS IS AN ENGLISH gundog which popularity has unaccountably bypassed in favor of other breeds. It was developed in the 19th century from crossings between the now-unknown Sussex Springer and the Cocker Spaniel. For some time during its early career in the show ring it was classified with the Cocker, then, having attained full breed status, lost it again during the 1950s and 1960s because numbers had fallen so low. Though it is still not numerous, the breed seems to be firmly established, thanks to the determined efforts of a handful of enthusiasts.

Characteristics

A well-balanced dog, noble, upstanding, and sporting, built for activity and endurance and combining beauty with utility and unusual docility. The head is strongly characteristic of the breed; the skull has a pronounced occiput (a visible bump at the upper back of the skull), the muzzle is long and lean. The eyes show a grave but not hard expression. The neck is long, strong, and muscular, set into long and sloping shoulders which give great activity and speed. The body is of moderate length, the chest deep, the back and loins strong and muscular. The tail, normally docked by one-third, is carried as an extension of the back, not elevated above it. Unusually, the standard specifies that the breed is unsuitable for city life. It is, however, a docile companion for an active country dweller.

> **Group**
> Retrievers, Flushing Dogs and Waterdogs (FCI).
> **Size**
> **Height:** 20 in. (51 cm). In AKC, bitches may be1 in. (2 cm) smaller.
> **Coat**
> **Color:** Liver and white or black and white, in either case with or without tan markings.
> **Texture:** Close, straight, and weather-resistant, without being coarse.

> **Group**
> Retrievers, Flushing Dogs and Waterdogs (FCI).
> **Size**
> **Height:** About 18 in. (45.7 cm).
> **Weight:** 40–55 lb. (18–25 kg).
> **Coat**
> **Color:** Black, liver, or roan, with or without tan markings.
> **Texture:** Flat or slightly waved, never curled but silky, glossy, and refined-looking.

English Springer Spaniel

SPANIEL, IRISH WATER

IRISH WATER SPANIELS represent a very old type of dog, found throughout Europe, which emerged in Ireland as a distinct breed probably as early as the 12th century. At this period and for some time afterward it was called by various names, including Shannon Spaniel, Rat or Whip-tail Spaniel, and Southern Irish Water Spaniel. From the 12th century until the emergence in 1834 of Boatswain, the man who was to help establish the modern breed, there are records of these distinctive dogs leaving Ireland as gifts. Nowadays, the Irish Water Spaniel is a gundog bred to work in shooting.

Characteristics

The Irish Water Spaniel slightly resembles a Standard Poodle, with a similar dense, curly coat, dropping ears and long, pointed muzzle. But this is primarily a working dog, never clipped into the extravagant styles that characterize the show poodle. It has powerful shoulders and a characteristic barrel-shaped ribcage which accentuates its rolling gait. The short unfeathered tail tapers to a fine point. Steady and reliable in the home as well as the field, the Irish Water Spaniel will take all the exercise you can give it.

Group
Retrievers, Flushing Dogs and Waterdogs (FCI).
Size
Height: Dogs 21–23 in. (53–58 cm), bitches 20–22 in. (51–56 cm).
Coat
Color: A rich, dark liver.
Texture: Should be composed of dense, tight, crisp ringlets free from woolliness and having a natural oiliness.

SPANIEL, SUSSEX

A CERTAIN MR FULLER, AIDED and abetted by Phineas Bullock, had a considerable hand in developing this distinctive breed of spaniel. The Sussex Spaniel emerged in days when breeding was organized in a very different way, utilizing large numbers of sturdy, well-trained dogs. Because conditions have now changed, and spaniels with a greater turn of speed and the ability to cover more ground have become increasingly popular, the Sussex Spaniel survives in dangerously low numbers, having to rely solely on the enthusiasm of a few devoted admirers.

Characteristics

The Sussex Spaniel is stocky and strongly built, with a characteristic rolling movement unlike that of any other spaniel. The head is broad and solid, almost like a scaled-down Clumber Spaniel. The large, hazel eyes have the soft expression common to most spaniels, but the wrinkles on the forehead give the Sussex a misleadingly worried frown; the large ears hang close to the head and are covered in soft, wavy hair. The whole body is strong and muscular, with strong bones in the legs. The tail is normally docked to a length of 5–7 in. (12.75–17.75 cm), but the dog still manages to wag it enthusiastically.

Group
Retrievers, Flushing Dogs and Waterdogs (FCI).
Size
Height: 15–16 in. (38–41 cm). In AKC, 13–15½ in. (33–39 cm)
Weight: About 50 lb. (23 kg). In AKC, 40–45 lb. (18–20.4 kg).
Coat
Color: Rich, golden liver.
Texture: Abundant and flat, with no tendency to curl and with ample undercoat.

Sussex Spaniel

SPANIEL, WELSH SPRINGER

HISTORY DOES NOT RECORD the advent of the Welsh Springer Spaniel as a distinct breed, though red and white spaniels similar to the modern Welsh are to be seen in many old sporting drawings and paintings. The standard for the breed confirms its ancient origin and refers to its old Welsh name of "Starter." The Welsh Springer is a first-class gundog and makes an excellent companion as well as an eye-catching show dog.

Characteristics

This is a very active dog in need of plenty of exercise—the first impression is one of compact strength and stamina. The head is fairly square with a slight dome, and the ears are shorter and less silky than the typical spaniel ears. The neck and shoulders are particularly strong, the chest deep and the hindquarters muscular. The tail is normally docked short, leaving the Welsh Springer to wag its rump merrily.

Group
Retrievers, Flushing Dogs and Waterdogs (FCI).
Size
Height: Dogs about 19 in. (48 cm), bitches about 18 in. (46 cm).
Weight: In FCI, 34–45 lb. (15.4–20.4 kg).
Coat
Color: Rich red and white.
Texture: Straight and thick, of a silky texture, never wiry or wavy.

WEIMARANER

THE WEIMARANER'S HISTORY goes back only to the beginning of the 19th century, when it was produced by crossing Bloodhounds with native German hunting breeds such as the Red Schweisshund; it became known simply as the Weimar Pointer. The Weimaraner is, therefore, one of the many breeds which talented German breeders produced in order to fulfill some particular purpose. In its early days it was used to hunt Europe's larger game, such as boar and deer, but it is now very much at home fulfilling the duties of a gundog accompanying modern sportsmen. The Weimaraner is not a kennel dog, being happier and working much better when living as part of the family. Its distinctive color and silent, effortless movement have earned it the popular name of "Gray Ghost."

Characteristics

The breed must be fearless, friendly, protective, and obedient. The Weimaraner is a medium-sized dog with considerable presence. Its head is moderately long and aristocratic; the eyes are unusually light, amber or blue-gray, and the ears are long and lobular, slightly folded and set high. The forelegs are straight and strong, and the hindquarters powerful. The body is square in outline with a level topline and sloping croup, deep chest, and moderate tuck-up. The tail is traditionally docked.

Group
Pointing Dogs (FCI).
Size
Height: Dogs 24–27 in. (61–69 cm), bitches 22–25 in. (56–64 cm). AKC dogs 25–27 in. (63.5–68.5 cm), bitches 23–25 in. (58.4– 63.5 cm). FCI dogs 25–27 in. (59–70 cm), bitches 23–25 in. (57–65 cm).
Coat
Color: Preferably silver gray, shades of mouse or roe gray.
Texture: Short, smooth, and sleek. There is a less popular long-haired type whose coat is 1–2 in. (2.5–5 cm) long on the body and whose limbs are feathered.

Weimaraner

Terriers

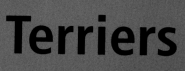

All dogs in this section are classed as Terriers by KC, AKC, and ANKC, and as Large and Medium-sized Terriers by FCI, unless otherwise stated.

AIREDALE TERRIER

THE AIREDALE IS BY FAR the largest of the terriers, and for that reason is sometimes referred to as the King of Terriers. In fact, the breed's size makes it something of an oddity, and both in origin and function it probably owes as much to the hound group as it does to the terriers. The Airedale was developed to combine some of the capabilities of terriers and hounds, terrier characteristics being inherited from the Old English Rough-Coated Black and Tan Terrier, and hound characteristics, including size, from the Otterhound. The breed's size, courage, and intelligence make it an excellent guard and police dog. It has also been used as a hunting dog for exotic game in many lands.

Characteristics

The Airedale is keen of expression and quick of movement. Its character is shown in the expression of the eyes and in the carriage of the ears and tail. The head is long and flat, the jaws deep, powerful, strong, and muscular. The eyes are dark, small, full of terrier keenness and intelligence, the neck clean and muscular set into long, well-laid-back shoulders. The forelegs are perfectly straight. The back is short, strong, and level, the chest deep but not broad, the loin and hindquarters muscular. The tail is set on high and carried gaily but should not be curled. The coat is shed twice a year and should be professionally stripped; in between times it needs daily brushing to maintain the characteristic neat appearance. The Airedale makes a loyal family pet, good with children and protective of its owner. Though unlikely to be the aggressor in a confrontation, it will react if provoked and requires firm early training to keep this tendency under control.

Size
Height: Dogs 23–24 in. 958–61 cm), bitches, 22–23 in. (56–59· cm). In AKC, dogs approximately 23 in. (58·cm), bitches slightly less.
Coat
Color: Tan with black or grizzle on a "saddle," on the top of the neck and on the top of the tail.
Texture: Hard, dense and wiry.

AUSTRALIAN TER-RIER

ONE OF VERY FEW TERRIER breeds that originated outside the British Isles. Although it was undoubtedly bred from old British breeds, it is impossible to say precisely which ones. The Australian's slightly old-fashioned appearance is probably closer to some of these old breeds than are their modern counterparts. Recognition came in 1892 with the formation of a club to look after the breed's interests, since which time it has achieved a modest popularity throughout the world.

Characteristics

The Australian Terrier is a rather low-set dog; it is compact and active with a long head, flat skull, soft topknot, and powerful jaw. The eyes are small, keen, and dark in color, and the ears are small, set high on the skull, pricked or dropped toward the front and fringed with long hair. The neck is inclined to be long in proportion to the body, with a frill of hair. The forelegs are perfectly straight, and are set well under the body, with a slight feather at the knee. The body is long in proportion to its height and the back is straight. The hindquarters have

Airedale Terrier

good strong thighs with hocks slightly bent. The tail is normally docked. A playful and extrovert dog, the Australian Terrier makes a very good family pet. It is also an alert house dog and will warn you—quite loudly—if there are any strangers approaching.

Size
Height: Approximately 10 in. (25.5 cm).
Weight: Approximately 14 lb. (6.3 kg). In AKC, 12–14 lb. (5.4–6.3 kg).
Coat
Color: There are two types: either blue or gray-blue, with tan on legs and face, and a blue or silver topknot ; or clear sandy or red, with a lighter topknot.
Texture: Straight hair 2–2½ in. (5–6 cm) long, of hard texture.

BEDLINGTON TERRIER

THIS IS ONE OF SEVERAL sporting terriers which come from the valleys of north-east England. The Bedlington's present name and its original name of Rothbury Terrier indicate precisely its place of origin. As a breed it owes much to the old rough-coated breeds which were kept as vermin killers by the sporting farmers and shepherds of Northumbria. Bedlingtons were developed with a longer leg, a longer, leaner head and a characteristic roached back, all of which suggest some Whippet blood, as does their ability to course a rabbit. The first club was formed in 1877, since which time the breed's original hardness and fighting qualities have been overlaid with a quiet, gentle disposition. In the hands of skilled trimmers its appearance has been transformed, and is very distinctive.

Characteristics

A graceful, lithe, muscular dog with no sign of either weakness or coarseness. The head should be pear- or wedge-shaped and the expression in repose mild and gentle, though not shy or nervous. When roused, the eyes should sparkle and the dog look full of temper and courage. Bedlingtons are capable of galloping at great speed. The movement is distinctive: rather mincing, light and springy in the slower paces, with perhaps a slight roll when in full stride. The Bedlington does not shed its coat, so may be a good choice for would-be dog-owners prone to allergies. But it needs daily brushing and regular clipping to keep it smart. Although devoted to its human family, the Bedlington is not altogether reliable with other dogs.

Bedlington Terrier

Size
Height: 16 in. (41 cm). In AKC, dogs 16–17½ in. (41–44 cm) and bitches 15–16½ in. (38–41.8 cm).
Weight: 18–23 lb. (8.2–10.4 kg). In AKC, 17–23 lb. (7.7–10.4 kg).
Coat
Color: Blue, liver, or sandy, or any of these colors with tan markings.
Texture: Very distinctive, thick and "woolly."

BORDER TERRIER

ANOTHER BREED THAT HAS origins in Northumbria which may retain a greater similarity to the ancient terrier stock than do its cousins, the Dandie Dinmont and the Bedlington. The Border Terrier was developed to run with hounds and to eject a fox from its earth, and so was an essential part of the system of fox control in the sheep-grazed hills of its homeland. The name derives from the connection with the Border Foxhounds, though neighboring packs also contributed to its development, as did other packs of foxhounds and other hounds since recognition in 1920. The breed retains close contact with its original purpose and is still much valued as a working terrier, though it is also at home in the show ring or by the fireside.

Characteristics

The Border Terrier is essentially a working terrier able to follow a horse; it must therefore combine activity with gameness. The head is a distinctive feature, resembling that of an otter, moderately broad in skull, with a short strong muzzle. The eyes are dark with a keen expression, the ears V-shaped and dropping forward close to the cheek. The neck is of moderate length, forelegs straight and not too heavy in bone. The body is deep, narrow, and fairly long, the hindquarters strong and racy. The tail is undocked, moderately short, and thick at the base. Bred for action and stamina, the Border needs a surprising amount of exercise for such a small dog. If you can provide this, it will make a good-natured and adaptable companion.

Size
Weight: Dogs 13–15½ lb. (5.9–7.1 kg), bitches 11½–14 lb. (5.1–6.4 kg).
Coat
Color: Red, wheaten, grizzle and tan, or blue and tan.
Texture: Harsh and dense and not over-long with a close undercoat. The skin must be thick; the American standard asks for a loose-fitting skin.

BULL TERRIER

AMERICA DIFFERENTIATES between white and colored Bull Terriers, but in England no such difference exists and they remain, white or colored, the same breed. The Bull Terrier is not of ancient origin, but was produced by crosses of the now-extinct English White Terrier with the type of Bulldog which existed in the early 19th century. The breed owes its development to James Hinks, a 19th-century Birmingham dog-dealer who, according to Rawdon Lee, writing in 1894, was quite prepared to test the quality of his show dogs in fights against other dogs. Not for nothing is the breed known as the gladiator of the terrier group, though breeders have now succeeded in producing a dog with all the old ability to fight but a much more sociable disposition. A Miniature Bull Terrier achieved recognition as a separate breed in Britain in 1943, but has yet to achieve the popularity of the larger version. Except with regard to size its standard is the same as for the Bull Terrier.

Bull Terrier

Characteristics

The Bull Terrier must be strongly built, muscular, symmetrical, and active, with a keen, determined, and intelligent expression. It should be full of fire and courage, but of even temperament and amenable to discipline. The head is a characteristic of the breed, being long, egg-shaped, and free from hollows or indentations. The eyes are narrow, triangular, and obliquely placed, black or as dark a brown as possible; the ears are small, thin, and erect. The neck is long, arched, and very muscular, fitting into strong and muscular shoulders. The body is well rounded, the back is short and strong, and the hindquarters are powerfully muscled. The tail should be short. Despite its pugnacious history and aggressive appearance, the Bull Terrier is affectionate with both adults and children and loves attention. White Bull Terriers are often born deaf, so you should always have a puppy's hearing checked before you go ahead and buy it. The problem seems to be less prominent in colored types, which were developed specifically to combat it.

Size
Height: The KC standard does not specify a height or weight, but both sexes should give an impression of "maximum substance." Miniatures should be no more than 14 in. (35.5 cm). In AKC, 21–22 in. (53–56 cm)
Weight: In AKC, 52–62 lb. (23.5–28 kg).
Coat
Color: White or colored. If colored, brindle is preferred; however, black, red, fawn, or tricolor are also acceptable.
Texture: Short, flat, even, and harsh to the touch with a fine gloss. The skin should fit the dog tightly.

CAIRN TERRIER

A DESCENDANT OF THE working terriers of Scotland and the Isle of Skye, the breed retains some of the appearance and characteristics of the older breeds, though it is no longer in demand as a working terrier. Its history is not well documented, so it is impossible to be sure to which modern breed it is closest. Authorities in the past often saw the Cairn as a short-haired Skye Terrier, but in the early 1900s, after a protest by Skye Terrier breeders, the name was changed to Cairn Terrier. As such, Cairns have achieved a considerable popularity.

Characteristics

This terrier should impress with its fearless and gay disposition, the general appearance of an active, game, and shaggy little dog, strong though compactly built, very free in movement and with a generally foxy appearance. It should stand well forward on its forepaws, and have a compact straight back of medium length with a deep rib-cage. The hindquarters are very strong, the tail short and well furnished with hair. A friendly, inquisitive, fun-loving companion, whose only potential fault is overprotectiveness of its owner. This can be overcome by early training and careful attention to socialization.

Size
Height: 11–12 in. (28–31 cm). In AKC, dogs 10 in. (25.4 cm), bitches 9½ in. (24 cm).
Weight: 14–16 lb. (6–7.5 kg). In AKC, dogs 14 lb. (6 kg), bitches 13 lb. (5.8 kg).
Coat
Color: Cream, wheaten, red, gray, or nearly black. Any of these colors may be brindled. The AKC standard allows any color except white.
Texture: Must be double-coated with a profuse, hard but not coarse outer coat, and a short, soft, close undercoat.

DANDIE DINMONT TERRIER

A BREED WHICH OWES ITS present name to a character in Walter Scott's *Guy Mannering*, but which was certainly in existence in the Cheviot Hills long before the book was published in 1815. The Dandie is a close relation of both the Border and Bedlington Terriers, and, although the three breeds are very different in overall appearance, the discerning eye can see some family resemblances. The Dandie Dinmont has never achieved a great popularity either as a show dog or as a companion, although it is intelligent and particularly good with children. It has a stubborn streak that responds well to firm handling.

Characteristics

A very distinctive breed with a strong and rather large head. The dark eyes, set wide apart, are full and round, the ears pendulous, falling close to the cheek. The neck is very muscular and well set into strong shoulders. The forelegs are short and very muscular, set wide apart. The body is long, strong, and flexible, the chest let well down between the forelegs. The hindquarters are set wide apart, the thighs well developed. The tail is short, carried a little above the level of the body.

Size
Weight: 8–24 lb. (8–11 kg), with the lower end of the range preferred.
Coat
Color: Pepper or mustard.
Texture: A mixture of hardish and soft hair, giving a coat which feels crisp to the touch but not wiry.

FOX TERRIER, SMOOTH

THE SMOOTH FOX TERRIER is undoubtedly the aristocrat of the terrier group, able to look back over a long history of work with hounds. At the beginning of the 20th century, it was among the most popular of companions and show dogs. This early popularity has meant that there is a considerable literature devoted to the breed, as well as a mass of carefully drawn illustrations which demonstrate that it has changed very little since the publication of Daniel's *Rural Sports* in 1801. So highly prized were Fox Terriers in the late 1800s that large kennels were maintained, and prices for a good specimen ran into several hundreds of pounds.

Characteristics

The dog must present a gay and active appearance and be compactly built, though not in any way coarse. The symmetry of the Foxhound may be taken as a model for the breed: he must stand like a cleverly made hunter, covering a lot of ground, yet with a short back. A friendly dog that makes an ideal pet, he needs to be carefully controlled in the country, where his hunting instincts are liable to get the better of him.

Size
Height: Not specified in KC. In AKC, dogs 15½ in. (39 cm) maximum, bitches proportionately shorter.
Weight: In KC and FCI, dogs 16–18 lb. (7.3–8.2 kg), bitches 15–17 lb. (6.8–7.7 kg). In AKC, dogs about 18 lb. (8 kg), bitches slightly less.
Coat
Color: White should predominate, with tan, black, or black and tan markings acceptable.
Texture: Straight, flat, smooth, hard, dense, and abundant.

Smooth Fox Terrier

FOX TERRIER, WIRE

THE EARLY FOX TERRIER BREEDERS, like the breeders of working terriers today, did not differentiate between smooth- and broken-coated dogs, the adage of "handsome is as handsome does" being applicable here. Both coats appeared in the same litter, but for companions and show dogs the smarter smooth coats were at first preferred. The wire coats followed them into the show ring about 25 years after the Smooth's debut. Nowadays, with better skills in trimming and presentation, it is the Wire which takes the high prizes.

Characteristics

As for the Smooth (see left), except for coat texture.

Size
Height: Dogs 15½ in. (39 cm) maximum, bitches slightly less.
Weight: Ideally dogs 18 lb. (8.25 kg), bitches slightly less.
Coat
Color: As for the Smooth.
Texture: Dense and wiry.

IRISH TERRIER

THE IRISH TERRIER SHARES much of the same origin as the Kerry Blue (see right), the other Irish terrier which has achieved distinction in the show ring. The breed made its show debut in 1879, but had been known and admired by the sporting gentry of Ireland for very many years before. Like so many terriers, it is hardy and adaptable, loyal, and makes an excellent guard.

Characteristics

Of all the fearless terrier breeds, the Irish is perhaps the one which comes closest to sheer recklessness, prepared to dash headlong after any adversary, oblivious to the consequences. It is even-tempered with people and completely trustworthy with children, but sometimes fiery with other dogs. It is active, lively, lithe, and wiry in appearance, entirely lacking in clumsiness. The head is long, the skull flat, the eyes dark, the ears small and V-shaped. The neck is of fair length, the shoulders fine, long, and sloping well into the back. The chest is deep and muscular, the body moderately long, the loins muscular and slightly arched, the hindquarters and thighs powerful. The tail is generally docked.

Size
Height: Dogs 19 in. (48 cm), bitches 18 in. (46 cm). In AKC and FCI, both sexes 18 in. (46 cm).
Weight: In AKC and FCI, both sexes 25–27 lb. (11.5–12 kg).
Coat
Color: Bright red, red-wheaten or yellow-red.
Texture: Hard and wiry, with a broken appearance.

KERRY BLUE TER-RIER

THE KERRY BLUE SHARES a common ancestry with the Soft-Coated Wheaten Terrier, and shares, too, a common birthplace among the mountains of Kerry, where it was developed to provide sport, security and companionship for the sporting farmers of that area. Nowadays, by careful breeding, skilful trimming, and painstaking presentation, it has been transformed into a very successful show dog, to a far greater degree than other Irish terriers. It is much more dandified than when it first appeared in the ring or lived the sporting life about the farms of Kerry.

Characteristics

The standard specifies that the Kerry Blue Terrier should exhibit a "disciplined gameness." It is a compact, powerful terrier showing gracefulness and an attitude of alert determination, with a definite terrier style and character. Typically it should be upstanding and well proportioned, with a well-developed and muscular body. The head is long and lean, the jaw is strong and deep, the eyes are dark, and the ears are small and V-shaped. The beard and eyebrows are prominent, while the hair on the rest of the head is kept short. The forelegs are straight and powerful, and the hindquarters are large and well developed. The body is short, with a deep chest. The topline is level, the tail set high and carried erect. As a pet, the Kerry Blue is quite demanding in terms of its exercise, food, and grooming requirements. Affectionate by nature, it also has a fiery temper that needs to be controlled by firm early training.

Size
Height: Dogs 18–19 in. (46–48 cm) at shoulder, bitches slightly less. In AKC, dogs 18–19½ in. (46–50 cm), bitches 17½–19 in. (44–48 cm).
Weight: Both sexes ideally 35 lb. (15.9 kg), though 33–37 lb. (15–16.8 kg) is acceptable for dogs, with bitches proportionately less. In AKC, dogs 33–40 lb (15–18 kg), bitches slightly less.
Coat
Color: Blue, with or without black points.
Texture: Soft, silky, plentiful, and wavy.

Kerry Blue Terrier

LAKELAND TERRIER

Lakeland Terrier

THE LAKELAND TERRIER WAS developed as a working terrier with the packs of hounds which hunt the rugged country in England's Lake District. It is to the north-western hunts of England what the Border Terrier is to the hunts of the north-east, and it is inevitable that during the development of both breeds there should be traffic between the two regions. Nowadays, unlike the Border, the Lakeland has split to produce two distinct types: those which are still used for work and which are to be seen in some numbers at terrier shows organized by hunts; and a much more refined and skilfully groomed type exhibited at Kennel Club shows where, in spite of its small numbers, the breed still achieves considerable success.

Characteristics

The Lakeland has a smart, workmanlike appearance with a gay, fearless demeanor. The skull is flat and refined, the eyes dark, and the ears moderately small, V-shaped, and carried alertly. The muzzle is quite long and covered with longer hair than the rest of the body. The neck is extended, the shoulders well laid back, forelegs straight and well boned. The chest is narrow, the back strong and moderately short. The hindquarters are strong and muscular, with hocks low to the ground. The tail is customarily docked to a medium length and is carried gaily. This is an immensely fun-loving, even naughty dog, bright, fearless, and affectionate. It has remarkable stamina and can take plenty of exercise. Its coat should be stripped professionally every six months, but between haircuts is easy to keep neat.

Size

Height: Not to exceed 14½ in. (37 cm) at the shoulder. In AKC, 14–15 in. (35.5–38 cm).
Weight: Dogs 17 lb. (7.7 kg), bitches 15 lb. (6.8 kg). In AKC, the standard for both is17 lb. (7.7 kg).

Coat

Color: Black and tan, blue and tan, red, wheaten, red grizzle, liver, blue or black.
Texture: Dense and weather-resistant, harsh with good undercoat.

MANCHESTER TERRIER

OLD PRINTS SHOW THAT a great many of the old terriers of different types were black and tan. As far back as 1570, Dr Caius was able to describe a Black and Tan Terrier breed, though lower to the ground and rougher-coated than this modern counterpart. The Manchester Terrier was developed for sport by the working people of Lancashire—people who did not follow the sports which required a great deal of money, but who looked to a day's ratting or rabbiting with their terriers for recreation. As well as all the instincts of other working terriers, the breed then needed a dash of speed which it might otherwise have lacked. It also had to live with its owner and share his home. Today the Manchester Terrier still makes an ideal house dog, being clean, and a good guard. It is surprising that the breed has not achieved a greater degree of popularity; perhaps its humble origins are less attractive than the exotic histories to which some breeds lay claim.

Characteristics

The Manchester Terrier is compact, with a long head, narrow in skull, with small, dark, sparkling eyes, and small V-shaped ears carried above the topline of the head. The neck is fairly long and free from throatiness. The forequarters are clean and well sloped, the forelegs straight and set well under the body. The body is short with a pronounced tuck-up. The tail is naturally short. Devoted to his human family, he adapts easily to either town or country life.

Size

Height: Dogs 16 in. (40–41 cm), bitches 15 in. (38 cm).
Weight: In AKC, there are two categories: 12–16 lb. (5.4–7.2 kg) and 16–22 lb. (7.2–9.9 kg). In FCI, dogs 18 lb. (8 kg), bitches 17 lb. (7.7 kg).

Coat

Color: Jet black and rich mahogany tan; the standard is precise in its description of the placement of the tan markings.
Texture: Short, smooth, and glossy.

NORFOLK AND NORWICH TERRIERS

Jack Russell Terrier

TWO OF THE SMALLEST of the terriers, but two which retain all their sporting instincts. Until 1964, the breed could have either drop or prick ears, but at that time the two types were separated, the drop-eared variety becoming Norfolk Terriers and the prick-eared Norwich Terriers. It is said that the breed was developed by Frank Jones, a horse-breaker from Cambridgeshire, who introduced his terriers to stables in the area where they earned their keep by killing rats. Indeed, in the early years of the 20th century the breed was known as the Jones Terrier. It was brought back almost from the point of extinction by Miss Macfie, a Sussex breeder, but even today it is not common.

Characteristics

Norfolk and Norwich Terriers have a lovable disposition, are not quarrelsome, have a hardy constitution, and are alert and fearless. They are small, low, keen dogs, compact and strong with a short back, good substance and bone. The skull is wide and slightly rounded, the muzzle wedge-shaped and strong. The eyes are oval, deep-set, and dark, giving an alert, keen, and intelligent expression. The ears of the Norfolk Terrier are V-shaped and drop forward, close to the cheek; those of the Norwich Terrier are similar in shape and size, but pricked up. The neck of both breeds is of medium length and strong, fitting into clean and powerful shoulders with short, powerful, and straight legs. The body is compact with well-muscled hindquarters. The tail is traditionally docked.

Size
Height: Ideally 10 in. (25–26 cm).
Coat
Color: All shades of red, wheaten, black and tan, and grizzle.
Texture: Hard, wiry, and straight, lying close to the body.

Norfolk Terrier

(PARSON) JACK RUSSELL TERRIER

CONTROVERSY HAS LONG surrounded the origins and status of this intelligent and efficient little terrier. It is said to have been developed by a 19th-century minister who felt that the ideal dog for fox hunting would be smaller than the conventional Fox Terrier, but would still have the stamina to follow the hunt all day and go into action when required. Although the Jack Russell has long been a popular companion and an easily identifiable breed, it was given an Interim standard by the Kennel Club only in 1990, is in the AKC's Miscellaneous Group, and is still not officially recognized in Europe.

Characteristics

The Jack Russell is essentially workmanlike in appearance, busy, active, bold, and outgoing. It needs a surprising amount of exercise for such a small dog and will run to fat if denied this. It is also highly intelligent, with a tendency to yap and become destructive if bored. The head is flat with a shallow stop, small, V-shaped, forward-drooping ears, and a strong, muscular jaw. The fairly deep-set, dark eyes should have an alert expression. The neck is muscular, the shoulders well laid back, the chest of moderate depth, and the back strong and straight. The hindquarters are strong and muscular, with the tail, which is customarily docked but not so short that it does not complement the body, set-on high.

Group
Miscellaneous (AKC). Not recognized by FCI.
Size
Height: Dogs minimum 13 in. (33 cm), ideally 14 in. (35 cm); bitches minimum 12 in. (30 cm), ideally 13 in. (33 cm).
Coat
Color: White, with or without markings in tan, lemon or white, or any combination of these colors. Markings should ideally appear on head and root of tail only.
Texture: May be either smooth- or rough-coated, but in either case the coat is harsh, close and dense.

SCOTTISH TERRIER

I T IS DIFFICULT TO BE PRECISE about the history of the Scottish Terrier because the name has long and variously been used to describe any one of several terrier breeds which originate in Scotland. Certainly the terriers of Scotland date back to the 14th century. Rawdon Lee, writing at the end of the 19th century, claimed that the Scottish Terrier was the original Skye Terrier. The original standard for the breed was drawn up in 1880 by J.B. Morrison and although the appearance of the breed has changed considerably since that time, this is a product more of differing methods of presentation than of significant changes to the dog itself. It is doubtful, however, whether modern terriers could do the job among the rocks of the Scottish hills for which their forebears were justly famous.

Characteristics

The Scottish Terrier is a sturdy, thick-set dog set on short legs, alert in carriage. The head gives the impression of being long for the size of dog and the naturally dignified demeanour is accentuated by the disapproving frown caused by the prominent eyebrows. The ears are neat, pointed, and erect. The muscular neck is of moderate length, set into long sloping shoulders. Forelegs are straight and well boned. The chest is fairly broad and hung between the forelegs, with well-rounded ribs carried well back. The back is short and muscular, and the topline is level. Hindquarters are powerful, with big and wide buttocks. The tail is of moderate length. Fearless defending his home, the Scottie is devoted to his adult family but aloof with strangers and not an ideal companion for young children.

Size
Height: 10–11 in. (25.4–28 cm).
Weight: 19–23 lb. (8.6–10.4 kg).
Coat
Color: Black, wheaten, or brindle of any color.
Texture: The undercoat is short, dense, and soft, the outer coat harsh, dense, and wiry.

SEALYHAM TERRIER

T HIS IS ONE OF THE VERY few breeds that owes its development to the work and inspiration of one man. Between 1850 and 1891 Captain John Edwardes of Sealyham in Haverford-west, Wales, set out to develop a strain of terrier which would measure up to his demanding standards in being able to hunt fox, otter, or even badger. There is no doubt that he succeeded in his aim and produced a tough, game, and strong strain of terrier which quickly became popular among those who shared his sporting interests. By 1910 the breed was appearing in the show ring and embarking on further development, which has now made it a very different animal from the one envisaged by Captain Edwardes, but one that makes a first-class watch dog.

Characteristics

The general appearance should be of a free-moving dog, with a slightly domed skull and long, powerful jaw. The eyes are dark and round, and the ears falling at the sides of the cheeks are rounded. The neck is fairly long, thick, and muscular, the forelegs short, strong, and straight. The body is of medium length with powerful hindquarters. The tail is carried erect. Like most terriers, the Sealyham needs firm early training to eliminate a stubborn streak and a willingness to fight another dog at the slightest provocation. Its luxuriant coat needs daily brushing and combing, and professional stripping at least twice a year if it is not to become scruffy. If you can cope with this, the Sealyham makes a loyal and affectionate pet.

Size
Height: Not to exceed 12 in. (31 cm). In AKC, 10–11 in. (25.5–28 cm).
Weight: Dogs ideally about 20 lb. (9 kg), bitches about 18 lb. (8.2 kg). In AKC, 22–25 lb. (10–11.5 kg).
Coat
Color: Mostly all white or white with lemon.
Texture: Long, hard, and wiry.

SKYE TERRIER

SOME AUTHORITIES ARGUE that the Skye Terrier and the present Scottish Terrier share common origins and that the modern Skye, with its extraordinary appearance, is a fairly recent development. In fact Dr Caius, writing in the 16th century, was able to describe the breed from the "barbarous borders fro' the uttermost countryes northward, which by reason of the length of heare, makes show neither of face nor of body."

Characteristics

The Skye Terrier is a one-person dog, distrustful of strangers, but not vicious in nature. The head is long with powerful jaws, the dark eyes are close-set and full of expression. Ears may be prick or drop and they should be fringed with hair. The neck is long and slightly crested, the shoulders are broad, the chest deep, and the forelegs short and muscular. The body is long and low to the ground, the hindquarters well developed and muscular. The tail should not be carried over the back. The American standard is precise about measurements of various parts of the body, including coat length. The lavish coat usually trails along the ground and tends to pick up mud, but this is easily brushed off once it is dry. Nevertheless, daily grooming is essential for this breed.

Size
Height: 10–10½ in. (25–26 cm); total length 41½ in. (103 cm). Bitches may be slightly smaller.
Coat
Color: Dark or light gray, fawn, cream, black, all with black points.
Texture: A soft, short, woolly, close undercoat is hidden by the long, hard, straight, flat topcoat which is such a characteristic feature of the breed.

Staffordshire Bull Terrier

STAFFORDSHIRE BULL TERRIER

ONE OF THE TWO gladiatorial members of the terrier group evolved to fight with other dogs or to bait bull, bear, or badger (see also Bull Terrier, page 48). The old breeds used for these savage sports were Mastiffs or Bulldogs which were too slow and ponderous for the 19th-century Corinthians, who introduced a dash of terrier blood to give speed and agility and so laid the foundations of the "Bull and Terrier" breed. By virtue of its association with the English Midlands this breed was to become the Staffordshire; James Hinks crossed it with the Old English White Terrier to produce the Bull Terrier. Only in 1935 was the Staffordshire recognized as a breed, but it is now one of the most popular show terriers and one to which the show ring has introduced no element of foppery.

Characteristics

The Staffordshire Bull Terrier should have great strength for its size and, although very muscular, should be active and agile. The head is short, the skull is broad, the cheek muscles are very pronounced, and the foreface is short and powerful. The eyes are round and should look straight ahead. Ears may be either rose or half-prick. The neck is short and muscular, set into wide, strong shoulders on straight, well-boned legs. Hindquarters should be well muscled. The tail is low set and carried like an old-fashioned pump handle. The breed still enjoys a good fight with other dogs—with people, however, particularly children, it makes a faithful companion and an excellent and fearless guard dog.

Size
Height: 14–16 in. (35.5–40.5 cm).
Weight: Dogs 28–38 lb. (12.7–17 kg), bitches 24–34 lb. (11–15.4 kg).
Coat
Color: Red, fawn, white, black, or blue, or any of these colors with white. May also be brindle, or brindle and white.
Texture: Smooth, short, and close to the skin.

WELSH TERRIER

THIS IS THE WELSH counterpart of the Lakeland Terrier, which in some ways it resembles. It was used to accompany the hunts in Wales in order to drive fox or otter from places of refuge. Until the turn of the century there appears to have been little distinction made between the Welsh and the Old English Black and Tan Terrier.

Characteristics

The Welsh Terrier has a gay, volatile disposition but is occasionally shy. It is affectionate, obedient, and biddable. The head is flat and rather wider between the ears than that of a Fox Terrier. The jaw is powerful, the eyes small and dark, well set-in. The ears are V-shaped, set fairly high, and are carried forward and close to the cheek. The neck should be of moderate length, slightly arched, and sloping gracefully into long shoulders set well back. The body is short, the forelegs straight and muscular, the hindquarters strong with muscular thighs. The tail is well set-on, but not carried too gaily.

Welsh Terrier

West Highland White Terrier

Size
Height: 15½ in. (39 cm).
Weight: 20–21 lb. (9–9.5 kg).
Coat
Color: Black and tan preferred.
Texture: Wiry, hard, very close, and abundant; should be double.

WEST HIGHLAND WHITE TERRIER

ACCORDING TO THE Malcolm family, the breed has its origins in Poltallock, Scotland, where for three generations the family bred these white terriers. Certainly the breed was called the Poltallock Terrier and the Roseneath Terrier, but it is likely that these places only concentrated on developing and refining a white strain of the old Scottish Terriers. In so doing, they produced a smart, courageous, and hardy little sporting dog, which is now much valued as a companion and has achieved considerable success in the show ring.

Characteristics

The general appearance is that of a small, game, and hardy terrier, possessed of no small amount of self-esteem. The breed is strongly built, deep in the chest, with a level back and powerful hindquarters. Movement is free, straight, and easy. The head is slightly domed, the jaws strong. The eyes, set wide apart, are of medium size and dark in color, giving a sharp and intelligent look. The ears are small and carried erect. The tail is 5–6 in. (12.7–15 cm) long, not docked, carried jauntily but not over the back.

Size
Height: About 11 in. (28 cm). The AKC prefers 10 in. (25 cm) for bitches.
Coat
Color: White.
Texture: Outer coat hard and free from curl, undercoat short, soft, and close.

Utility

All breeds in this section are classified as Utility by the Kennel Club, and as Nonsporting by the AKC and ANKC, unless otherwise stated.

BOSTON TERRIER

Bulldog

THIS AMERICAN BREED was the result of crosses between imported English Bulldogs and terriers made in the 1870s by Robert C. Hooper and William O'Brien of Boston. They were first exhibited as Round Heads or Bull Terriers, but, as a distinct and stable type developed, the name was changed to Boston Terrier. In 1891 the first breed club was formed in America, and in 1893 the breed was recognized by the AKC.

Characteristics

The Boston has a gentle disposition and is eminently suitable as a companion and as a house pet. It is smooth-coated, short-headed, compactly built and well balanced. The head is square, muzzle short, eyes large and round. The ears are carried erect and may be cropped in countries where this operation is not illegal. The neck is of fair length and the body deep, with a good width of chest. The shoulders are sloping, the back short, the loins short and muscular. Forelegs are set moderately wide apart, straight, and well muscled; hindlegs have strong, muscular thighs. The tail is short, fine, and tapering and may be straight or screw.

Group
Companion and Toy Dogs (FCI).
Size
Weight: Not exceeding 25 lb. (11.4 kg). In AKC divided into three classes: under 15 lb. (6.8 kg), 15–20 lb. (6.8–9.1 kg) and 20–25 lb. (9.1–11.5 kg).
Coat
Color: Brindle with white markings preferred, though black with white markings is acceptable.
Texture: Short, smooth, bright, and fine.

BULLDOG

THIS STURDY SYMBOL of the British character was originally used for bull-baiting, a sport which began in the early 13th century and continued until it was made illegal in 1835. The Bulldog as a distinct breed had evolved by the mid-17th century from crosses between Mastiffs and more active terriers, and was then more like a Boxer or an old-type Staffordshire Bull Terrier. After bull-baiting became illegal the breed evolved to its present exaggerated form.

Characteristics

The general appearance is of a thick-set dog, low in stature but broad, powerful, and compact. The head is strikingly large in proportion to the dog's size. The face is extremely short, the muzzle very broad, blunt, and inclined upward. The tail is short and screwed, the forelegs bowed. The Bulldog's pugnacious appearance masks a loving personality; generally good-natured with children, the dog will quickly become devoted to and very protective of its family. However, the characteristic squashed face can sometimes lead to a tendency to drool excessively and even to more serious breathing problems. The Bulldog cannot breathe quickly, and for this reason it must never be allowed to become overheated. This is very important if you have to leave the dog in a car on a warm day. Park in the shade and make sure your pet has plenty of air.

Group
Pinscher and Schnauzer, Molossians and Swiss Mountain Dogs and Cattle Dogs (FCI).
Size
Weight: 55 lb. (25 kg) for a dog, 50 lb. (22.7 kg) for a bitch. In AKC, 50 lb. (22.7 kg) for a dog, 40 lb. (18 kg) for a bitch.
Coat
Color: Various shades of brindle, red, fawn, fallow, white or pied, with or without a black mask or muzzle.
Texture: Fine in texture, short, close and smooth.

CHOW CHOW

IT IS POPULARLY AND erroneously accepted that the Chow Chow was produced as a source of food in China. In fact the Chow as we know it today is very much a product of Western breeding and selection from dogs imported from China in the late 18th century, which showed the unique blue-black tongue and characteristic scowling expression.

Characteristics

A powerfully built dog, leonine in appearance with a proud, dignified bearing, loyal yet aloof, and with a stilted gait. The head is large and broad, the ears small, thick, and rounded, the eyes small and dark. The body is short, compact, and strong. The tail is carried well over the back. Because it is not a playful dog, the Chow Chow is perhaps not an ideal companion for children.

Chow Chow

Group
Nordic Sledge Dogs (FCI).
Size
Height: Dogs 19–22 in. (48–56 cm), bitches 18–20 in. (46–51 cm).
Coat
Color: Whole colored black, red, blue, fawn, cream, or white, shaded, but not in patches or parti-colored. Back of legs and under tail often lighter.
Texture: Abundant, dense, straight, and standing out from the body. Outer coat rather coarse with a soft, woolly undercoat.

DALMATIAN

Dalmatian

THE DALMATIAN IS SAID to have originated in Dalmatia on the Adriatic coast, although spotted dogs are found in many parts of the world. However, the breed has been established for such a long time in Britain, where it was used as a carriage guard, that it can perhaps be recognized as a British breed. In America, its affinity with horses and carriages earned it a place with the horse-drawn fire engines, and it became known as the Firehouse Dog.

Characteristics

The most obvious feature is the spotted coat. Dalmatians should also be strong, muscular, active, and of good demeanor. Shyness is considered a major fault. They are graceful in outline, elegant, and capable of great endurance. Dalmatians have great freedom of movement, exhibiting a smooth, powerful, rhythmic action with a long stride which enables them to cover considerable distances. Sadly, a cute and cuddly image, fostered through films, novels, and advertisements, in part contradicts the fact that the Dalmatian is a big, strong dog in need of firm control and plenty of exercise.

Group
Scenthounds (FCI).
Size
Height: Dogs 23–24 in. (58·5–61 cm), bitches 22–23 in. (56–58·5 cm). In AKC, 19–23 in. (48–58 cm) for both sexes. In FCI, dogs 21½–24 in. (55–61 cm), bitches 19½–23 in. (50–58 cm).
Weight: In FCI, dogs 55 lb. (24·9 kg), bitches 49½ lb. (22·4 kg). In AKC, both sexes maximum 53 lb. (24 kg).
Coat
Color: Pure white, evenly covered with separate, well-defined, black or liver spots.
Texture: Short, hard, and dense, sleek and glossy in appearance.

FRENCH BULLDOG

French Bulldog

THIS BREED HAS DESCENDED from Bulldogs introduced from Britain into France, probably at the end of the 19th century. Seventeenth-century paintings show dogs very like the present-day Frenchie, although this does not necessarily mean that they are any relation of the breed. Whatever its origins, there can be no doubt about the great speed at which this stylish miniature Bulldog swept to popularity among the fashion-conscious French.

Characteristics

A French Bulldog should be sound, active and intelligent, of compact build, medium or small-sized, with good bone. The head is massive, square and broad, with a domed forehead and loose skin forming symmetrical wrinkles. The bat ears are distinctively different from the ears of other Bulldog breeds. Having a less squashed-in face than the English Bulldog, the Frenchie is less prone to breathing problems. It is playful, intelligent and loves human company.

Group
Companion and Toy Dogs (FCI).
Size
Weight: 28 lb. (12.7 kg) for dogs, 24 lb. (10.9 kg) for bitches. In AKC, there are two classes: under 22 lb. (10 kg) and 22–28 lb. (10–12.7 kg). In FCI, 17½–31 lb. (7.9–14 kg).
Coat
Color: Brindle, pied, and fawn.
Texture: Fine, smooth, lustrous, short, and close.

JAPANESE AKITA

THE NAME AKITA INU means "large dog," and this breed developed from the largest of the Spitz dogs which descended from the polar regions to the cold mountainous areas of northern Japan many hundreds of years ago. Originally a fighting dog, the Akita was later used for hunting such formidable prey as black bear, wild boar, and deer. Today this is the most popular breed in Japan and is increasing in popularity elsewhere. Over 1,300 Akitas were registered with the Kennel Club in 1997, which puts the breed on a par with such household names as the Basset Hound and the Standard Poodle.

Characteristics

A dog with great strength of character, an excellent guard but also an affectionate pet, with great loyalty to his owners. The overall impression is one of power and substance, but also of dignity and quiet reserve; this is a breed that tends to dominate other dogs. It has a large, broad head with prick ears and strong jaws; a strong, muscular body and a full tail, carried over the back and dipping down below the level of the back in a full or double curl.

Group
Working (AKC). Nordic Sledge Dogs (FCI). Utility (ANKC).
Size
Height: Dogs 26–28 in. (66–71 cm), bitches 24–26 in. (61–66 cm).
Weight: In AKC, 75–110 lb. (34–50 kg) or more.
Coat
Color: Any color, with well-defined markings that may include a mask or blaze.
Texture: A straight, coarse outer coat over a soft, dense undercoat.

Japanese Akita

JAPANESE SPITZ

THIS DESCENDANT OF THE Spitz breeds was taken to Japan in the early years of the 20th century, where it was bred to produce a more toy-like dog. It was then taken to Sweden, and thence to Britain, where it has been seen only since the 1970s but is fast gaining in popularity. Although its lavish coat requires careful and regular grooming, the striking appearance of the Japanese Spitz—and its affectionate disposition—will amply reward this effort.

Characteristics

The muzzle is pointed, and the ears are erect and pointed. The tail is richly fringed and curls up and over the back. The forequarters and hindquarters are well proportioned. The body is compact and the general appearance is handsome. The Japanese Spitz is characterized by great courage as well as an intelligent and cheerful nature.

Group
Nordic Sledge Dogs (FCI).
Size
Height: Dogs 12–14 in. (30–36 cm), bitches slightly smaller.
Coat
Color: Pure white.
Texture: The straight outer coat stands away from the body—it is long except on the face and legs, and there is a profuse mane and tail. The undercoat is short, soft, and abundant.

KEESHOND

THE BREED SHARES ORIGINS with its close neighbor, the Pomeranian, and is named after a Dutch patriot, Kees de Gyselaer of Dordrecht. It was adopted as a mascot of the Patriotten during the revolutionary times of the 18th century. The breed had long existed as a watch dog used on the barges of Holland, but has its origins among other more northerly Spitz breeds—the Samoyed, the Norwegian Elkhound, and the Finnish Spitz, among others. Since its rise to popular recognition some two centuries ago, the breed has changed little and is still easily identified in the paintings and drawings of the period. However, political changes as well as advances in the design of barges reduced the breed's popularity. In 1920 the Baroness van Hardenbroek began to breed Keeshonds and was responsible for making the breed well known and admired once more.

Characteristics

The Keeshond has a short, compact body, alert carriage, and a fox-like head. The well-feathered tail is curled over the back in the typical Spitz manner.

Movement should be clean and brisk, and temperament bold. The appearance of this handsome dog amply repays the effort required to keep its coat in immaculate condition. The Keeshond's natural exuberance needs to be kept in check by early training. It makes a friendly companion and a good domestic guard, with a tendency to be a one-person dog.

Group
Not recognized by FCI, which does not differentiate it from the German Wolfspitz, a breed which is not recognized outside Europe.
Size
Height: Dogs 18 in. (45.7 cm), bitches 17 in. (43.2 cm). In AKC, up to 19 in. (48 cm).
Weight: AKC 55–66 lb. (24.9–30 kg).
Coat
Color: A mix of black and any shade of gray, with pale gray or cream undercoat.
Texture: Dense and harsh, standing away from the body with a thick, soft undercoat, never silky or wavy.

Keeshond

LHASA APSO

IN TIBET, THE LHASA APSO'S homeland, this breed is known as Abso Seng Kye, the Bark Lion Sentinel Dog, a name which sums up its function. The Apso is one of four breeds now justly popular in the West, which for very many years acted as guards within the precincts of the lamaseries in and around the sacred city of Lhasa. This task is one for which the Apso's intelligence, alertness, acute hearing, and distrust of strangers aptly fit it.

Characteristics

The Apso is a solid little dog with a cheerful and assertive character, yet it can be wary of strangers. It carries an abundance of coat, with hair completely covering its face and body. The ears are pendent and heavily feathered. The tail is also well feathered, high-set, and carried over the back. The coat needs a lot of attention, but the Lhasa is otherwise easy to look after, requiring little exercise and not much to eat. It should be properly socialized at an early age, but then makes a playful and affectionate pet.

Group
Companion and Toy Dogs (FCI).
Size
Height: Dogs 10 in. (25.4 cm), slightly smaller for bitches.
Coat
Color: Golden, sandy, honey, dark grizzle, slate, smoke, parti-color, black, white, or brown.
Texture: Straight and hard, not woolly or silky, long and with a dense undercoat.

POODLE, MINIATURE

OF LATER ORIGIN THAN the Standard Poodles and used exclusively as a companion. The standard is the same as for the Standard Poodle (see right) except for the following:

Size
Height: Under 15 in. (38 cm) but not less than 11 in. (28 cm). In AKC, the minimum is 10 in. (25.4 cm). In FCI, the permitted range is 13¾–17¾ in. (34.8–45 cm).

POODLE, STANDARD

ORIGINATING IN FRANCE, the Poodle was used as a gundog over a wide area, including France, Germany, and Russia. Its adaptability, intelligence, and unusual appearance soon led to its being used for a wide variety of purposes, as well as in the production of other gundog breeds.

Characteristics

A very active, intelligent, and elegant dog with a good temperament, carrying itself proudly. The head is long and fine with almond-shaped eyes, and the chest is deep and moderately wide. The back is short and strong. The tail is normally docked. Poodles are often chosen as pets by those who are normally allergic to dogs, as they do not shed their hair and lack the distinctive "doggy" smell. The "lion clip" usually seen on show dogs requires careful and skillful grooming, probably performed by a professional. Away from the show ring, frequent brushing and combing combined with regular clipping will keep a Poodle looking neat. The Standard Poodle is a big dog requiring lots of exercise and plenty of play between walks.

Group
Companion and Toy Dogs (FCI).
Size
Height: 15 in. (38 cm) and over. In FCI, 17¾–21½ in. (45–54.5 cm).
Weight: In AKC, 45–70 lb. (20–32 kg).
Coat
Color: All solid colors—white, cream, browns, apricots, blacks, silver, or blue.
Texture: Very profuse and dense and of harsh texture.

Standard Poodle

SCHIPPERKE

Miniature Schnauzer

THE GENERAL APPEARANCE of the Schipperke strongly suggests a Spitz breed. Indeed the breed was originally called Spitske. However, when it is allowed to retain its tail, the carriage seems to suggest a relationship with the other European herding breeds. The Schipperke is descended from the same herding dogs which produced the Belgian Shepherd Dog (Groenendael), the latter remaining as herders and Schipperkes becoming smaller watch dogs. Probably Schipperkes can be credited with taking part in the first organized dog shows when, in 1690, a show was held at the Grand Palace of Brussels for dogs owned by Guild workmen. It was not until 1888 that the breed's name was changed to Schipperke, which in Flemish means "little captain," a reference as much to the Schipperke's air of self-importance as to its association with the barges of the Flemish canals.

Characteristics

The general appearance of the Schipperke is of a small, intensely lively animal with a sharp expression, always on the alert. The head is distinctly foxy with small, rather oval, dark brown eyes and sharply pointed, stiffly erect ears. The shoulders are surprisingly muscular and the topline slopes down to comparatively slim hindquarters. The Schipperke makes an alert house dog as well as a faithful, intelligent companion.

Group
Sheepdogs (FCI).
Size
Weight: About 12–16 lb. (5.4–7.3 kg). In AKC, up to 18 lb. (8 kg). In FCI, large dogs 11–20 lb. (4.9–9 kg), small dogs 6½–11 lb. (2.9–4.9 kg), miniatures under 6½ lb. (2.9 kg).
Coat
Color: Black preferred. Other whole colors are permissible in Britain, though not in America.
Texture: Abundant, dense, and harsh, smooth on the head, ears and legs, but erect and thick round the neck, forming a mane and frill, and with a good culotte on the back of the thighs.

SCHNAUZER

KNOWN IN NORTH AMERICA as the Standard Schnauzer, this may be regarded as the forerunner of the three Schnauzer breeds: Miniature, Standard, and Giant (in Britain the Giant Schnauzer is classified as a Working Dog—see page 70). It is of German origin with a long history dating back to the 15th and 16th centuries. In its veins may run Poodle blood, some Spitz, and some Pinscher blood, but the Schnauzer has long been a distinctive breed used in its various sizes as a vermin killer, a yard dog and a most effective guard. Larger types were once much used as army dogs, and in all its roles the breed has shown itself to be adaptable, trainable, and intelligent.

Characteristics

A powerfully built, robust, sinewy, nearly square dog with a temperament which combines high spirits, reliability, strength, endurance, and vigour. Its legs are very straight, giving an upright appearance. Although the coat is short and neat over the body, the legs are covered in longer hair, and the face has prominent eyebrows and a pronounced beard and moustache.

Group
Working (AKC). Pinscher and Schnauzer, Molossians and Swiss Mountain Dogs and Cattle Dogs (FCI). Utility (ANKC).
Size
Height: Dogs ideally 19 in. (48.3 cm), bitches 18 in. (45.7 cm).
Coat
Color: All pepper and salt colors, or pure black.
Texture: Hard and wiry, with a dense undercoat.

SCHNAUZER, MINIATURE

The standard is the same as for the Schnauzer except for the following:

Group
Terrier (AKC).
Size
Height: Dogs 14 in. (35.6 cm), bitches 13 in. (33 cm). In AKC, 12–14 in. (30.4–35.6 cm).
Coat
Color: All pepper and salt colors, or pure black, or black with silver markings.

SHAR PEI

Right: Shih Tzu
Below: Shar Pei

LISTED AS THE RAREST DOG in the world in *The Guinness Book of Records* as recently as 1980, the Shar Pei has been brought back from the verge of extinction, largely thanks to an enthusiastic breeder in California, from where it was introduced into the UK in the latter part of the 20th century. Although it has been given only an Interim standard by the Kennel Club, it has established itself so quickly that in 1997 there were almost 1,000 registrations. In fact, this is a very ancient breed, known as a fighting dog in China at least 2,000 years ago.

Characteristics

A solid, muscular dog with a square head, and a tapering tail set very high on the body and carried in a kink over the back. The breed's most distinguishing features are its very loose, wrinkled skin and its frowning expression. Although Shar Pei at their best are affectionate companions, rapid breeding from a limited stock has developed some faults of temperament, notably that the ancient fighting qualities may re-emerge in inappropriate circumstances. When buying a Shar Pei, therefore, it is even more important than usual to ensure that the dog originates from sound stock.

Group
Pinscher and Schnauzer, Molossians and Swiss Mountain Dogs and Cattle Dogs (FCI).
Size
Height: 18–20 in. (46–51 cm).
Weight: In AKC, 45–55 lb. (20.5–25 kg).
Coat
Color: Black, red, fawn, or cream. Lighter colors have a dark muzzle and dark rings round the eyes.
Texture: Short and bristly, with no undercoat.

SHIH TZU

RECORDS DATING FROM AD **624** show that dogs were given as tribute to the Tang Emperor by K'iu T'ai; paintings and carvings show these dogs, and others offered in later tributes, to have been very like the modern Shih Tzu. Whether the breed, also known as the Chrysanthemum Dog, originated in Tibet or in some part of the Byzantine Empire is not known. These self-important little dogs, favored because of the close association between the Buddha and his pet dog, preceded their royal masters about the Chinese court and by their barking warned lesser mortals to avert their eyes from the personifications of the Sun and Sons of Heaven. Shih Tzu means "lion dog," a reference more to its courage than its appearance.

Characteristics

The Shih Tzu is a very active, lively, and alert dog with a distinctly arrogant carriage. Although classified as a Toy in many parts of the world, this is an independently minded, extrovert breed that craves fun and activity rather than pampering. Its most attractive features are the long, luxuriant coat and the hair growing upward from the muzzle, giving the characteristic "chrysanthemum" look. The head is broad and round, wide between the eyes with a short, square muzzle. The eyes are large, dark, and round, but not prominent. The body is sturdy and muscular. The tail is heavily plumed and carried well over the back.

Group
Toy (AKC). Companion and Toy Dogs (FCI). Nonsporting (ANKC).
Size
Height: Not more than 10½ in. (26.7 cm). In AKC, 8–11 in. (20–28 cm).
Weight: The ideal weight is 10–16 lb. (4.5–7.3 kg), but up to 18 lb. (8.1 kg) is acceptable. In AKC, 9–16 lb. (4–7.25 kg) is ideal, but a maximum of 19 lb. (8.5 kg) is permitted.
Coat
Color: All colors are permissible. The AKC standard prefers a white blaze and tail tip.
Texture: Long and dense but not curly, with a good undercoat.

TIBETAN SPANIEL

THROUGHOUT ANCIENT history the rulers of China, Tibet, and neighboring countries showed great interest in the small breeds of dogs which inhabited their courts and which were their constant companions, serving as food tasters, as status symbols, and even having religious significance. Dogs were exchanged between the courts, some from Tibet moving to China, with possibly the Happa becoming the ancestor of the Pekingese, and the Carla becoming the ancestor of the Tibetan Spaniel. Other dogs very similar to the Tibetan Spaniel were also found in Japan and South Korea and these too may have contributed to the formation of the breed.

Characteristics

The Tibetan Spaniel is cheerful, intelligent, and aloof with strangers. The luxuriant coat may make it look like a lapdog, but do not be fooled—this is a spirited, independent breed. The head is small in proportion to the body and proudly carried, the skull domed, the muzzle short, the mouth slightly undershot. The tail is set high, richly plumed, and carried in a gay curl over the back when the dog is moving.

Group
Companion and Toy Dogs (FCI). Toy (ANKC).
Size
Height: About 10 in. (25.4 cm).
Weight: Ideally 9–15 lb. (4.1–6.8 kg).
Coat
Color: Any color or combination of colors.
Texture: Double coat, silky in texture and not overcoated. Males in particular are encouraged to grow a profuse mane.

TIBETAN TERRIER

LEGEND PLACES THIS breed's origins in the Lost Valley of Tibet and, given that its history stretches back 2,000 years, legend may be as reliable as supposed fact. Tibetan Terriers were regarded as companions which brought luck to their owners and had religious significance. In Tibet they were called "Luck Bringers" or "Holy Dogs" and were kept purely as companions and symbols of status. Why in the West they are called terriers, with which group they have no affinity whatsoever, is hard to say. But they are healthy, tough, and affectionate, and make ideal companions.

Characteristics

The general appearance is rather like that of an Old English Sheepdog in miniature, with a long coat covering the entire body and a fringe of hair falling forward over the eyes. The hindlegs are slightly longer than the forelegs, so the loin is slightly arched. The body is compact and powerful for its size. The tail is of medium length, set fairly high, and carried in a gay curl over the back; it is very well feathered and often has a kink near the end.

Group
Companion and Toy Dogs (FCI).
Size
Height: Dogs 14–16 in. (35.6–40.6 cm), bitches slightly smaller.
Weight: In AKC, average 22–23 lb. (9.9–10.4 kg), but may be 18–30 lb. (8–13.6 kg).
Coat
Color: Any color except chocolate or liver; white, golden, cream, gray or smoke, black, parti-color, and tricolor are all acceptable.
Texture: Double-coated, the undercoat of fine wool and the top coat profuse (not silky or woolly), long, and either straight or waved.

Tibetan Terrier

Working

All breeds in this section are classified as Working by the Kennel Club and AKC, as Utility by the ANKC, and as the rather unwieldy Pinscher and Schnauzer, Molossians and Swiss Mountain Dogs and Cattle Dogs by the FCI, unless otherwise stated.

BERNESE MOUNTAIN DOG

THIS IS ONE OF A NUMBER of European working breeds developed from herding dogs left behind by Roman legions. Switzerland is home to four varieties of mountain dogs, but it is the breed developed in the canton of Berne which, because of its rich, black and tan, silky coat, is the most distinctive. By the late 18th century the Bernese had degenerated, but was rescued by Franz Schertenlieb and Professor Albert Heim, so that by the 1900s a breed club was founded.

Characteristics
The Bernese Mountain Dog is well balanced, active, and alert, combining sagacity, fidelity, and utility. The skull is flat with a well-defined stop, the eyes dark, hazel brown, and full of fire, and the ears V-shaped, set-on high, and in repose hang close to the head. The body is rather short and compact, the chest broad and with a deep brisket. The forelegs are straight and muscular, the loin strong, and the hindquarters muscular with well-developed thighs. The tail is carried low. An obedient, affectionate dog, the Bernese is an ideal family pet for those able to cope with it—this is a big dog with a hearty appetite, a love of exercise, and a fine coat that needs frequent grooming.

Size
Height: Dogs 25–27½ in. (64–70 cm), bitches 23–26 in. (58–66 cm).
Coat
Color: Jet black with russet-brown markings on face, legs, and chest, and a white blaze, white chest, and preferably white feet.
Texture: Soft and silky with bright, natural sheen, long, and wavy not curly.

BOUVIER DES FLANDRES

THIS IS ONE OF A small group of Flemish drovers' dogs used partly for herding cattle and partly as guards. After the First World War, in which they had acted as ambulance and messenger dogs, very few animals survived, but an army vet had saved one dog, Nic, who was to become the father of virtually the entire breed. Bouviers are now used as police and army dogs.

Characteristics
A compactly bodied, powerfully built dog of upstanding carriage and alert, intelligent expression, giving an overall impression of strength. The head is large and square with a shaggy beard and moustache, the body and legs solid, well muscled, and heavy-boned. The tail is normally docked. Of a calm and gentle disposition, this dog is very protective of

Group
Herding (AKC). Sheepdogs (FCI). Working (ANKC).
Size
Height: Dogs 25–27 in. (62–68 cm), bitches 23–25½ in. (59–65 cm). In AKC, dogs 23½–27½ in. (59.7–69.8 cm), bitches a minimum of 22¾ in. (57 cm). In FCI and ANKC, dogs 25½ in. (65 cm), bitches 24½ in. (62 cm).
Weight: 77–88 lb. (35–40 kg) for dogs, 60–77 lb. (27.2–35 kg) for bitches.
Coat
Color: Fawn to black, including brindle. A white spot on the chest is allowed.
Texture: Rough, tousled, and unkempt in appearance, the coat is capable of withstanding the hardest work in the most inclement weather. Topcoat harsh, rough, and wiry, undercoat fine and soft.

home and family but is friendly enough to make an excellent pet. The untidy-looking coat is easy to look after and the Bouvier needs less exercise than many other dogs of his size.

BOXER

A GERMAN BREED, this is one of several European dogs which have their origins in the mastiffs of Southern Europe and which in the Middle Ages were developed as hunting dogs. Nowadays Boxers are used mainly as police dogs and guard dogs. During the First World War this breed, in common with others of Germanic origin, went through a period of unpopularity, but the Boxer's virtues as a companion and guard dog soon restored it to favor.

Characteristics
A medium-sized sturdy dog of square build with a short back, strong limbs and short, tight-fitting coat. Clean and hard in appearance, with a firm, springy stride. The head is square and short, a distinctive feature of the breed, with skin forming deep wrinkles. In America the

Left: Bouvier des Flandres   Right: Bullmastiff

ears may be cropped, but in Britain, where cropping has long been illegal, the ears lie flat and close to the cheeks. The mouth is normally undershot, though the teeth of the underjaw should not be seen when the mouth is closed. Although the Boxer needs firm early training and plenty of exercise, it makes a devoted pet and an enthusiastic playmate.

Size
Height: Dogs 22½–25 in. (57–63 cm), bitches 21–23 in. (53–59 cm). In FCI, dogs 24 in. (61 cm), bitches 23 in. (59 cm).
Weight: Dogs 30–32kg (66–70lb), bitches 25–27kg (55–601b). In FCI, 25kg (55lb) for bitches.
Coat
Color: Fawn or brindle, with or without white markings.
Texture: Short, shiny, lying smooth and tight to the body.

Boxer

BULLMASTIFF

SHAKESPEARE COMMENDED the British mastiffs as being very valiant creatures of unmatchable courage. The Bullmastiff is a 19th-century development of these ancient breeds, the product of a cross between mastiffs and terriers to produce a smaller, more active dog. It was used as and often referred to as the Gamekeepers' Dog and because it often worked at night was also sometimes called the Night Dog. A sagacious guard and one feared by even the boldest poacher, the Bullmastiff is quick enough to catch the fastest runner and capable of throwing down and holding the strongest of intruders. Officially recognized as a breed in 1924.

Characteristics
The Bullmastiff's temperament combines high spirits, reliability, activity, endurance, and alertness. It is a powerfully built dog, showing great strength but not cumbersome. The head is large and square, and the skin wrinkles when the dog becomes interested in something. The neck is well arched and very muscular, the chest broad and deep, the back short and straight. Hindquarters are wide and muscular. Like all very strong dogs, the Bullmastiff needs to be well disciplined, but will then make an intelligent and devoted companion and excellent house dog.

Size
Height: Dogs 25–27 in. (63·5–68·5 cm), bitches 24–26 in. (61–66 cm).
Weight: Dogs 110–130 lb. (50–59 kg), bitches 90–110 lb. (41–50 kg). In AKC, bitches 100–120 lb. (45·3–54·3 kg).
Coat
Color: Any shade of brindle, fawn, or red. A black muzzle is essential.
Texture: Short and hard, lying flat to the body.

DOBERMAN

THIS BREED IS THE SECOND most popular breed in the U.S., where it is known as the Doberman Pinscher (*Pinscher* is the German for terrier), although Britain has adopted the shortened name. It is of such recent origin that it can be traced to the person who first bred it, Louis Dobermann, a German tax collector. Between 1865 and 1870 he set about producing a first-class guard dog based on the concept of a giant terrier, combining agility with strength, speed, and great intelligence. So well did he succeed that the Doberman is now sometimes too quick and too intelligent for those who seek to control it. Such a dog demands the highest standards of its handlers.

Characteristics

A medium-sized dog with a well-set body, muscular and elegant, proud carriage and bold alert temperament, compact and tough with light, elastic movement. Neither shyness nor viciousness is characteristic of the breed. The head is long and clean, and the eyes are deep and almond-shaped. The ears may be erect or dropped; they may be cropped in countries where the operation is not banned. The body is square, and the back is short and firm. The tail is normally docked.

Size
Height: Dogs ideally 27 in. (69 cm), bitches 25½ in. (65 cm). A height is not specified in AKC.
Weight: In FCI, dogs 88–99 lb. (40–45 kg), bitches 70–77 lb. (32–35 kg).
Coat
Color: Black, red, brown, or blue with rust-red markings which must be sharply defined. White markings of any kind are undesirable.
Texture: Smooth-haired, short, hard, thick, and close-lying.

DOGUE DE BORDEAUX

THE DOGUE DE BORDEAUX may lay claim to being the national dog of France and is increasing in popularity elsewhere, although it is not yet recognized by the Kennel Club or the AKC. It entered France with the Romans 2,000 years ago and for centuries was highly successful fighting bears, bulls, and others of its own kind.

Characteristics

In appearance the breed is very similar to the English Mastiff and is descended from the same stock as other European mastiff breeds. It has a massive head with pronounced wrinkles, powerful legs, shoulders, and hindquarters, and a medium-length tapering tail. Nowadays, it makes an excellent watch dog as it is vigilant, faithful, and has great strength. Loving and devoted to its human family, it is still likely to fight with other dogs.

Size
Height: 27½–30 in. (70–76 cm).
Weight: 120–145 lb. (54.3–65.7 kg).
Coat
Color: Apricot, silver, fawn, or dark fawn-brindle with black points.
Texture: Smooth and short.

GIANT SCHNAUZER

The standard is the same as for the Schnauzer (see page 63) except for:

Size
Height: Dogs 25½–27½ in. (65–70 cm), bitches 23½–25½ in. (60–65 cm).

GREAT DANE

IN SPITE OF ITS NAME the breed has no close association with Denmark. Indeed because drawings of very similar dogs were found on Fourth Dynasty tomb walls, some people put its origins in Egypt, but it was in Germany that the breed was developed and achieved popularity. Great Danes were favored by Bismarck and were used to hunt wild boar. In spite of its present group classification the Great Dane's original work was that of a hound.

Characteristics

Great Danes should be very large, very muscular, strongly though elegantly built.

Left: Doberman

The head is carried high and the whole outline should be elegant. Size, however, is of paramount importance. This is one of the most good-natured of breeds, devoted to both adults and children. An ideal companion if you have the room and don't mind your pet taking up all the space in front of the fire.

Group
Non-sporting (ANKC).
Size
Height: Minimum for an adult dog 30 in. (76 cm), for a bitch 28 in. (71 cm). In FCI, 31½ in. (79.5 cm). In AKC 30–32 in. (76–81 cm) or over preferred.
Weight: Minimum for an adult dog 120 lb. (54 kg), for a bitch 100 lb. (46 kg).
Coat
Color: Brindle, fawn, blue, black, or Harlequin (white with black or blue patches).
Texture: Very short and thick, smooth and glossy.

MASTIFF

ONE OF THE ANCIENT mastiff breeds of Europe with origins in the warrior dogs which fought alongside their masters to resist the Roman legions invading Britain in 55 BC. The Romans recognized the dogs' great courage and carried them back to Rome to take part in gladiatorial contests against bulls, bears, lions, and tigers. The breed was so greatly admired that mastiff-like dogs, generally called "dogues," eventually gave their particular name to all domestic dogs. The present-day English Mastiff is largely based on the strain which, since 1415, had been bred at Lyme Hall, near Stockport in Cheshire, and the Duke of Devonshire's strain which was kept at Chatsworth, Derbyshire.

Characteristics
A large, massive, and robust dog with a symmetrical and well-knit frame, combining grandeur with good nature and courage with docility. The Mastiff has a square, powerful-looking head, strong teeth, heavy muscular shoulders and hindquarters, and a long, tapering tail. Despite its strength, it has a calm temperament and is affectionate and protective toward its owner. It needs plenty of space and has a hearty appetite.

Size
Height: Not specified in KC, though both height and substance are desirable and must be in proportion. In AKC, minimum height for dogs is 30 in. (76 cm), for bitches 27½ in. (70 cm).
Weight: In AKC, 175–190 lb. (79–86 kg).
Coat
Color: Various shades of fawn, including fawn brindle. The muzzle, ears, and nose should be black, with black also round and between the eyes.
Texture: Short and close-lying, but not too fine over shoulders, neck, and back.

NEAPOLITAN MASTIFF

MANY OF THE European mastiff breeds are of ancient origin and the Neapolitan is no exception: although it made its European appearance in the show ring only after the Second World War, it is descended from the Roman fighting dogs. It has an Interim standard with the Kennel Club.

Characteristics
The Roman writer Columella described the breed and said it should be black "so that during the day a prowler can see him and be frightened by his appearance. When night falls the dog, lost in the shadows, can attack without being seen." The head is so massive that it seems to be the most important part of the body. The ears fall toward the front, the brilliant and penetrating eyes are black or gray, the chest is deep and hairy, the hind-legs powerful. The loose-fitting skin round the head and the sagging dewlap give it a rather mournful expression. Like many dogs originally bred for fighting, the Neapolitan Mastiff is devoted to and fiercely protective of its family.

Group
Not recognized by AKC.
Size
Height: Dogs 26–29 in. (65–75 cm), bitches somewhat less.
Weight: 110–154 lb. (50–70 kg).
Coat
Color: Black, blue-gray, or brown varying from fawn to red. Browns may also be brindle.
Texture: Dense and smooth.

Left: English Mastiff

NEWFOUNDLAND

Left: Newfoundland

Top right: Siberian Husky

Below right: St Bernard

THE NEWFOUNDLAND BREED was primarily developed not, as is often suggested, as a canine lifeguard, but as a draught dog, big and strong enough to pull carts or carry heavy loads. However, its affinity with the fishermen of Newfoundland made it a superb water dog, and its loyalty and great intelligence have enabled it to save the lives of many people in danger of drowning. Early prints suggest that the breed has its origins among the huskies of northern Canada; other writers have argued that its blood carries that of Pyreneans or French Boarhounds. Whatever its origins, there can be no dispute that the breed is today a most magnificent and aristocratic animal.

Characteristics

Newfoundlands should have an exceptionally gentle and docile nature and, although strong and massive of body, should also give the appearance of being active. The broad, solid head has a short muzzle, deep-set dark brown eyes, and small ears lying close to the head. The neck, shoulders, and hindquarters are all very strong, the chest deep, and the feet large and webbed. Movement should be free, possibly with a slight rolling gait. This breed makes a particularly devoted companion for those who have the space to accommodate it and the time to give it the exercise it needs.

Size
Height: Average for dogs 28 in. (71 cm), for bitches 26 in. (66 cm).
Weight: Dogs 140–150 lb. (64–69 kg), bitches 110–120 lb. (50–54 kg). In AKC, 130–150 lb. (59–68 kg) for dogs, 100–120 lb. (45–54 kg) for bitches. The AKC standard states that although large size is desirable, it should not be achieved at the expense of balance, structure, or correct gait.

Coat
Color: Dull jet black, chocolate, or bronze, or "Landseer" (white with black markings).
Texture: Flat and dense, coarse, oily, and water-resistant.

ROTTWEILER

YET ANOTHER OF THE European mastiff breeds which probably have their origins among the dogs which guarded and helped drive the herds of cattle accompanying the Roman armies. The town of Rottweil in what is now Germany was founded by the Romans and was an important cattle-trading center in the 12th century. In such circumstances it is not surprising that a distinctive breed of working dog developed. The Rottweiler Metzerhund was an integral part of the region's prosperity until its use declined with the coming of the railways and mass transport of cattle. At the beginning of the 20th century a club was formed to protect the Rottweiler and, soon after, its qualities earned it a place in police work. The breed's ability as a guard dog is still recognized; its courage, strength, and forbidding aspect make it a marvelous guard for those who have the ability to control it.

Characteristics

The Rottweiler is a compact dog, well proportioned and powerfully built to permit great strength, maneuverability and endurance. Its bearing displays boldness, while its tranquil gaze manifests good nature and devotion. The head is distinctive, broad, of medium length, with well-muscled cheeks and moderately wrinkled. The neck, forelegs, and hindquarters are particularly muscular. Movement should be supple giving an impression of strength, endurance, and purpose. Although wary of strangers and in need of firm discipline, this dog can also make a loyal and affectionate pet.

Size
Height: Dogs 25–27 in. (63–69 cm), bitches 23–25 in. (58–63.5 cm). In AKC, dogs 23¾–27 in. (60–68.5 cm), bitches 21¾–25¾ in. (54.5–65 cm). In FCI, dogs 23½–27 in. (60–68 cm), bitches 21½–25 in. (55–63 cm).
Coat
Color: Black with clearly defined tan markings on cheeks, muzzle, chest, and legs, as well as over the eyes and under the tail.
Texture: Coarse and flat, with a medium-length topcoat.

ST BERNARD

T HE ST BERNARD'S ancestors were probably brought to Switzerland by invading Roman armies. These dogs were crossed with native dogs to produce the Talhund and Bauernhund which, by the 11th century, were in common use on Swiss farms. At the beginning of the 18th century, a passing reference to rescue dogs, working from the hospice founded by Archdeacon Bernard de Menthon, implies that rescue work was a well-established part of the dog's uses, although a hundred years earlier the hospice appears not to have possessed any dogs.

Characteristics
The head of the St Bernard is massive and round with an expression of benevolence, dignity, and intelligence. The muzzle has a well-developed dewlap. The body is broad and muscular throughout, set on strong, well-boned legs. The gait should be easy and unhurried. Although this is a delightful dog, particularly good-natured and trustworthy, it is also enormous, needing lots of space, exercise, and food, plus a considerable amount of grooming.

Size
Height: The taller the better, as long as it is in proportion. In AKC, a range of 25½–27½ in. (64–69 cm) is given as a minimum.
Weight: In AKC, 110–200 lb. (50–91 kg) or more. The AKC and FCI standards both specify a more delicate build for bitches.
Coat
Color: Orange, mahogany-brindle, or red-brindle with white markings; or predominantly white with markings in one of these colors. Black face and ears.
Texture: Rough specimens have a dense, flat coat; smooths have a close, hound-like coat.

SIBERIAN HUSKY

T HIS IS A BREED FORGED in the hardest-imaginable environment among the Chukchi people who inhabited the frozen wastelands of north-eastern Asia. The Chukchi were nomadic hunters who depended for their survival on the strength, speed, courage, intelligence, and toughness of the dogs they had developed by rigorous selection. So well did they succeed that, when the breed was matched in Alaska against the very much bigger native dogs, the Siberians demonstrated a considerable superiority. They continue to give sterling service to humans venturing into the hostile Arctic and Antarctic wastelands.

Characteristics
The general appearance is of a medium-sized working dog, quick and light on its feet and graceful in action. The moderately compact, well-furred body, erect ears, and brush tail suggest its northern heritage. Its characteristic gait is smooth and effortless; its body proportions reflect its power, speed, and endurance. The Siberian is still basically a working dog, with strength, stamina, and need for exercise; but it is friendly and affectionate to all humankind and has a great love of life, making it a most rewarding companion if you are able to control it.

Group
Nordic Sledge Dogs (FCI).
Size
Height: Dogs 21–23½ in. (53–60 cm), bitches 20–22 in. (51–56 cm).
Weight: Dogs 45–60 lb. (20–27 kg), bitches 35–50 lb. (16–23 kg).
Coat
Color: All colors, from black to pure white, with a variety of markings.
Texture: Double, of medium length; the undercoat dense and soft, the overcoat straight and smooth-lying, never harsh or standing straight away from the body.

Pastoral

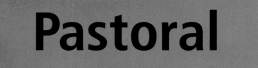

All breeds in this section are classifed as Pastoral by the Kennel Club, Herding by the AKC, Sheepdogs by the FCI, and Working Dogs by the ANKC, unless otherwise stated.

Belgian Shepherd Dog

AUSTRALIAN CATTLE DOG

FROM IMPORTED STOCK Australia has produced two distinctive and impressive working breeds, the Kelpie (see page 80) and the Cattle Dog. The Cattle Dog has been known as the Australian, Blue, or Queensland Heeler, *heeler* being an old British word applied to cattle dogs. In its veins runs the blood of several working breeds which have combined to produce this superlative cattle dog. Two now-extinct breeds, the Black Bobtailed Sheepdogs and the Smithfield Drover, as well as dingoes, Kelpies, Smooth Collies, and Dalmatians have all contributed to its make-up. Although popular in Australia and recognized by the AKC and FCI, the breed has only an Interim standard with the KC.

Characteristics

This is a sturdy, compact working dog that needs plenty of exercise to keep it in good, hard condition. It tends to be suspicious of strangers, but is a loyal and protective companion to those it knows. The head is broad and wedge-shaped, the ears pricked, and the eyes dark. The neck is exceptionally strong, the chest broad, and the loin powerful. Hindquarters are broad and powerful. The tail is long, carried and furnished like a fox's.

Size
Height: Dogs 18–20 in. (46–51 cm), bitches 17–19 in. (43–48.2 cm).
Weight: AKC 35–45 lb. (16–20.5 kg).
Coat
Color: Blue, blue mottled, or speckled, with or without other markings; or red speckled.
Texture: Hard, straight, weather-resistant topcoat with short, dense undercoat.

BELGIAN SHEPHERD DOG

THE HERDING DOGS OF mainland Europe are all closely related and share several strong family characteristics. However, it was not until Professor Reul, at the end of the 19th century, embarked on a study of these dogs, then generally simply referred to as Chien de Berger, that the various local breeds were accorded separate recognition. Among the three basic types recognized by Professor Reul was one with rather long, black hair. The principal breeder of this type was Monsieur Rose of Groenendael, whose stock was all descended from a single black pair, Petite and Picard D'Uccle, black being a color not traditionally favored by the Belgian shepherds. From this pair developed the Groenendael, one of four types now recognized by the Kennel Club and gaining in popularity worldwide. The other three are the Lakenois, the Malinois, and the Tervueren, and the four differ from each other only in color and coat texture. The AKC does not recognize the Lakenois, although the Canadian Kennel Club does.

Characteristics

The breed should be intelligent, courageous, alert, and faithful, protective of the person and property of its owners, but it should show no viciousness by unwarranted attack. The Belgian Shepherd is a well-balanced, square dog, elegant in appearance with a pronounced proud carriage of the head and neck. The head is strong, the ears stiffly erect, the topline slopes from withers to croup, the chest is deep but not broad. The forelegs are straight and strong, set into long and oblique shoulders; the hindquarters are broad and heavily muscled. The tail is long and undocked.

Size
Height: Dogs 24–26 in. (61–66 cm), bitches 22–24 in. (56–61 cm). In FCI, the ideal height for a dog is 24½ in. (62 cm), for a bitch 23 in. (58.4 cm).
Coat
Groenendael
Color: Black, with or without some white.
Texture: Long, straight, and abundant, of medium harshness. Longer in males than in females. The undercoat should be extremely dense.
Lakenois
Color: Reddish fawn with black shading.
Texture: Harsh, wiry, not curly, about 2½ in. (6 cm) long all over body.
Malinois
Color: Red, fawn, or gray with black overlay.
Texture: Short, thick, close to the body, with dense undercoat.
Tervueren
Color: Red, fawn, or gray with black overlay.
Texture: Long, straight, and abundant, of medium harshness. Longer in males than in females. The undercoat should be extremely dense.

BRIARD

Briard

THE BRIARD COMES FROM one of several ancient sheepdog breeds which probably reached Europe with the Mongol invaders and developed into different and localized breeds. This one is from France. By 1809, Abbé Rozier was able to differentiate between the Berger de la Brie (Briard) and the de la Beauce, the difference being in coat length. A club was formed in France in 1900 to protect the breed, and by 1930 an agreed standard had been adopted. The breed came to Britain after the First World War and to America in 1922.

Characteristics

A strong and substantially built dog, fitted for field work, lithe, muscular, well proportioned, alert, and active. The square, strong head has a powerful muzzle and long hair forming a beard and moustache; the prominent eyebrows hang over the eyes. The body is longish with muscular hindquarters and well-boned legs. The dog's appealingly shaggy appearance can easily become messy if not regularly groomed; it also needs a lot of exercise, but is a delightful and playful companion with no hint of aggression in its make-up.

Size
Height: Dogs 24–27 in. (62–68 cm), bitches 23–25½ in. (56–64 cm). In FCI, both sexes may be ½ in. (1 cm) smaller.
Coat
Color: Black, with or without some white hairs; fawn, with or without dark shading; or slate gray.
Texture: Long, slightly wavy, stiff and strong, with a dense undercoat.

COLLIE, BEARDED

THIS COLLIE HAS VERY similar origins to the Rough Collie (see page 78) but remains a little nearer to its original appearance and uses. The breed was not recognized in Britain until 1944, since which time it has achieved considerable popularity and built an impressive record as a show dog. Most, if not all, modern winning Bearded Collies are descended from a single individual champion called Jeannie of Bothkennar.

Characteristics

A good temperament is an essential of the breed, which should be alert, lively, and self-confident. This is an active dog with a long, lean body, strong without giving a heavy appearance. The face should have a quizzical expression. Movement should always be free and active. A cheerful and adventurous dog, the Bearded Collie, or Beardie, makes an ideal family pet for those who are able to give it plenty of exercise.

Size
Height: Dogs 21–22 in. (53–56 cm), bitches 20–21 in. (51–53 cm).
Weight: AKC, 40–60 lb. (18–27 kg).
Coat
Color: Slate gray or reddish fawn, black, blue, all shades of gray, brown, and sandy, with or without white Collie markings.
Texture: Must be double: the undercoat soft, furry, and close, the outercoat hair strong and flat, free from woolliness or any tendency to curl. Sparse hair on the ridge of the nose, longer on the sides. A long beard is a characteristic of the breed.

Bearded Collie

COLLIE, BORDER

ARGUABLY THE WORLD'S finest sheepdog, the Border Collie is now found wherever sheep are kept in appreciable numbers, and in environments very different from those in which it originated—in the hills of southern Scotland. By the mid-19th century the breed was already well established, and for many years in Britain has had its own stud book and registration system. However, its great popularity as a companion, its use in working and obedience trials (for which its considerable intelligence and desire to please make it an extremely popular choice), and a growing interest in the breed as a show dog made it desirable that it should be recognized as a breed by the Kennel Club. This recognition was granted in the 1970s, but enthusiasts on both sides of the Atlantic still encourage a strong emphasis on the dog's working qualities.

Characteristics

A well-proportioned dog with a smooth outline which shows quality, grace, and balance, with sufficient substance to convey the impression that the dog is capable of enduring long periods of active duty. Very intelligent, loyal to its owner, and at all times well disposed toward the stock with which it works. This is a very intelligent breed which needs to be kept active, as it is likely to become destructive if allowed to get bored.

Size
Height: Dogs ideally 21 in. (53 cm), bitches slightly less. In AKC, 18–20 in. (46–51 cm).
Weight: AKC 30–45 lb. (13.5–20.5 kg).
Coat
Color: A variety of colors, provided white does not predominate.
Texture: May be either smooth or moderately long, in both cases with dense topcoat and undercoat.

Rough Collie

COLLIE, ROUGH

THIS BREED ORIGINATED, like the other three collie breeds, Smooth, Border, and Bearded, in the dark-colored herding dogs of Scotland, from which the name is derived, *col* being Anglo-Saxon for black. For centuries they carried out their arduous work herding sheep on the northern hills, with only local recognition. In 1860, however, Queen Victoria visited Balmoral for the first time, saw the dog, fell in love with it, and so assured its future popularity. This understandably changed the breed, bringing with it a greater emphasis on elegance and beauty and less on working ability.

Characteristics
The standard seeks to protect the breed's working ability by asking for a strong and active dog, free from coarseness. It places great emphasis on the sweetness of the expression, a product of the shape of the head, size, and shape of eyes, and position and carriage of the ears. The body is slim but muscular, and the gait effortless with plenty of drive. The Rough Collie needs a lot of grooming but makes an excellent pet. Wary of strangers, it is devoted to its own family.

Size
Height: Dogs 22–24 in. (56–61 cm), bitches 20–22 in. (51–56 cm). In AKC, 2 in. (5 cm) higher.
Weight: Not specified in KC. In AKC, dogs 60–75 lb. (27.2–34 kg), bitches 50–65 lb. (22.6–29.4 kg).
Coat
Color: Three recognized colors, sable and white, tricolor, and blue merle, each with white markings.
Texture: Very dense, the outer coat straight and harsh, the undercoat soft, furry, and very close. Mane and frill very abundant, mask smooth, legs well feathered, and the hair on the tail profuse.

COLLIE, SMOOTH

The standard is as for the Rough except:

Size
Weight: Dogs 45–65 lb. (20.5–29.9 kg), bitches 40–55 lb. (18–25 kg).
Coat
Texture: Hard, dense, and smooth.

GERMAN SHEPHERD DOG (ALSATIAN)

A BREED WHOSE ORIGINS and uses are indicated by its name. The first breed club, the Verein für Deutsche Schäferhund, was formed in 1899. By 1926 it was the most popular dog in Britain, where it was called the Alsatian Wolf Dog. Thoughtless breeding and ignorant handling contrived to give the breed a dubious reputation which only the worst specimens deserve. Of the best, it is difficult to praise too highly the intelligence and sagacity, resourcefulness, and desire to please, but all these virtues must be in the hands of an owner able to develop and control them.

Characteristics
The characteristic expression of the German Shepherd Dog gives the impression of perpetual vigilance, fidelity, liveliness, and watchfulness, alert to every sight and sound; fearless, but decidedly suspicious of strangers. This breed possesses highly developed senses. It is well proportioned, showing great suppleness of limb, and has a long, strongly boned body with plenty of muscle. Obviously capable of endurance and speed and of quick, sudden movement, its gait is supple, smooth, and long-reaching.

Hungarian Puli

Size
Height: 25 in. (62.5 cm) for dogs, 23 in. (57.5 cm) for bitches. In AKC, 22–26 in. (55–65 cm) for both sexes.
Weight: In AKC, 75–95 lb. (34–43 kg).
Coat
Color: Black, or a black saddle with tan or gold to light gray markings.
Texture: Smooth, double texture: thick, close, woolly undercoat and close, hard, straight, weather-resistant outer coat.

HUNGARIAN PULI

T HIS BREED ORIGINATED in the herding dogs brought into Hungary by invading Magyars. It was used to herd and drive sheep. The distinctive thick coat developed because of the harsh weather the Puli had to endure.

Characteristics
A medium-sized breed, vigorous, alert, and active, to the point of being distinctly

German Shepherd Dog

bouncy. By nature, Pulis are affectionate and loyal, but, being excellent guards, are suspicious of strangers. The construction of the Puli is not exaggerated in any way, the head is of medium size, and the neck is strong and muscular and of medium length. The chest is deep and fairly broad, and the body of medium length, straight, and level. The tail is carried over the back. Be warned, however: this is not a breed for those who do not enjoy grooming their dog.

Group
Working (AKC).
Size
Height: Dogs 16–17½ in. (40–44 cm), bitches 14½–16 in. (37–40.6 cm). AKC dogs about 17 in. (43 cm), not to exceed 19 in. (48.2 cm), bitches 16 in. (40.6 cm), not to exceed 18 in. (45.7 cm).
Weight: Dogs 28½–33 lb. (13–15 kg), bitches 22–28½ lb. (10–13 kg). In AKC, 18–39 lb. (8–18 kg).
Coat
Color: Black, white, various shades of gray, and apricot. The black may appear "rusty," or it may show some white hairs.
Texture: The coat is characteristic of this and related breeds and hangs in tight, even cords.

KELPIE

THE KELPIE APPEARS TO have emerged, having been developed from crosses between imported herding dogs, as a distinct breed in the 1870s, and itself produced the smaller and more aggressive Australian Cattle Dog (see page 76). Nowadays the Kelpie works side by side with the ubiquitous Border Collie on the huge sheep farms of Australia where its keen sight, scenting powers, and hearing make it highly valued.

Characteristics

A tough and muscular dog, rather fox-like in appearance with a strong, arched neck, moderately long back, and bushy tail carried low. Devoted to those it knows, and a committed worker, it is likely to be suspicious of strangers.

Group
Not recognized by KC or AKC.
Size
Height: Dogs 18–20 in. (45.7–50.8 cm), bitches 17–19 in. (43–48.2 cm).
Weight: 25–45 lb. (11–20.5 kg).
Coat
Color: Black, black and tan, red, red and tan, fawn, chocolate, or smoke-blue.
Texture: Short, straight, thick, and harsh to the touch.

OLD ENGLISH SHEEPDOG

THE BREED WAS PROBABLY developed, if it did not originate, in the West of England, by using either indigenous herding breeds such as the Bearded Collie or, less likely, imported stock such as the Russian Owtchow. This breed was used not so much as a herding dog but as a drovers' dog for driving sheep and cattle to market. Drovers' dogs were tax-exempt if docked; hence the tailless outline of the Old English Sheepdog and its popular nickname of "Bobtail."

Old English Sheepdog

Characteristics

The Old English Sheepdog is a strong, compact-looking dog, profusely coated all over, very elastic in a gallop, but when walking or trotting it has a characteristic ambling or pacing movement. The bark should be loud with a peculiar "bell-like" ring to it. The head is large and rather squarely formed, and the jaw is fairly long and strong. This is a most faithful breed; it is intelligent, playful, and excellent with children. However, daily grooming is an essential requirement if its coat is not to become knotted and scruffy-looking.

Size
Height: Dogs 24 in. (61 cm) and upward, bitches 22 in. (56 cm).
Weight: In AKC, 66 lb. (30 kg) or more.
Coat
Color: Any shade of gray, grizzle, blue, or blue merle, with or without white markings.
Texture: Profuse and of good hard exture, not straight but shaggy and free from curl. The undercoat should be a waterproof pile.

Kelpie

PYRENEAN MOUNTAIN DOG

THIS HUGE DOG, known in North America as the Great Pyrenees, is a descendant of the Southern European herding and guard breeds, originating in the mountains situated on the borders of France and Spain. It was the guard dog of the region, protecting the flocks against wolves, bears, and thieves. The Chien de Berger des Pyrenées, a smaller version, is used as the herding dog. The Pyrenean Mountain Dog is an impressive animal, and in 1675 captured the interest of the then Dauphin of France who brought some examples of the breed to the court in Paris.

Characteristics

The Pyrenean is serious in play and at work. It should exemplify gentleness and docility even to the point of self-sacrifice. It is a dog of immense size, great majesty, keen intelligence, and a kindly expression. Soundness of temperament is of the

Samoyed

greatest importance in this breed. The head is large, the body is powerful and muscular, and the tail is an attractive plume carried in a circle above the back when the dog is alert.

SAMOYED

JUST AS THE SALUKI may lay claim to being the oldest of the Mediterranean sighthounds, so the Samoyed is probably the oldest of the Northern Spitz breeds. Originally bred as a guard for herds of reindeer, the breed also acted as companion, guard, and sled dog. It shared the hard life of the Sayantsi people in ancient times, and more recently accompanied the polar explorers Nansen, Shackleton, Scott, and Amundsen on their expeditions. The Samoyed's strength, stamina, and hardiness are belied by its child-like good nature and soft, fairy-tale appearance.

Characteristics

The Samoyed is intelligent, alert, and full of action, but above all displays affection toward all humankind. It should be strong, active, and graceful, with a muscular back of medium length allowing liberty of movement. The chest is deep and well sprung, the neck is proudly arched, the front is straight, and

the loins are exceptionally strong, giving an impression of great endurance. The head is powerful and wedge-shaped, the eyes almond-shaped with an intelligent expression. The ears are erect and thick, covered inside with hair. The tail is long and profusely coated, carried over the back when alert, but sometimes dropped when at rest. Its gorgeous coat needs a lot of care, but this is a cheerful, fun-loving companion that will amply repay the effort involved. If necessary, the Samoyed's boisterous love of life can be kept under control by obedience classes.

Group
Working (AKC). Pinscher and Schnauzer, Molossians and Swiss Mountain Dogs and Cattle Dogs (FCI). Utility (ANKC).
Size
Height: Minimum for dogs 28 in. (70 cm), bitches 26 in. (65 cm). In AKC, dogs 27–32 in. (68.5–81 cm), bitches 25–29 in. (63.5–73.6 cm).
Weight: Minimum for dogs 110 lb. (50 kg), bitches 90 lb. (40 kg). Taller dogs should be heavier but in proportion, giving an impression of strength. In AKC, dogs 100–140 lb. (45.3–63.5 kg), bitches 90–115 lb. (40.8–52 kg). In FCI, 100–120 lb. (45.3–54.5 kg).
Coat
Color: All white or principally white, with markings of badger, gray, or pale yellow.
Texture: Created to withstand severe weather, with a fine undercoat and thick overcoat of coarser hair.

Group
Working (AKC). Nordic Sledge Dogs (FCI). Utility (ANKC).
Size
Height: Dogs 20–22 in. (51–56 cm), bitches 18–20 in. (46–51 cm). In AKC, dogs 21–23½ in. (53.3–60 cm), bitches 19–21 in. (48.2–53.3 cm). In FCI, dogs 21 in. (53.3 cm) minimum, bitches 18 in. (45.7 cm) minimum.
Weight: In AKC, 50–65 lb. (22.5–29.5 kg). In FCI, dogs 44–66 lb. (19.9–29.9 kg), bitches 37½–55 lb. (16.9–24.9 kg).
Coat
Color: Pure white, white and biscuit, cream. Silver tips on the outer coat.
Texture: A thick, close, soft, and short undercoat, covered with an outer coat of straight, harsh hair, which grows straight away from the body providing protection against extreme cold.

SHETLAND SHEEP-DOG

THE SHETLAND SHEEPDOG, in spite of exhibiting a considerable degree of similarity to the larger Rough Collie, is not a miniature version of that breed but a separate breed produced in response to the peculiar demands of the hard climate and terrain of the isolated northerly islands off the shores of Scotland. These islands have produced distinctive and hardy breeds of small sheep and ponies, and the Shetland Sheepdog falls into the same category. It is undoubtedly of ancient origin but, owing to lack of records, we know little of its history before it was recognized by the Kennel Club in 1914.

Characteristics
The Sheltie should be instantly appreciated as a dog of great beauty, intelligence, and alertness. It should be affectionate and responsive toward its owner, but may be reserved in its attitude to strangers. The head is refined, a long, blunt wedge tapering from ear to nose, with the tips of the ears dropping forward. The lavish coat disguises a muscular body—this is a tough and active little dog. It is easily bored, however, and does tend to yap.

Size
Height: Dogs ideally 14½ in. (37 cm), bitches 14 in. (35.5 cm). In AKC, 13–16 in. (33–40.6 cm).
Coat
Color: Tricolor, sable, blue merle, black and white or black and tan.
Texture: Must be double: the outer coat of long hair of harsh texture and straight, the undercoat short and close. The mane and frill should be abundant, the forelegs well feathered, and the hindlegs with profuse trouserings.

SWEDISH VALL-HUND

BOTH THE RESEMBLANCE and the similar function in life argue for some shared ancestry between the Vallhund and the Corgi. The fact that both have distinct Spitz characteristics seems to indicate origins in Scandinavia. Like the Corgi, however, this Swedish breed, also known as the Vasgotaspets, has only recently been recognized, in 1948.

Characteristics
The breed is low-slung, long in the body, small and muscular. The carriage and expression indicate vigilance, courage, and energy. The tail is naturally short, not docked, and should not exceed 4 in. (10 cm) in length. Cheerful, friendly, and a natural show-off, eager to be the center of attention, the Vallhund is also a good guard and enjoys lots of exercise.

Group
Not recognized by AKC. Nordic Sledge Dog (FCI).
Size
Height: Dog 13–13¾ in. (33–35 cm), bitch 12-13 in. (31–33 cm).
Weight: 25–35 lb. (11.4–15.9 kg).
Coat
Color: Shades of gray or reddish yellow or reddish brown.
Texture: Of fair length, hard and dense, the undercoat fine and tight.

Swedish Vallhund

WELSH CORGI, CARDIGAN

THE BREED SHARES A common heritage with its more popular cousin from Pembrokeshire (see right).

Characteristics

Apart from the fact that the Pembroke lacks a tail and the Cardigan has a good full one, the two share considerable and obvious similarities. The Cardigan's tail is moderately long and set in line with the body, closely resembling the brush of a fox. The Cardigan is also slightly larger, with not such a sharp head, and larger ears. Although less popular than the Pembroke, the Cardigan is the more reliably even-tempered of the two breeds.

Size
Height: 12 in. (30 cm).
Weight: Dogs 22–26 lb. (9.9–11.7 kg), bitches 20–24 lb. (9–10.8 kg). In AKC, 28–30 lb. (12.5–13.5 kg) maximum for both sexes.
Coat
Color: Any color, with or without white markings, provided that white does not predominate.
Texture: Short or medium, and of hard texture.

WELSH CORGI, PEMBROKE

PEMBROKE CORGIS ARE universally familiar because of their long association with the British Royal Family, but they have an unaristocratic history. The two breeds of Corgi, the Pembroke and the Cardigan, and the Lancashire Heeler, were developed as specialist cattle dogs sometime during the 12th century. The Corgi is said to have been brought to Britain from Holland by Flemish weavers who settled around Haverfordwest in West Wales. This would do much to explain the Corgi's distinct Spitz characteristics which, crossed with the Old Black and Tan Terriers, may have produced the more lightly built Black and Tan Heelers. In recent times, the Pembroke has become firmly established as a house dog and show dog.

Characteristics

The Corgi is low-set, strong, sturdily built, and active, giving an impression of substance and stamina in a small space. It is, in fact, not a small breed but a medium-sized breed on short legs. The head is foxy, the neck and body fairly long. A deep rib-cage, a firm level topline and a short loin add to the impression of strength. The legs are short, forearms slightly turned inward, and hindquarters moderately angulated. The tail is normally docked as short as possible, though some puppies are born without a tail. Like all dogs bred to work, Corgis require plenty of exercise and run quickly to fat if this is not supplied. Although friendly and outgoing the Pembroke can be snappy and uses its powerful bark freely. It needs to be firmly trained.

Size
Height: Approximately 10–12 in. (25.5–30.5 cm).
Weight: Dogs 22–26 lb. (10–12 kg), bitches 22–24 lb. (10–11 kg). In AKC, 24–28 lb. (11–12.5 kg) for both sexes.
Coat
Color: Red, sable, fawn, black and tan. May have white markings on legs, chest, and neck.
Texture: Short or medium length and of hard texture.

Above: Cardigan Corgi
Left: Pembroke Corgi

All breeds in this section are classed as Toys by the KC, AKC, and ANKC, and as Companion and Toy Dogs by the FCI, unless otherwise stated.

AFFENPINSCHER

DOGS WHICH LOOK very like modern Affenpinschers are to be seen in many paintings dating from the 14th century, but it was not until the end of the 19th century that the breed attracted enough attention in Germany, its country of origin, to be scheduled at shows. It is closely related to the Smooth Miniature Pinscher (see page 91).

Characteristics
Facially the Affenpinscher has a strong resemblance to a monkey and also has some of that animal's mischievousness and humor. The face is flat with round, forward-looking, dark eyes. The teeth fit closely together and many dogs are slightly undershot. The ears are small and pointed; in America they may be cropped. The body is short, compact, and square with a docked tail, and it is set, fore and rear, on straight legs.

Affenpinscher

> **Group**
> Pinscher and Schnauzer, Molossians and Swiss Mountain Dogs and Cattle Dogs (FCI).
> **Size**
> **Height:** In KC, 9½–11 in. (24–28 cm). In AKC, less than 10 in. (25 cm). In FCI and ANKC, 10–11 in. (25–28 cm).
> **Weight:** In KC, 6½–9 lb. (3–4 kg).
> **Coat**
> **Color:** Usually black, but black and tan, red, gray and other mixtures are permitted in North America.
> **Texture:** Short and dense, hard and wiry. The head should carry a good crop of whiskers.

AUSTRALIAN SILKY TERRIER

THE SILKY TERRIER MAY be regarded as a second-generation Australian since it is said to have originated from a cross between the Australian Terrier and imported Yorkshire Terriers. It is just as likely to be a smaller, silkier-coated variation of the Australian, retained and bred for its attractive appearance and disposition, and valued by urban dwellers for its easy adaptation to city life. Only in 1955 did the breed come to be known by its present name, having previously been called the Sydney Silky. In its homeland it has been recognized as a distinct breed since the early years of the 20th century. It was first exhibited in 1907, had its original standard drawn up in 1909, and was recognized in America in 1959. In Britain the few imports have yet to achieve much popularity, perhaps because of its similarity to the Yorkshire Terrier, but in its home country the Silky is recognized as an ideal pet—energetic, intelligent, and affectionate. The breed has an Interim standard with the Kennel Club.

Characteristics
The Australian Silky Terrier is a lightly built dog of pronounced terrier character and spirited action. The head is strong, wedge-shaped, and moderately long. The ears, V-shaped and pricked, are set high and carried erect; the eyes are small and dark, with a piercingly keen expression. The body is long for the size of the dog, low-set, and covered with a silky coat of medium length. The tail is normally docked.

> **Group**
> Large and Medium-sized Terriers (FCI).
> **Size**
> **Height:** Ideally 9 in. (23 cm); bitches may be slightly less.
> **Weight:** About 8–10 lb. (4 kg). In FCI, 9–11 lb. (4–4.9 kg).
> **Coat**
> **Color:** A rich mixture of blue and tan or gray-blue and tan. The topknot is silver or fawn.
> **Texture:** Flat, fine in texture, glossy, and silky.

BICHON FRISÉ

ITALIAN TRADERS RETURNING from the Canary Islands in the 14th century brought with them some of the small and very attractive little dogs which they had found on the islands. The dogs were probably descended from the Old Barbet or Water Spaniels from which the original name of Barbichon was derived. This was later contracted to "Bichon" or

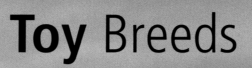

Toy Breeds

Bichon Frisé

changed to "Teneriffe" and the breed began to gain favor in the Royal Courts of Europe. After the French Revolution, Bichons became fashionable as circus dogs, but by the 19th century much of their popularity had been lost. After the First World War the breed's potential was again recognized and, in 1933, the present name was adopted, since which time the breed has regained much of its former standing.

Characteristics

The Bichon is sturdy and lively with a stable temper, has a stylish gait and an air of dignity and intelligence. The skull is broad and somewhat round with a dense topknot. The ears are dropped and covered with long, flowing hair; the large, round eyes are dark and expressive. The neck is rather long and carried proudly behind the erect head. The body is broad and muscular for the size of the dog. The tail is covered with long, flowing hair, carried gaily and curved to lie on the back. The legs are straight and strong-boned.

Group
Non-sporting (AKC).
Size
Height: 9–11 in. (23–28 cm). In AKC up to 12 in. (30 cm).
Coat
Color: Solid white with a dark pigment underneath.
Texture: Very distinctive—profuse, silky, and loosely curled, with an undercoat.

CAVALIER KING CHARLES SPANIEL

THE CAVALIER KING CHARLES SPANIEL is a re-creation of the toy dog favored by King Charles II in the 17th century. In its early days, the breed—popular throughout Europe and painted by Rubens, Rembrandt, and also of course Gainsborough—resembled the modern King Charles Spaniel (see page 90), but over the next two centuries it became smaller and more snub-nosed. Impetus to recreate this attractive toy spaniel in its original form came from a Mr Eldridge, an American, who in 1920 offered prizes of $40 (£25) for Blenheim Spaniels possessing "long faces, flat skulls, no inclination to be domed, no stop and a beauty spot in the center of the forehead." By 1928, a club had formed and the breed was established.

Characteristics

The breed is active, graceful, has a sporting character, and is free in action. Large, dark eyes are set into an almost flat skull, with long, well-feathered ears hanging down. The body is small and well balanced, and the tail is well feathered and jaunty, though not carried too high. The Cavalier makes a delightful companion, eager to please. Although it likes comfort and is never happier than when curled up by the fire, it is also fond of outdoor activities and a good run.

Group
Retrievers, Flushing Dogs and Waterdogs (FCI).
Size
Height: In AKC, 12–13 in. (30–33 cm).
Weight: 12–18 lb. (5.4–8 kg); may be 2 lb. (1 kg) less in AKC.
Coat
Color: Black and tan, ruby (rich red), Blenheim (chestnut and white), tricolor.
Texture: Long, silky, and free from curl, with ample featherings.

Cavalier King Charles Spaniel

CHIHUAHUA

THE ORIGINS OF THE world's smallest breed of dog are shrouded in mystery. Certainly its immediate origin was the Mexican state after which it is named, but whether it arrived there via trade routes with China and Japan or was developed by the native Aztecs or Toltecs, it is impossible to say. The first Chihuahua to be registered by the AKC was Midget in 1904, though there had been reliable references to Mexico's little dogs for the previous twenty-five years. Before that there existed neither archeological remains nor reliable references to help establish the history of the breed.

Characteristics

There are two types—Smooth-coated and Long-coated. The most obvious characteristic of either is its extremely small size. The distinctive head is round with an "apple dome" skull. The eyes are full and round, though not protruding, and the ears large, set at an angle of about 45°. The dog is alert and swift with a saucy expression, small with a dainty, compact appearance coupled with a brisk and forceful personality. Chihuahuas can be delicate, prone to stomach upsets, and prefer two or three small meals a day to one large one. The Smooth-coated in particular is also susceptible to the cold.

Size
Weight: Up to 6 lb. (2.7 kg) with 2–4 lb. (1–1.8 kg) preferred. In AKC, 1–6 lb. (0.5–2.7 kg) preferred.
Coat
Color: Any color or mixture of colors.
Texture:
Long-coat: Long, soft, and either flat or slightly waved. There is a pronounced ruff, and feathering on ears, feet, legs, and hindquarters. The tail should be long and full as a plume.
Smooth-coat: Smooth, soft, close, and glossy.

CHINESE CRESTED DOG

HAIRLESS DOGS exist in many parts of the world, such as Africa, Turkey, China, and Mexico. Whether all such breeds share a common origin, or whether each is a mutant produced from a local breed, is impossible to say. Even in Mexico the Mexican Hairless Dog has been called the Chinese Hairless, because it possibly originated in China.

Size
Height: Ideal for dogs 11–13 in. (28–33 cm), for bitches 9–12 in. (23–30 cm). In AKC, only the maximum heights are specified.
Weight: Not over 12 lb. (5.5 kg). In AKC, 5–10 lb. (2.25–4.5 kg).
Coat
Color: Any color or combination of colors.
Texture: The crest on the head is long and flowing. The tail should carry a plume on the last two-thirds of its length. Furnishings on feet should not extend above the knee on the forelegs, and hock on the hind-legs. The skin should otherwise have no large patches of hair and should be fine-grained and smooth. In Powder Puffs, the undercoat is covered by a soft veil of long hair.

Chinese Crested Dog

Characteristics
A small, active, graceful dog, medium- to fine-boned with a smooth hairless body, having profuse hair on feet, head, and tail only. There is also a "Powder Puff" variety that is covered entirely with long hair. The skull in both types is slightly rounded with a fairly long muzzle, the eyes round and set wide apart, the ears large and upstanding. The tail is carried over the back or looped. Despite their small size, they make alert and intelligent guard dogs as well as good companions.

GRIFFON BRUXEL-LOIS

ORIGINALLY THE GRIFFON was a humble adjunct of stables, used to keep down vermin and as an effective early-warning system of unauthorized intrusion. It probably has origins in the more ancient Affenpinscher, but certainly owes a debt to a number of other breeds, including Black and Tan Terriers, Pugs, and Yorkshire Terriers. Although small and toy-like, the Griffon retains many of its terrier characteristics and makes a happy and playful pet.

Size

Height: In AKC, 7–8 in. (17.5–20 cm).
Weight: Ideally 6–10 lb. (2.7–4.5 kg), although both as small as 5 lb. (2.2 kg) and as large as 11 lb. (4.9 kg) are acceptable. AKC: 8–10 lb. (3.6–4.5 kg) is ideal, with 12 lb. (5.41 kg) the maximum permissible. In FCI, there are two categories: small Griffons should not weigh over 6½ lb. (2.9 kg); large Griffons should weigh over 6½ lb. (2.9 kg), with a maximum weight of 11 lb. (4.9 kg) for dogs and 10 lb. (4.5 kg) for bitches.

Coat

Color: Red, black, or black and rich tan.
Texture: Smooth variety—short and tight. Rough variety—straight and wiry, ideally with no undercoat.

Characteristics

The Griffon is a smart little dog with a pert, monkey-like expression. It is well balanced, square in outline, lively, and alert. The head is large and rounded, the eyes also large and round. The body is short and sturdy and the hindquarters very muscular for such a small dog. The tail is normally docked. There are two types of coat, rough and smooth, which occasionally occur in the same litter.

ITALIAN GREY-HOUND

A BREED OF ANCIENT origin which was certainly widely known and admired among the civilizations located around the Mediterranean 2,000 years ago, but which probably achieved its peak of popularity in 16th-century Italy and later in the courts of James I, Frederick the Great, and Catherine the Great. It is the smallest of the sighthounds, though its fragile proportions preclude any active participation in the chase. The Italian Greyhound is prized today—as it always has been—for its elegance, sweet nature, great beauty, small size, and the ease with which it is kept.

Characteristics

A miniature greyhound, very slenderly made and of great elegance, with a high-stepping and free action. The skull is long, flat, and narrow, the muzzle very fine; the eyes are rather large, bright, and full of expression, the ears rose-shaped, soft, and delicate. The neck is long, gracefully arched, and set into long, sloping shoulders. Forelegs are straight with small delicate bones, hindquarters carry muscular thighs. The chest is deep and narrow, the back curved and drooping to the hindquarters. The tail is rather long and fine, carried low.

Group

Sighthounds (FCI).

Size

Height: In AKC, 13–15 in. (33–38 cm). In FCI, 12.4–15 in. (31.5–38 cm).
Weight: In KC, 6–10 lb. (2.7–4.5 kg). In FCI, maximum 11 lb. (4.9 kg). In AKC, there are two categories, up to 8 lb. (3.5 kg) and over 8 lb. (3.5 kg).

Coat

Color: Black, blue, cream, fawn, or red, all with or without white markings. All white is also acceptable.
Texture: Thin and glossy, like satin.

JAPANESE CHIN

LIKE SO MANY OF THE toy breeds that originated in the Orient, the Japanese Chin, sometimes called the Japanese Spaniel, has long been associated with the royal courts. Its ancestors probably arrived in Japan as gifts from the Chinese Emperor to his Japanese counterpart. It is interesting to note that the breed was introduced into Britain in just the same way, as a gift to Queen Victoria. The Chin makes an excellent and attractive companion, but one with a mind of its own.

Characteristics

A lively little dog of dainty appearance, smart compact carriage, and profuse coat. It is stylish in movement, lifting the feet high, and carries its plumed tail over its back. The head is large in proportion to the size of the dog, with a broad and rounded skull, and very short muzzle. The body is squarely and compactly built, wide in the chest. The legs are profusely feathered. The tail is set high and profusely feathered, closely arched or plumed over the back.

Size

Height: In FCI, dogs average 30.4cm (12in).
Weight: 4–7 lb. (1.8–3.2 kg), the daintier the better, provided the dog is well balanced and sound. In AKC, there are two categories, over and under 7 lb. (3.2 kg). In the smaller category, the smaller the better.

Coat

Color: Black and white, or red and white.
Texture: Profuse, long, soft, and straight, of silky texture, free from curl or wave.

Left: Griffon Bruxellois

KING CHARLES SPANIEL

A TOY SPANIEL WHICH derives its name from its popularity at the court of King Charles II, which was so great that few portraits of the period seem to be without such a dog reclining on milady's lap or peeping from behind a chair. Though it was Charles II who gave his name to the breed, toy spaniels had been popular for some time before. Mary, Queen of Scots, was fond of them and one even accompanied her to her death. When this breed emerged in the 17th century, it was more like the modern Cavalier (see page 87), but has become smaller over the years. In North America this breed is also known as the English Toy Spaniel.

Characteristics

The King Charles's head is large for the size of the dog, with large dark eyes full of expression, a short snub muzzle and long, pendulous, well-feathered ears, set low and lying close to the cheeks. The body is stocky and well muscled, proportioned like a miniature spaniel.

Size
Height: In AKC, 10–10½ in. (25–26 cm).
Weight: 8–14 lb. (3.6–6.3 kg). In AKC, 9–12 lb. (4–5.4 kg).
Coat
Color: Black and tan, tricolor, Blenheim (white with chestnut patches), or ruby (self-colored chestnut red).
Texture: Long, silk,y and straight.

LÖWCHEN (LITTLE LION DOG)

FROM THE MIDDLE AGES, dogs very like the modern breed of Löwchen appeared in paintings, and Lion Dogs are described by Thomas Bewick, writing around 1800. Whether the modern Löwchen is the same as these dogs is a matter for conjecture, since it seems fairly unlikely that the older types had to be clipped in order to produce their lion-like appearance.

Characteristics

A small, intelligent dog with an affectionate and lively disposition combining all the good qualities of a companion dog. The head is short and broad, the skull flat between the ears, and the body well proportioned. Löwchen are traditionally clipped in the lion clip, leaving a profuse mane over the head and shoulders, and feathering on the feet.

Group
Miscellaneous (AKC).
Size
Height: 10–13 in. (25–33 cm).
Coat
Color: Any color or combination of colors.
Texture: Fairly long and wavy, but not curly.

MALTESE

THIS BREED HAS BEEN known in the Mediterranean islands probably since the time of the Phoenicians. Certainly it has existed very much in its present form since, at the time of the Apostle Paul, Publius, the Roman Governor of Malta, owned a Maltese which was described by the poet Martial as being "more frolicsome than Catulla's sparrow… purer than a dove's kiss… gentler than a maiden… more precious than Indian gems." Throughout the intervening years, the breed has attracted the admiration of successive writers, and its extraordinary grace and beauty

Size
Height: Not over 10 in. (25.5 cm). In FCI, dogs 8–10 in. (20–25.4 cm), bitches 7¾–9 in. (18.9–22.8 cm).
Weight: In AKC, under 7 lb. (3 kg), 4–6 lb. (1.8–2.7 kg) preferred. In FCI, 6½–9 lb. (2.9–4 kg).
Coat
Color: Pure white, but slight lemon markings are acceptable.
Texture: The coat should be of good length, but not so long as to impede movement, of silky texture and straight. It should not be woolly or crimped. There should be no woolly undercoat.

Maltese

Papillon

PAPILLON

ARGUABLY PAPILLONS, or their Miniature Spaniel progenitors, appear in more paintings by artists such as Rubens, Watteau, Boucher, and Fragonard than any other breed of dog. As companions to the ladies of the courts of Europe, these elegant little creatures led a noble existence. Today they have lost none of their elegance, charm, and vivacity. They have also, to a large degree, retained the toughness that they inherited from their gundog ancestors.

Characteristics

The Papillon is a dainty, balanced little dog which should have an attractive, slightly rounded head with a finely pointed muzzle and round, dark eyes showing an alert, lively expression. The bearing should be alert, and the movement sound, light, and free. The ears should be large, rounded at the tips, heavily fringed, and carried obliquely like the spread wings of a butterfly, hence the name Papillon, which is French for butterfly. The body should be long and well formed. The tail is a luxuriant plume arched over the back.

> **Size**
> **Height:** 8–11 in. (20–28 cm).
> **Weight:** In FCI, there are two classes, below 5½ lb. (2.4 kg) and over 5½ lb. (2.4 kg) to 10 lb. (4.5 kg) for dogs and 11 lb. (4.9 kg) for bitches.
> **Coat**
> **Color:** White with patches which may be any color except liver. A tricolor must be black and white with tan over the eyes, on cheeks, inside ears, and under the tail.
> **Texture:** Abundant and flowing, but without undercoat, long, fine, and silky, with a profuse frill on the chest. Short and close on skull, muzzle, and front part of the legs.

have found it a place in the courts of Ancient Greece and Egypt, and in that of Queen Elizabeth I.

Characteristics

The breed should be sweet-tempered and very intelligent, smart, lively, and alert. The profuse white coat covers a well-made little dog with dark brown eyes, long pendant ears, and a short solid body. The tail is well arched over the back, and feathered.

MINIATURE PINSCHER

CONTRARY TO POPULAR misconception the Miniature Pinscher is not a small Doberman; its original name "Red Pinscher" referred to the breed's resemblance to small forest deer. It has existed for several centuries in Germany and Scandinavia, where it was valued as a very alert watch dog. It was, however, only during the early years of the 20th century that it began to find international favor.

Characteristics

This is structurally a well-balanced, sturdy, compact, elegant, short-coupled, smooth-coated toy dog, naturally well groomed, proud, vigorous, and alert. Its high-stepping gait, its fearless animation, complete self-possession, and spirited presence differentiate it from other toy dogs. The head is narrow, the ears upstanding, cropped in countries where the operation is not forbidden. The body is compact and muscular, the tail set high and normally docked short.

> **Group**
> Pinscher and Schnauzer, Molossians and Swiss Mountain Dogs and Cattle Dogs (FCI).
> **Size**
> **Height:** 10–12 in. (25.5–30.4 cm). In AKC, 11–11½ in. (27.9–29 cm) is the ideal.
> **Weight:** In AKC, 10 lb. (4.5 kg).
> **Coat**
> **Color:** Black or blue; chocolate with tan markings; or solid red.
> **Texture:** Smooth, hard and short, straight and lustrous, closely adhering to and uniformly covering the body.

PEKINGESE

IN ANCIENT TIMES the Pekingese was the sacred dog of China, its presence and appearance recorded in intricately carved statues of ivory, jewel-studded wood or cast in bronze or precious metals. Certainly during the Tang Dynasty in the 8th century these "Foo Dogs" were already highly prized, carefully bred, and jealously guarded. The Foo Dogs were of three types: the strongly built Lion Dogs, the golden Sun Dogs, and the tiny Sleeve Dogs. Their introduction to the West came after the Imperial Palace in Peking had been looted; part of this loot was a fawn and white Pekingese which passed into the hands of Queen Victoria. Lord Hay and the Duke of Richmond had other Chinese Pekingese.

Characteristics

The Peke should be a small, well-balanced, thick-set dog with great dignity, a fearless carriage, and an alert, intelligent expression. The head is massive for the size of the dog, the skull broad, wide, and flat between the ears and eyes. The nose is very short and broad, well wrinkled with a firm underjaw, giving a flat profile. The eyes are large, clear, dark, and lustrous, the ears heart-shaped and carried close to the head, with long profuse feathering. The body is short with a broad chest, falling away behind, lion-like with a distinct waist. The forelegs are short, thick, and heavily boned, bowed but firm at the shoulder. Hind-quarters are light but firm and well shaped, absolutely sound, giving a slow, dignified, rolling gait in front, with a close gait behind.

Size
Weight: Dogs not over 11 lb. (5 kg), bitches not over 12 lb. (5.5 kg). The dog should be surprisingly heavy when picked up. In AKC, a maximum of 14 lb. (6.3 kg), with a medium size preferred.
Coat
Color: All colors and markings, except albino and liver.

Texture: Long and straight with a profuse mane forming a frill round the neck, and profuse feathering on ears, legs, thighs, toes, and tail, which is carried over the back. The top coat should be rather coarse with a thick undercoat.

POMERANIAN

POSSIBLY THE SMALLEST of the Spitz breeds, but one which retains all the courage and character of its larger cousins. During the last hundred years the Pomeranian has been reduced in size, but seems to have avoided many of the problems often associated with miniaturization. It is no longer used to herd sheep, but remains an alert house dog, capable of warning of the presence of intruders with a surprisingly deep bark, giving the impression that a larger animal is on duty.

Characteristics

The Pomeranian is a short-coupled, compact dog, alert in character and deportment. The head is fox-like in shape and expression, the eyes bright and dark in color, the ears small and erect. The shortness of the neck and body are accentuated by the characteristic Spitz ruff and curled tail. Movement is smooth and free.

Size
Height: In FCI, 27.9cm (11in) maximum.
Weight: Dogs 4–4½ lb. (1.8–2 kg), bitches 4½–5½ lb. (2–2.5 kg). In AKC, 3–7 lb. (1.3–3 kg), ideally from 4–5 lb. (1.8–2.2 kg). In FCI, not more than 7½ lb. (3.3 kg).
Coat
Color: Any solid color with or without lighter or darker shadings of the same color, but not black or white shading.
Texture: Double-coated: a short, soft, thick undercoat with a longer, coarse, harsh-textured outer coat.

Pekingese

POODLE, TOY

THE STANDARD IS the same as for the Standard Poodle (see page 62) except for the following:

Group
Non-sporting (ANKC).
Size
Height: Below 11 in. (28 cm). In AKC, not more than 10 in. (25.4 cm). In FCI, less than 13¾ in. (34.8 cm).

PUG

THE PUG IS ANOTHER OF the toy breeds with roots in ancient China, where it has flourished for the past 2,000 years. Many carvings were made of Pugs in Netsuke, which show how little the breed's appearance has changed. Though very much a toy dog, the Pug has all the characteristics of some of the Eastern mastiff breeds which it so closely resembles. In Europe, its fortunes were based on its being taken up as a political mascot. It was associated with the Dutch House of Orange after it saved the life of William, Prince of Orange, by warning of Spanish intruders. Josephine, Napoleon's wife, was so captivated by the breed that

Size
Height: In AKC, 10–11 in. (25.5–27.5 cm).
Weight: 14–18 lb. (6.3–8.1 kg).
Coat
Color: Silver, apricot, fawn, or black. Paler colors should have clearly defined black mask and ears.
Texture: Fine, smooth, soft, short, and glossy, neither hard nor woolly.

Pug

she was able to ignore its history of royal patronage and chose Pugs as her companions during her husband's imprisonment. She even contrived to get her pet to carry messages to Napoleon.

Characteristics
A square little dog, giving an impression of considerable substance packed into small size. The head is round, massive, and deeply wrinkled, the muzzle short and blunt, the eyes very large, bold, and dark. The body is short but wide in the chest. The forelegs are strong and straight, the hindquarters muscular. The tail is curled tightly.

YORKSHIRE TERRIER

ALTHOUGH BY VICTORIA'S reign the Yorkshire Terrier, with its diminutive size and glamorous coat, had become a fashionable pet, its ancestry is much more humble. Originating among the Scottish Terriers, it was taken up in the 1840s by Yorkshire weavers who wanted a sporting little terrier for ratting expeditions or for competition in the rat pits. It was popular perhaps because of its attractive coat which owed something in texture to the Skye Terrier and in color to the now-extinct Waterside Terrier. The breed in those days weighed anything up to 20 lb. (9 kg) with 10 lb.

(4.5 kg) being regarded as an ideal but, when killing rats ceased to be part of its purpose in life, the size was further reduced.

Characteristics
The general appearance should be that of a long-coated terrier, very compact and neat, the carriage conveying an air of importance. The head is rather small and flat, the eyes dark and sparkling, and the ears V-shaped and carried erect or semierect. The forelegs are straight, the body very compact with a good loin and level topline. The coat is the important characteristic of the breed, and the standard lays down precise requirements as to length and shading on different parts of the body. The tail, normally docked to medium length, is covered in hair and carried quite high. A tough little dog with a lot of character, the Yorkie can hold its own in an encounter with a much larger dog. It makes a spirited, outgoing, and delightful companion, enjoying a good walk as much as any of the larger terriers.

Group
Large and Medium-sized Terriers (FCI).
Size
Weight: Up to 7 lb. (3.1 kg).
Coat
Color: A dark steel blue with rich bright tan markings.
Texture: Long and perfectly straight, not wavy, glossy and of a fine silky texture.

Part Three

Physiology and Behavior

It will help you to understand more about your dog if you know something about how his body works and the basic instincts that make him behave the way he does.

THE MUSCULOSKELETAL SYSTEM

A DOG'S SKELETON VARIES from that of a human in a number of ways which explain the different movements it is able to make. The size and shape of individual bones may vary from breed to breed, although the essentials do not. The skull of the Bulldog, for example, is thick and solid while that of the Borzoi is long and much less massive.

The dog's neck contains seven vertebrae, known as cervical vertebrae. The first (the atlas) allows the head to nod up and down, and the second (the axis) permits the atlas and the head to rotate enabling the dog to turn its head on one side. The rest of the neck vertebrae allow the dog to bend its neck and look behind much more efficiently than a person can.

There are thirteen pairs of ribs. Those at the front of the chest are joined at their lower ends to the sternum or breastbone, but the final pair are not. The thoracic vertebrae, the ribs, and the sternum form what is commonly known as the rib cage, which encloses the heart and the lungs. The rib cage allows a significant amount of movement between the ribs themselves so that the lungs can expand and contract to permit breathing.

At the upper end of each front leg is a triangular bone called the scapula or shoulder blade. This is attached to the chest by muscles that allow the greatest freedom of movement backward and forward but very little sideways. The lower end of the scapula is fitted with a cup or socket that allows the top end of the next bone, the humerus, to form a highly mobile shoulder joint.

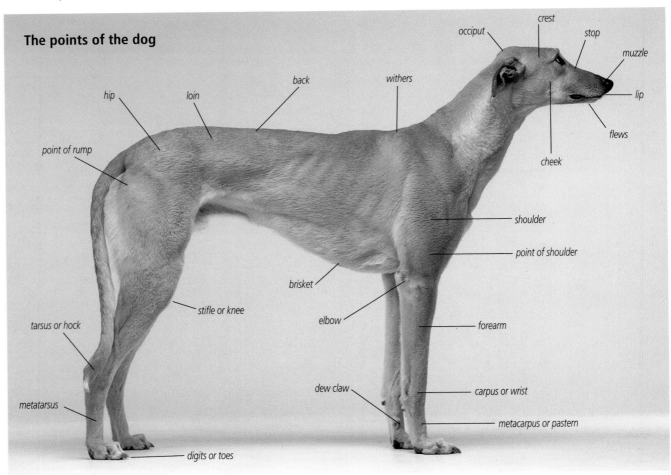

The points of the dog

hip · loin · back · withers · occiput · crest · stop · muzzle · lip · flews · cheek · point of rump · shoulder · point of shoulder · brisket · forearm · stifle or knee · elbow · tarsus or hock · dew claw · carpus or wrist · metatarsus · metacarpus or pastern · digits or toes

The dog's foreleg is similar in construction to a human arm; the elbow joint has a comparable "hinge" action. The wrist, foot, and "fingers" consist of a number of small bones; the third "finger bone" is covered by the dog's claw. The smallest, inside digit is known as the dew-claw but is often absent.

The hind leg is attached to the skeleton by means of the bony pelvic girdle. On either side of this girdle is a small depression called the acetabulum, which forms the cup for the femur or thigh bone. This is the hip joint. The femur forms the knee or stifle joint with the tibia and its smaller partner, the fibula. The hind foot has the same bone structure as the front one, but the dew-claw is an even rarer occurrence.

Ligaments and muscles control the working of the joints, and nerve cells carry impulses from the dog's brain to the muscles and body organs. Different muscles have very different functions, but all act in the same manner by contracting or relaxing. The heart beats because its muscles regularly contract and relax. The muscles of the chest constantly work to expand the rib cage, drawing fresh air into the lungs, and to release it, pushing spent air out.

The locomotor muscles, which provide the means by which a dog moves its limbs, are attached to the various bones. As the individual muscles contract, so they draw together the bones to which they are attached. Similarly, as they relax they allow the bones to move apart. In this way the joints are flexed or extended, the limbs are moved, and progress in any direction is achieved.

Every part of the body of a dog, and every bodily function, is controlled by the brain, which contains the majority of the nerve cells in the body. From these cells messages are transmitted to the tissues throughout the body. These communication links are located first in the spinal cord. At various points along the length of the spinal cord, bundles of nerve processes leave the cord, pass through the spinal column between the vertebrae, and travel onward to the muscles and organs.

These nerve bundles carry messages in both directions. Messages from the brain control functions, instructing a muscle to contract, for example, or a gland to discharge its contents. Others "report back" to the brain, keeping it informed of what is happening all over the body. If, for example, a dog's skin is inflamed, a message indicating pain will be transmitted to the brain, which may then "instruct" a leg to scratch the area concerned. If a nerve is seriously damaged, the message will not get through. The result of this will be loss of feeling and motor paralysis.

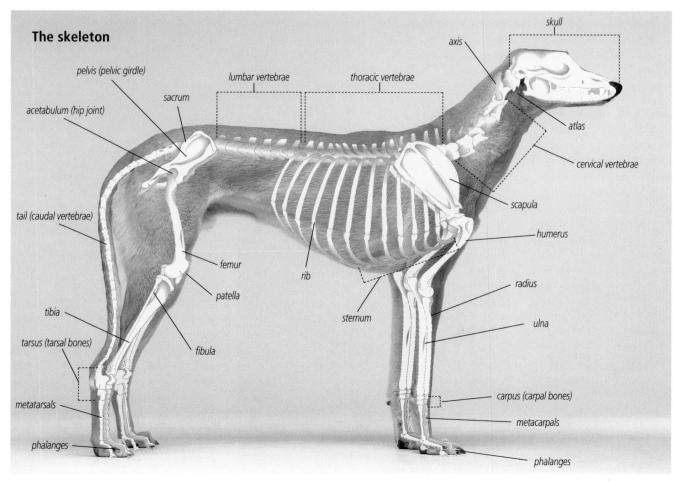

The skeleton

skull

axis

pelvis (pelvic girdle)

lumbar vertebrae

thoracic vertebrae

sacrum

atlas

acetabulum (hip joint)

cervical vertebrae

scapula

tail (caudal vertebrae)

humerus

femur

radius

rib

patella

tibia

ulna

sternum

tarsus (tarsal bones)

fibula

metatarsals

carpus (carpal bones)

metacarpals

phalanges

phalanges

THE DIGESTIVE, RESPIRATORY, AND CIRCULATORY SYSTEMS

SIMPLY PUT, THE ALIMENTARY canal is a tube of varying size which runs from the mouth at one end to the anal opening at the other. Food enters via the mouth, passes through the tube, where it is digested and all the available nutrients are extracted; what remains is then excreted as waste.

The tongue is one of the first bodily parts by which a dog derives its nutrition. It is used for lapping fluids and licking up particles of food. In the mouth the food is softened for swallowing, aided by the addition of saliva from three pairs of salivary glands that empty into the mouth.

The teeth serve the important function of cutting up meat into pieces of a size suitable for swallowing. Every dog, from the Peke to the German Shepherd, should have the same number of teeth—twenty-eight. The side of each jaw should have three incisors, one canine, and four pre-molars in both upper and lower sets. There are two molars in the upper jaw but three in the lower.

From the mouth, the food proceeds into the oesophagus or gullet, which passes down the neck and chest into the abdomen and stomach. There, acids and enzymes work on the food, preparing it for passage through the pylorus, a ring-shaped muscle around the hind end of the stomach, and into the small intestine where the useful parts of the food are absorbed into the bloodstream.

The small intestine is the longest section of the alimentary canal and sits coiled up within the abdomen. In fully grown dogs it is capable of dealing with a large quantity of food at a time, which is why they need to be fed only one substantial meal a day. After everything of value has been extracted from the contents of the small intestine, the rest moves on into the large intestine, where excess fluid is removed. What is left then passes into the rectum and finally out through the anus as feces.

Near to the first part of the small intestine is the pancreas gland, which produces two important substances. One is insulin, a deficiency of which causes sugar diabetes; the other is trypsin, an insufficient quantity of which will lead to chronically soft fecal excretion.

The liver has a great number of functions. It sits in the front of the abdomen and its main task is to aid the digestion of food that is taken from the stomach and the small intestine. It also produces bile, which assists in the digestive process and is stored in the gall-bladder.

The urinary tract provides the means by which a dog voids most of the liquid waste. The starting point is the two kidneys, which receive all the blood that has been carried to other parts of the body, and act as a sophisticated filter. The waste matter they remove, now in the form of urine, passes down the ureter to the bladder, where it is temporarily stored. Periodically a sphincter muscle at the hind end of the bladder is relaxed, and the urine flows out through the urethra. In the dog it passes directly outside through the penis. In the bitch the urethra empties into the hind part of the vagina, and urine is then passed out of the body through the vulva.

The skin and the lungs also play an important role in expelling waste products from the body, the first by direct transmission into the atmosphere, and the second by the breathing out of waste gases via the trachea.

In order to stay alive a dog needs to have an effective means of drawing

Left: Water is as vital to a dog's survival as it is to a human's. Make sure your dog always has a bowl of fresh, clean water.

Right: A Border Collie pup chewing on a piece of meat. Chewing helps prevent a buildup of plaque on the teeth.

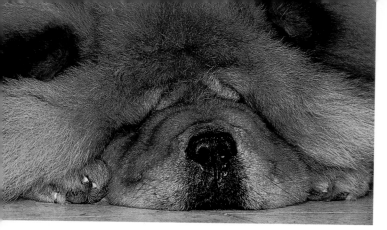

The structure of the dog's nasal passages accounts for its keen sense of smell. This is apparent even in comparatively short-muzzled dogs such as the Chow Chow.

oxygen into its body and ridding itself of waste gases. Air is drawn into the two lungs via the nostrils and the area at the back of the mouth (the pharynx), through the larynx, to the trachea or wind-pipe. The trachea, which consists of a series of cartilaginous rings, passes down the neck and enters the chest. Once inside the chest the trachea divides into two bronchi, one leading to each lung. Each bronchus in turn splits into a series of smaller air passages called bronchioles. Through this system air is drawn into the functioning cells of the lungs, where the oxygen is diffused into the dog's bloodstream. Waste gases such as nitrogen and carbon dioxide are transported in the bloodstream back from the body to be exhaled into the atmosphere.

The nostrils take air through the nasal cavities and thus over the highly specialized cells that register the sensation of smell. There are two main reasons why the dog has such a powerful sense of smell. First, it has a greater length of nasal passage than most other animals; and, second, within the nose it has bones known as turbinates that are shaped something like a scroll. This extra bone area means the dog has a greater number of scent cells than humans do.

Within the larynx are situated the vocal cords. A dog with a sore throat can become just as hoarse as a human, and the sound of its bark is noticeably altered. The technique of panting is another function connected with the respiratory system. Panting serves a useful purpose, drawing cold air in over the tongue and passing it out again, taking moisture with it. It thus reduces the dog's body heat by evaporation.

The circulatory system consists of the heart and the two systems of blood vessels: the arteries, which receive a rich supply of oxygen from the lungs and carry it away from the heart to "feed" the organs and muscles; and the veins, which bring oxygen-depleted blood back again. The further from the heart an artery is, the smaller it becomes. The smaller arteries are called arterioles, and the tiniest are capillaries. The blood in the arteries is pumped along by the beat of the heart. In most arteries it is possible to feel the effect of each heart-beat in the form of a pulse.

Arterial blood is usually redder than venous blood because it contains a greater, more useful supply of oxygen.

The darker, more maroon-colored, venous blood is returned to the heart via the venules and veins and finds its way back to the lungs, where it is re-oxygenated. Venules and veins are generally wider than arteries, have thinner walls, and do not pulsate. The function of the blood is to carry nourishment to every cell in the animal's body and to remove waste products. So every cell of tissue, bone, muscle, organ, or skin has an arteriole bringing a constant supply of oxygenated blood, as well as a corresponding venule carrying waste-bearing blood back to the lungs for regeneration.

The spleen, which lies alongside the stomach, helps in the process of filtering out old blood cells and producing new ones, but in older dogs most of these functions are carried out by other tissues such as bone marrow.

GENETICS

Left: Selective breeding over a number of generations produces features that distinguish one breed from another. The Pug is characterized by its small size, sturdy body, very short muzzle, and prominent eyes.

Right: The Bernese, the German Shepherd, and the St Bernard are all large dogs, but selective breeding accounts for the variations between them in size, shape, and coat.

GENETICS IS THE SCIENCE of heredity, which means the transmission to offspring of the characteristics that are inbuilt in previous generations of animals and plants. Inherited characteristics may be physical, mental, or temperamental. They may be greatly modified by the environment, to the extent that an inherited tendency may never manifest itself because of over-riding factors which arise during growth.

The sum total of an animal's make-up is a combination of inherited and acquired characteristics, the latter resulting from environmental factors and such things as accidental or deliberately imposed features of its rearing from conception. There is an important distinction between truly inherited features and congenital abnormalities. A congenital disease or abnormality arises when the fetus in the womb is developing. An animal may be born with a defect already apparent, but this is not necessarily an inherited problem. It may be acquired by accident prior to birth.

Genes are the hereditary material in reproductive cells. They are carried in thread-like chromosomes. Each species has a specific number of chromosomes, which occur in pairs. The dog has thirty-nine pairs of chromosomes. Chromosome pairs are alike in gene content, and genes are also carried in pairs. While it is often possible to correlate one pair of genes with one inherited characteristic, most characteristics depend on the interaction of genes. One pair of genes may also affect more than one characteristic.

The pairing of genes is responsible for the phenomenon of dominance and recessiveness. Each individual has only two genes of each kind, one derived from his or her father, and one from his or her mother. Each gene may be either dominant or recessive to its pair. A simplified example is the genes for eye-color. The gene for brown eyes is dominant, the gene for blue eyes is recessive. If an animal receives genes for blue eyes and for brown eyes from its parents, it will have brown eyes because of the dominance of

that gene. It will have blue eyes only if the gene for blue eyes is passed on from both parents.

This leads to further conclusions. A blue-eyed animal has genes for blue eye-color alone and it is known as homozygous for that characteristic. If a brown-eyed individual has one gene for blue eyes and one for brown, it will be known as heterozygous for eye-color. It is impossible to tell the difference between a heterozygous and a homozygous brown-eyed individual by physical examination, but the heterozygous dog may pass the recessive blue-eyed gene on to its offspring and, if the other parent passes on a similar gene, the pair may produce blue-eyed offspring, even though both are brown-eyed.

The population of dogs available for breeding may be regarded as a population of genes—a phenomenon known as the gene pool. The long-term objective of a breeder is to alter, by selection, the frequency with which genes occur. He or she gambles on breeding an outstanding perhaps that of the Cavalier King Charles Spaniel, which closely resembles the small spaniels that originally became fashionable during the reign of Charles II. Over time, the King Charles Spaniel became smaller, and it was only in the 1920s that an American breeder decided to "recreate" the original breed. By promoting the selection for larger King Charleses with longer faces and flatter skulls, he was able to produce the modern Cavalier. Many toy breeds have been selected for their daintiness, so that the modern dog is much smaller than his 19th-century predecessors would have been; similarly, giant breeds have been deliberately made larger over the years.

individual but calculates on improving the overall standard of the breed and particularly of his or her own line of dogs. Individuals with undesirable characteristics should be eliminated from the breeding program and individuals carrying desirable traits should be selected. For health reasons alone, one should never breed from an animal with hip dysplasia, for example, or one that suffers from epilepsy.

An animal's appearance alone may be a poor guide to its ability to reproduce its own characteristics. A knowledge of the animal's ancestry can help. Line-breeding and family breeding are diluted forms of in-breeding—the breeding of closely related individuals. The more closely related the animals of a particular line are, the more reliably will they reproduce their characteristics (whether good or bad). For this reason, close in-breeding demands the greatest of care.

Many of today's pedigree dogs are the result of generations of selective breeding. The most famous example is

SOCIAL INSTINCTS

THE DOG'S BEHAVIOR IS WELL adapted to the needs of humans. As a pet it has become our friend and companion, and as a working animal it can be trained to perform a wide range of useful tasks. Unlike the cat, which seems to choose when to give companionship, the dog is unquestioning and reliable in both giving and receiving affection.

The dog, like its ancestor the wolf, is essentially a pack animal. Pack behavior can be seen if a group of dogs live together or come together for a period. They will stay close to each other and do the same type of things at the same time. Some individuals are dominant and an order of "rank" is formed. If you have

more than one dog, or if you introduce a new individual into an established group, there may be some minor conflict at first while they sort themselves out, but once the "pecking order" is established everyone will know his or her place and settle down in it.

For owners the most important consequence is that the human family becomes the dog's pack. It is essential that the owner and not the dog is the one that dominates; otherwise the dog will

cause problems. If the dog is submissive to its owner it will give respect and affection, and will learn, with training, to respond to commands. The dog is content in such a relationship since to live in a pack is natural to it, and no disadvantage attaches to the fact that the dog is not the leader.

There are a number of ways in which a dog's "pack" instinct is relevant to your training program. For example, pet behaviorist David Appleby publishes a good behavior guide whose suggestions include:

• Don't let your dog sleep on the bed. If you do, it will think it can dominate you. In the wild, only subordinate animals offer to share their sleeping quarters.
• Don't feed your dog scraps from the table, or give it food you have been eating. In the wild, only subordinate animals willingly share their food.
• If your mealtime and the time when you want to feed your dog coincide, eat first and feed the dog later.
• Don't let your dog sit on the furniture or on your lap. In the dog's eyes, height equals dominance.
• Always make your dog give way to you in a doorway. If it is lying in your way, don't be tempted to step over or round it—make it move.

Since a dog is highly social it needs to learn how to live with others. Research in the United States suggests that this learning is confined to a brief period at puppy stage—most conditioning is done

Left: Dogs and cats can co-exist amicably if the dog understands that the cat is not to be chased. Restrain your puppy so that it gets this message.

Right: Children are naturally attracted to puppies, but can overwhelm them with attention. If you teach small children not to pick puppies up, grab them by the tail, or stroke them too vigorously, peace should prevail.

Left: If you already have a dog when you get a new puppy, they will need to get used to each other. Let them meet on neutral ground, away from food or sleeping quarters, and let them investigate one another quietly.

Right: Always eat your own meal before feeding your dog, and don't feed it scraps from your plate. This will help the dog to understand that you are the boss.

by the time the puppy is about twelve weeks old. The best time to remove a puppy from its mother and litter-mates seems to be about six to eight weeks of age. The puppy will then become used to people and will still mix well with other dogs. If a puppy is removed any earlier it may become too close to humans and be overly dependent. On the other hand, the researchers found that if puppies were left with their mother and litter-mates and did not have their first human contact until they were about 13 weeks old or more, they could never adjust well to people. They stayed fearful, withdrawn, and almost incapable of being trained.

The most important stage in the development of normal behavior therefore occurs before the age of 12 weeks. In the first four weeks of life a pup's development is rapid, but its behavior is basic and concerned mostly with eating and sleeping. The eyes open at the earliest after ten to fifteen days and the senses of hearing and smell improve about the same time. From about four weeks a pup becomes much more active and will start to play with its litter-mates. This marks the start of the process when a pup learns to live with others. This is why is it vitally important to socialize your dog, both with people and with other dogs. Although it is not allowed to go out or to meet other dogs until it has had all its vaccinations, it can meet other people if they come to it. Invite people of all ages. If you don't have children, introduce the puppy to the children of your friends and neighbors. Invite some older people so that it learns that not everyone wants to play all the time.

Once its vaccinations are complete, take your puppy with you to the post office or to shops where it is allowed in. Take it to obedience classes, not only for training, but to meet other people and other dogs. Get it used to being around strangers, so that it learns to behave in a friendly but not overly excited way. From the end of this phase basic behavior changes little, except that the puppy matures and becomes more responsive to being trained. The sexual behavior of adult dogs is discussed on page 136.

SENSES

THE WAY IN WHICH A DOG interprets the world is very different from the responses of a human being. A dog's sense of smell is far superior to that of a human, and is evident in the way a dog uses its nose while out for a walk or when investigating an object it has found. It is thought that a dog's sense of smell is at least a hundred times more powerful than a human's, and possibly more for certain scents.

A dog's hearing is also superior to that of a human. Dogs seem to be more sensitive to some sounds, especially those at high frequencies. Hence the use of "silent" dog whistles, audible to the dog but not to the human ear. This probably also explains the ability of a dog to detect

Right: Cocking the head is a way of turning the ears in the direction of a sound. The pricked ears also serve to indicate attentive interest.

Below: The one sense in which dogs are inferior to humans is daytime vision. They do not see color well—the white ball in the grass stands out better than the red one.

the arrival of a particular car, or distinguish the footsteps of its owner, well before these sounds can be recognized by human senses. A dog's mobile ears help to pinpoint the source of a sound, since they can be directed toward it.

In vision, the dog is inferior to humans, at least during the day. There is some controversy as to whether dogs are color-blind or not. They probably have some color vision but it is not very good. Compared with a person, a dog has much less visual acuity and sees only moving objects well. At night, however, a dog sees better than a human being. The way a dog's eyes light up in the glare of car headlights is an indication of this. Light is reflected from a layer at the back of the animal's eye and passes through the light-sensitive retina twice, doubling sensitivity. Dogs have better peripheral vision, giving a larger visual field. So not only can they hear someone approaching from behind better than we can, but they are also able to see them sooner.

A dog's hearing is believed to be sufficiently acute to recognize its owner's car or footsteps. This Cairn Terrier clearly knows that a welcome person is about to arrive.

This may be accompanied by a hunched, guilty-looking posture, the meaning of which is unmistakable.

Communication by body language is complex, and confusion can arise since fear and submission, or excitement and aggression have components in common. Some breeds, by virtue of ear shape or lack of tail, are unable to communicate visually as well as others can. However, no one who has seen the wagging rump of an excited Cocker Spaniel can be left in much doubt as to its meaning.

The use of smell is very important. When two dogs first meet they usually smell each other's face and then their inguinal regions. Scent plays a significant part in territory. When a male dog cocks his leg to mark a prominent object while out on a walk, he is deliberately masking the smell of dogs that have recently passed by. Scratching with the back feet, seen mainly in male dogs after defecation, leaves a chemical signal, known as a pheromone, from special glands between the toes. Feces may be used as scent markers, and a dog has anal glands that secrete a mixture of chemicals. Dogs also sometimes roll in foul-smelling substances. The strong odor may give extra social status. A bitch in heat gives off special smells from the vagina, also present in the urine, which indicate her sexual status.

Sounds used include barking, whining, and howling. Barking is usually done in order to gain attention, and was probably originally encouraged for watch dogs during domestication. Whining, often indulged in when a dog is left alone, is a distress call aimed at the owner, hardly ever at another dog. Howling is probably a warning sound used to protect a territory.

Communication between dogs is impressive. Sounds, body signals, and chemical smells are all employed. Facial and body expressions indicate feelings. The eyes are also important. The stare, for example, is a threat signal usually given only by a dominant dog to a submissive one. If a person stares at a dog it will usually look away and perhaps roll on its side or back, indicating submission. Occasionally, a dominant dog will respond aggressively to a stare and will need to be reminded by vocal commands who is the head of the household.

The way the ears are held is an important indicator of expression. Ears held back against the head show submission or fear. Erect ears indicate alertness. These expressions will almost always be combined with some indication from the mouth and lips as well as from the body. Certainly dogs bare their teeth as a sign of aggression, but some also do it to indicate pleasure, almost as if they were smiling. A tail held high usually indicates alertness. A wagging tail probably indicates excitement, and a tail held low may mean fear or a position of submission.

PLAY AND AGGRESSION

MOST DOGS ARE extremely playful, even once they have grown up. A dog uses a classic pose, often called the "play bow," to start play. The head and front quarters drop to the ground, the hindlegs remain upright with the hindquarters in the air, and the tail is held high. This indicates that what follows will be play. It is important for one dog to communicate this to another, because during play the normal relationships between dominant and submissive individuals will be temporarily abandoned. A dominant animal may sometimes fall on its side in a submissive gesture to a smaller dog in order to encourage play.

Play is first seen in young puppies aged about a month, when play fights act as a rehearsal for adult behavior, building muscles and improving coordination and reaction times, which would all have been essential when the dog's ancestors had to hunt in order to survive. It is not known exactly why adults continue to play. In the domestic dog, playfulness was probably encouraged by human companions during the period of domestication, but even in the wild some animals still occasionally indulge in play.

Right: Even the gentlest pets retain their wild ancestors' protective instincts about food and resent your interference.

Below: Even small puppies play-fight, building up muscles, improving agility, and establishing rank.

Some dogs are often described as aggressive, but aggression is not a single type of behavior. There are probably about eight varieties of aggression that may be exhibited by dogs, and all have different causes that can be isolated.

Predatory aggression or the catching of prey is seen when a dog chases a bird, a rabbit, or even a cat. This type of aggression is never normally directed at humans. If a dog is taught to attack a person, as police dogs are, this is an

Play-fighting usually involves one of the dogs making a gesture of submission to show that this is only play. Rolling over on the back is an admission of the other dog's superiority.

example of trained aggression and will not occur without a spoken command.

Territorial aggression is more commonly directed at humans, usually in the form of a threatening posture. A dog may defend its territory against its own species as well as against people. This behavior is usually seen in dominant dogs, or if the owner is absent for a period, when the dog may assume territorial dominance. Postmen may especially notice this. If they wear a distinctive uniform and retreat, the dog will be encouraged to threaten again next time in defense of its territory. Male dogs tend to be more territorial than females.

Fear-induced aggression probably accounts for many of the dog bites that are suffered by children. Dogs who are not used to children may be frightened by a child rushing up with outstretched hands. What is intended as a friendly gesture can easily be interpreted otherwise by the animal. Keeping a close eye on children if there is an unfamiliar dog about is a sensible precaution. Pain-induced aggression is similar, except that the dog reacts to a genuinely painful stimulus. Dogs that have been injured may therefore snap unexpectedly and should be handled gently—or muzzled if necessary.

Some male dogs are especially prone to getting into fights with other males. This appears to have something to do with the male sex hormones. A mother protecting her puppies may also sometimes be aggressive. This is comparable, if only because she is in a special hormonal state at this time.

The final type of aggression results from competition for something desirable, such as food or even affection from the owner. In the wild, most competitive fights would soon be resolved by signals, such as threats followed by submission. In the case of pet dogs, however, the protection offered by an owner to an underdog may interfere with the natural resolution of such conflicts.

Being on the lead often makes an inadequately socialized dog more assertive since it may feel the presence of its owner strengthens its position.

Part Four

Care of the Dog

To get the most from a new family pet it is necessary to know how to train it so that it will be a social asset and a pleasure to its owners. It is also essential to know how to care for it so that it becomes a happy and healthy member of your family.

CHOOSING A PUPPY

THE DECISION TO HAVE A DOG should be a family one. It is not one that can be made lightly and without a great deal of thought. The dog, when you get it, will become an integral part of your family and is likely to remain so for many years. It is important, therefore, that every member of the immediate family should want a dog and be prepared to accept the duties that responsible ownership entails.

Christmas is never a good time to introduce a puppy into a family, especially when children are around. There are too many other things demanding the owner's attention which make it difficult for a puppy to settle and be properly cared for and appreciated at this time of year. Late spring and early summer have the advantage of fine weather and make house-training easier. But it is grossly unfair and unsettling to introduce a dog (of any age) into the household and then, two or three weeks later, to put it into a kennel while the family goes on vacation.

If you decide to have a puppy, you should not buy one less than eight weeks old. (Indeed, a respectable breeder will not sell you a puppy younger than this.) It should be fully weaned and wormed. Having a puppy in the house is similar to looking after a new baby, as it requires regular feeding, play, sleep, and training. Anyone who tells you that a puppy is no trouble has never looked after one properly, but the pleasure of the task brings its

When you have a choice of puppies, opt for a healthy-looking, outgoing individual with bright eyes and a shiny coat.

own reward. If you choose an adult dog it will take a little longer than a puppy to adapt to your way of life, but on the plus side it should be house-trained and will not need to be fed so frequently.

If you want a pure-bred dog you can choose from more than 150 breeds. It is very important to select one that is suitable for your circumstances and whose needs you will be able to satisfy. Avoid the temptation of being swayed by the appearance of dogs you have seen on TV

Dogs come in many shapes and sizes—find out as much as possible about a breed's needs before you choose a puppy. This is a Doberman and a Chihuahua.

• *How much time can you give to your dog?* If you are out all day, it may be wise to reconsider altogether and get a cat. Even if you have more time to spare, some breeds like more company than others and will be bored and possibly destructive if left on their own too long.

• *How much exercise can you give it?* Don't buy a big breed if you cannot spare the time or are not healthy enough for long walks; and don't forget that some smaller breeds, such as Border Collies and even tiny Yorkshire Terriers, require a surprising amount of exercise.

• *How much experience with dogs do you have?* If you have never owned one before, you may not be able to control a strong-willed breed such as a Boxer or Doberman.

• *Do you want a male or a female?* Some people say that females are more affectionate, but can you cope with them being "in heat" twice a year?

• *Do you want a long-haired or a short-haired breed?* An Afghan or a Lhasa Apso may look gorgeous, but you are buying a pet, not an accessory, and keeping these breeds clean and tidy, never mind glamorous, requires a daily commitment to grooming.

commercials or in glossy magazines.

It is no use thinking about a Great Dane, Afghan Hound, Old English Sheepdog, or German Shepherd if you live in an apartment or small town house. These dogs need plenty of room. By the same token if you live in the country and are looking for a companion for long walks a Pekingese is not for you. If you want a playmate for your children and they are at the "toddler" stage, most of

the breeds classified as toys would be unsuitable as they are too much of a temptation for a small child to pick up. A puppy can be easily dropped—and does not like the experience. Children have to be taught how to treat a dog properly. They must not, for example, squeeze a puppy as if it were a teddy bear. A larger, tougher breed would be more suitable for young children. Other questions you should consider include:

Pedigree Pet Foods produce a useful questionnaire called Select-a-Dog (accessible only through the internet at www. waltham.com) to help you choose the breed that is best suited to you. The magazine *Dog Monthly* has an illustrated Pedigree Puppy Buyers' Guide in which breeders and breeders' associations advertise; they also have a monthly feature on an individual breed, which emphasizes the show aspects but also gives some indication of its suitability as a pet, its grooming, and exercise needs, etc.

Puppies like these Corgis show at a glance that they are healthy, alert, clean, and carefully looked after. This is the sort of quality you should expect from any reputable breeder.

Always buy a pure-bred dog from a respectable breeder. The Kennel Club will be able to put you in touch with the breed society, which will provide you with a list of breeders in your area. Write or telephone the breeder to see if he or she has puppies available—a successful breeder's puppies may well be booked up in advance. Be patient. It is worth waiting for the right pet. Once you know that the breeder has puppies for sale, make an appointment to see them and when you go, take only immediate members of the family with you, as too many people will confuse the issue. Be suspicious of anyone who does not want you to visit, or who is unwilling to let you meet the mother of the puppies or to see the kennel or room in which they were reared. Breeders are busy people who may not welcome you if you turn up out of the blue without an appointment, but good ones are also proud of the conditions in which they keep their dogs.

Expect to be interviewed quite rigorously by the breeder about your circumstances, how much you know about looking after a dog, and why you want this particular breed. Breeders like to know that the puppies they have carefully raised are going to the right homes. They have a reputation to uphold and may refuse to sell you a puppy at all if they consider you "unsuitable." But this firm approach should reassure you about the quality of the dog you are buying. A puppy from such a source will be a planned puppy. The stud dog will have been carefully chosen, the bitch will have had the best possible care, and the puppy reared to the highest standard.

You will probably be able to visit when the litter is about three or four weeks old, and choose the puppy you want from those not yet spoken for. You will then return to collect it when it is about eight weeks old. If this is inconvenient—for example, because of a previously planned holiday—the breeder may agree to "run the puppy on" for a few weeks until you are able to give it all the attention it needs.

When making your choice, look for a confident, enquiring puppy, a lively youngster with bright, sparkling eyes, a shiny coat, and a moist nose free from mucus. It should be a "firm" puppy, not one whose ribs stick out, or whose tummy is disproportionately large. Discount a sluggish-looking puppy and choose an extrovert instead. A puppy should be a mixture of appeal, mischief, curiosity, sensitivity, playfulness, and, when asleep, serenity.

The breeder will supply you with recommendations about feeding, and with the puppy's vaccination certificates, Kennel Club registration certificates, and pedigree. If the course of vaccinations is not complete, he or she will make sure that you know what others the puppy is going to need, and when.

Breeders sometimes have older dogs that they are willing to sell for a very reasonable sum to a good home. Nearly always these dogs will give many happy years of companionship and love. They are ideal for people who feel a puppy may be too exuberant.

It has never been a good idea to buy a puppy from a pet shop or a "puppy farm." Fortunately, legislation that came into force in Britain January 2000 has made a serious attempt to control the worst practices of these farms. Under the new laws, any breeder who produces five or more litters a year will need to be licensed, and the conditions of the licence insist that no bitch shall be mated before she is twelve months old; no bitch shall have more than one litter per year or more than six in total; and no bitch shall be bred after she is eight years old. The breeder must also keep—and produce on demand—proper records, and his or her premises are liable to regular inspection by both the local authority and a vet. Breach of the licensing regulations will involve heavy penalties and the revoking of the license.

If you choose a mongrel or "crossbreed," it will obviously be much cheaper than a pedigree dog, and if you acquire your pet from a dogs' home or rescue center you will have the satisfaction of knowing that you are taking on an animal in great need of a secure and loving family. But be warned: if you buy a puppy without knowing anything about its parents, you can have no idea how big it is going to grow, or what personality traits it is likely to develop. Rescue centers sometimes know why a dog has had to be relocated, so do find out if you can. Dogs that have been abandoned or ill-treated by their previous owners may

have behavioral problems that take time and patience to correct. Others may have faults of temperament that make them unsuitable for your circumstances, too.

If you know someone whose bitch has had puppies accidentally, you will have the security of knowing the size and state of health of the mother and seeing

the conditions in which the puppies were reared. In all these cases, you should apply criteria similar to those for choosing a pedigree puppy—try to pick out one that looks healthy, happy, and confident. Most people find that the best possible pet is the one that is outgoing enough to choose them.

CARING FOR A NEW PUPPY

THE BEST TIME TO COLLECT YOUR puppy is in the morning; this gives it time to settle into its new surroundings before the loneliness of the night begins. If you are going by car, remember that this may be the puppy's first outing and the first time away from its litter-mates. Take some old towels, newspaper, and paper towels in case it is carsick. Any animal may experience stress when moved from one environment to another, and dogs are no exception.

When you get home, take the puppy into the kitchen. First associations are important and the kitchen, usually warm and with a lingering smell of food, makes a happy introduction to new surroundings. A house pet will always live in the house, but it is a good idea to keep any puppy indoors until it has received its initial training and is mature, even if it is going to live in an outdoor kennel as an adult.

The puppy should have its own sleeping quarters. A bed in a draft-free area in the kitchen or utility room is necessary. When you first bring a puppy home, a cardboard carton, with a piece cut out of the front to allow easy access, or a crate lined with newspaper and a piece of old blanket, is ideal. Gradually, as the dog grows older this can be replaced by a bed. There are a variety of dog beds on the market and it is a matter of personal preference which one you select.

The old wicker-basket type is hard to keep clean and tends to harbor dust and dirt. New plastic beds in bright colors can be lined with a choice of the special washable-pile polyester-fur fabrics which are veterinary-approved. Dogs love this type of bedding. These beds are inexpensive and easy to keep clean, as they can be wiped over inside and out daily with a wet cloth and disinfectant. They come in a variety of sizes.

A canvas-base, camp-type bed strung between metal supports with its own attractive washable cover will blend in with any décor. These are available from small to Great Dane size. Some of the small smooth-coated dogs such as Chihuahuas or Italian Greyhounds, which feel the cold, appreciate the hooded, padded material beds into which they can snuggle and hide. These beds are machine-washable. Still another hygienic type of bed, in every size, is the

Confining your puppy to a spacious playpen is one way of giving you a break from wondering what it is up to.

Below: If you have more than one puppy from the same litter, it is great fun watching them develop their own personalities.

Right: Synthetic, washable, fur-like fabric makes a cosy blanket into which a puppy can snuggle. Buy at least two pieces so that your dog always has a warm, clean bed while one is in the wash.

one filled with polystyrene beads which takes on the shape of the dog. Whichever type you use, remember to clean it out daily and make sure it is in a warm, draft-free area of the house.

For dogs that are kept outside, a good weatherproof outbuilding with a comfortable bed is ideal. Make sure the building has a window that gives light and ventilation during warm weather. If the floor is concrete, the bed should be raised from the floor. A large wooden box especially designed as a dog bed with wooden blocks attached to the bottom and filled with shredded paper is very acceptable.

Purpose-built kennels, with enclosed runs attached to them, are available on the market. Most of these are constructed of wood, and are therefore easy to scrub down and keep clean.

Sleep and periods of rest away from the excitement of human companionship during the day are of great importance to a growing dog, so put the puppy firmly in its box for a rest after each meal.

Above: Puppies don't like to mess in their own beds. From about three weeks, they leave their "nest" to use the paper.

Right: When you take your puppy into the yard to relieve itself, always use the same spot. Don't be impatient.

The best plan at night is to surround the bed with clean newspaper. Play with the new puppy until it is sleepy, then take it outside for a final elimination. Put it in the bed, place a loud ticking alarm clock nearby to simulate the mother's heartbeat, turn out the light and leave your pet to sleep. It may give a few whimpers at first but will soon settle down.

House-training is achieved through patience and persistence. Dogs should be trained where to defecate. Never slap a puppy for being dirty. As far as daytime habits are concerned, house-training can usually be achieved within a week. The puppy should be taken to the same spot in the yard first thing in the morning, preferably immediately after it awakens, again after each feed, drink, and nap, and last thing at night. When the puppy is taken to the selected spot the command "Be quick!" should be repeated several times while it sniffs around. Once it has obliged, spoken praise such as "Good boy!" or "Good girl!" will soon start to

register in the puppy's mind. It is important to remember that this comes under the heading of schooling. It is a serious matter and in no circumstances should you indulge in playing with the puppy on these occasions until *after* the object of the exercise has been achieved.

If you live in an apartment, you may prefer to "paper-train" your dog. This involves placing several sheets of newspaper in a convenient position. When you wish the puppy to relieve itself, just adopt the procedure outlined above. A word of warning, however. Many a "paper-trained" pup takes a greater than usual interest in *any* piece of newspaper after this training. A newspaper left lying open

on the floor, a table, or chair invites use.

Most breeders will give you a diet and instruction sheet when you buy a puppy, and this diet should be followed as closely as possible. You may upset the puppy's stomach if you change his diet the moment you bring him home. If you want to change it (perhaps because the breeder's choice of food is too expensive), do so very gradually, introducing your preferred food little by little, so that the puppy has a chance to get used to it. For more information on diet, see pages 126–127.

The general rule with puppies is to feed little and often—four times a day for an eight-week-old—then as the dog

Always praise a puppy when it relieves itself in the right place, whether in the yard or on newspaper. This helps reinforce the message.

grows older decrease the number of meals but increase the amount, until at six months of age the animal is on two meals a day, and by a year is down to one substantial meal a day. Very small dogs, and larger breeds with sensitive stomachs such as the Borzoi, should continue to have two or three moderately sized meals a day even in adulthood.

While the dog must be allowed to enjoy its own home, it will appreciate it all the more if it knows what it may use. If there is a room you don't want him to go into, or if you never want him to go upstairs, say "No!" firmly whenever he wanders in that direction, and if necessary pick him up and bring him back to somewhere he is allowed to be. Praise and pat him when he does what you say and he will soon get the message. Always use the same words when giving a command. A sharp "No!" or "Down!" in a tone that expects to be obeyed will achieve a hundred times more than a despairing "Oh, Timmy, don't do that." Remember a puppy doesn't have a wide vocabulary and although it will soon learn to recognize a few words it is responding more to your tone of voice than to what you are actually saying.

The theory of setting your puppy ground rules applies to toys, too. If you give him a slipper to play with, how can you expect him to understand that he mustn't pick up any shoes and slippers left lying about? One of the most satisfying toys for a puppy is an old sock knotted into a "dolly" which he can easily carry around in his mouth and shake. It will provide him with endless enjoyment.

Give your dog its own feeding bowl and always feed it at the same time and in the same place.

EXERCISE

THE AMOUNT OF EXERCISE a dog needs each day depends on the breed and the living circumstances—and remember that you considered the amount of exercise your dog would need before you chose that breed. Like a human, your dog needs an adequate amount of exercise if it is to remain healthy and happy.

If you have a large fenced-in yard or run and your dog is allowed to run freely several times a day, further exercise is unnecessary. Toy breeds that have a yard in which to run require very little else. If you have a medium-sized or large dog and a small yard, however, or if you have

Right: A puppy's first collar should be loose enough for you to tuck your fingers into it. Hold it gently but firmly to get him accustomed to being restrained.

Below: Don't let children indulge puppies, or let puppies break rules when playing with children. Supervise play between them to ensure good behavior on all sides.

any breed and no yard at all, you must exercise your dog. It will need short walks to relieve itself (if it cannot do so at home) at least first thing in the morning, in the middle of the day, and last thing at night. One of these walks should be converted into a long one—ideally first thing in the morning, particularly if

you are then going to leave it on its own while you go to work, as it will be tired, more likely to sleep while you are away, and less likely to become bored and destructive.

Puppies obviously need less exercise than fully grown dogs. This is particularly so with large breeds, as they take

longer to mature, and you can do permanent damage to their legs and joints if you over-exercise them. As a general rule, smaller dogs mature at between 12 and 18 months, large breeds not until they are two years old, and with some giant breeds you need to be careful until they are about three. For the same reason, you should not let puppies go up and down stairs, or jump on and off furniture.

Bear in mind that if you are able to let an active young dog off the lead, it will probably run two or three times as far as you walk. If you are restricted to walking on the lead, a medium-sized breed such as a Golden Retriever will appreciate a walk of 3–4 miles a day, and a large and energetic breed such as an Alaskan Malamute would view that as a minimum. This means a good hour at a brisk walking pace. Some small dogs such as Dachshunds, Corgis, and most terriers will also take all the walking you can give them once they are fully grown (and will quickly run to fat if under-exercised).

Dogs should never be let out on the street on their own, or left to roam without supervision. The ideal dog is one which follows on the lead when in a built-up area, and enjoys its freedom, but is ready to return to heel at once when in the open country. Certainly it is essential that the dog is taught that there are times when its freedom has to be restricted. It is a most important part of the training program.

Using a long lead will give your dog some freedom but still keep it under control when something else attracts its attention.

Puppies will soon learn to behave themselves on a lead, and to obey simple commands such as "Sit!," "Stay!," and "Heel!."

Every dog should learn to walk properly on a lead. Some puppies take immediately to a collar and lead; others need more patience and encouragement. Puppies should start lead training at an early age. As soon as the prescribed time after the final vaccination has elapsed, they can be taken out for walks. First lessons can take place in the garden and gradually be increased. After five or six lessons and a lot of praise it should be happy to go on the lead.

A puppy's first collar should be a lightweight one, fastened securely yet loose enough for you to insert two fingers between the neck of the dog and the inside of the collar. At first the dog may be irritated by the collar and scratch and try to remove it, but if you put the collar on just before feeding or play time it will soon become distracted and forget about the source of the irritation.

Once your puppy has become accustomed to the collar, go into the garden and attach a light lead. Keep the lead very slack and start walking, at the same time calling the puppy by name. If it starts to move in another direction, keep the lead slack and go with it, but continue talking to it. This is to get it used to the feel of a lead attached to the collar and to someone controlling the other end of the lead.

The puppy may sit down and decide it does not like this "game." Such a response, or lack of response, should be met with encouragement and the offer of a titbit as a reward when the puppy eventually decides to move.

You may find, especially with the larger breeds, that they are so confident they start to pull. This must be checked immediately and in such cases it is advisable to teach the dog to "heel." Walking at heel means the dog walking on your

Left: Lots of people are frightened of big dogs. If you own a breed that is perceived as aggressive, it is better for everyone to muzzle it when you take it out for a walk.

Below: If you have access to woodland or unspoiled countryside, you and your dog can have as much exercise as you like in healthy and invigorating surroundings.

left side with its head close to your leg. He must also walk at your pace. If it pulls give the lead a sharp jerk telling it to "heel." When it is again in the desired position walking in pace with you, slacken the lead. Your dog will soon learn that if it leaves that position by going too fast or too slow it will receive an uncomfortable jerk.

There are a wide variety of collars and leads available. The choke chain used to be very popular but has rather fallen from favor because of potential damage to the dog's larynx; the half-check, which has a double chain over the back of the dog's neck but leather at the throat, is now considered safer. Small docile dogs can be taken for walks with a non-adjustable lead clipped to their collar. If you want your dog to be able to roam considerable distances but still be under your control, expandable Flexi-leads whose length is adjusted by a button on the handle are ideal. The Halti is half-collar, half-muzzle, useful for restraining dogs that pull on the lead. If there is the remotest possibility that your dog will bite, put a muzzle on it when you take it out. This is also a sensible precaution if you own a dog that other people may perceive as fierce, such as a Boxer, a Doberman, or a Rottweiler.

TRAINING

A WELL-BEHAVED DOG is a source of enormous pleasure, a badly behaved one a source of irritation to all around it. This means that some basic training is essential.

Very few people want their pets to leap through hoops like circus performers, or to turn into submissive whimpering neurotics at the sound of their voice, but in order to be an acceptable member of a social group (i.e., your family), your dog should learn to respond promptly to such simple commands as "No!," "Sit!," "Stay," and "Come."

Initially all training should be done by the same person, to ensure that commands are consistent. Whether your new pet is a puppy or an older dog, it can easily become confused by different tones of voice or if what pleases one person does not satisfy another. Training a dog

Left: Make your dog sit at every curbside even if there is no traffic. Then, if it get out on its own, it is less likely to run out into the street and be involved in an accident.

Below: Having someone else holding the dog and releasing it when you call teaches it to respond to your commands.

requires patience and self-control. It is not necessary to spank or punish a dog when it disobeys—the tone of the human voice is sufficient to make it feel ashamed—but it is essential to give lavish praise when you are pleased with your pet. The learning process should be enjoyable both for the dog and for its owner.

Let your dog master one thing at a time and do not make the mistake of trying to teach it too much at once. Make sure it fully understands each stage of a new exercise before proceeding further. Keep training sessions to ten minutes at most, but start with periods of two or three minutes and increase the time gradually. Always end a lesson by giving an order that the dog understands, so that it earns praise and the lesson ends on a happy note. Repetition and praise feature strongly in any training program. Most experts now believe that giving edible treats is a perfectly acceptable way of rewarding your dog. At first you can reward your puppy every time it obeys the simplest command, then gradually cut down on the number of treats as it becomes more used to the training. If you use this method and your puppy is getting a lot of treats, remember to include them in your calculations of its daily food intake and cut down one or

two of its meals to compensate.

The first thing your dog will learn is its name. It is important that you talk to your dog when it is with you, using its name repeatedly so that it quickly comes to recognize it. The next command is "No!" This means "Stop it now!" If the puppy is chewing something or doing something that you want it to stop, say "No!" and repeat the instruction followed by the puppy's name. This should all be done in a commanding tone of voice. If it does not desist, repeat the command and use your index finger to show what you want the dog to stop doing. When it stops, praise it and try to distract it by encouraging it to occupy itself in some other way.

Many puppies indulge in "catch me if you can" games when called. This can be overcome by attaching a thin cord to the dog's collar and letting it trail behind when the animal is off the lead. If the dog tantalizes you just out of reach, the game can soon be stopped by putting your foot on the trailing cord and giving a sharp tug accompanied by the command "Heel!" Praise the dog when it obeys.

To teach a small dog to sit, it is usually sufficient to say "Sit!" while putting your hand over its rump, and very gently pushing it down. With a larger dog it is sometimes necessary to put one hand on the hindquarters and the other on the chest. When this has been mastered, the follow-on command is "Stay!," with "No!" then "Stay!" being used when the dog starts to rise.

Start your training at home. When your dog has mastered the art of coming, sitting, and staying on command, try issuing these commands without warning when it is running loose in the garden. When it can be relied on to obey such

A well-trained dog will walk closely to heel and obey visual as well as verbal commands.

commands in these circumstances, try using them when you are out for a walk. This will probably be more difficult at first, because the dog will be distracted by all that is going on around it, but patience and persistent firmness should win through in the end.

Do not let your dog jump up on people, either at home or outside. Teach it to welcome you with its four feet on the ground. To discourage a large dog from jumping up, repeat the word "Down!" If it persists raise your knee so that you catch it on the chest or brisket as it jumps, at the same time saying "Down!" The technique is slightly more difficult with a small dog. In this case use your hand to push the dog down, firmly but gently, saying "Down!" as you do so.

SENSIBLE OWNERSHIP

Always make sure your dog has plenty of fresh air if you have to leave it in the car, even on a cool day. On sunny days, park somewhere that will remain in the shade.

MOST COMMUNITIES HAVE obedience training classes that will help you help your dog to act in a responsible way in society (ask your vet or breed society, or look for advertisements in your local library). The Kennel Club runs a Good Citizen Dog Scheme and the AKC a Canine Good Citizens program, both of which teach dogs the rudiments of good manners and obedience without the competitiveness to be found in more advanced obedience classes. But even before you reach this stage there are some elementary points that the responsible dog-owner should keep in mind.

• Do not let your dog foul the pavement when it is out for a walk. If it starts to defecate, put it into the gutter immediately. Disposable plastic scoop bags are available which fit easily into the pocket and can be disposed of in a suitable place after use. Some local governments have designated their area a "pick up" zone, which means that you can be fined for not clearing up after your dog. At home, encourage it to use the same corner of the yard to relieve itself, so that you do not have to spend your time clearing up after it or be careful where you walk in your own back yard.

• Parks and beaches have long been favorite exercising and playing areas for dogs, but a little thought needs to be given to the other people using these places. Dogs should not be permitted to use children's play areas as toilets, and there are few things more annoying to sunbathers than a dog who races out of the sea and shakes itself all over them, or pelts them with sand because it has decided to have a dig.

• No matter where you live, never take your dog for a walk without a lead. It should be allowed to run loose only in an area completely cut off from traffic. It is all too easy for a dog to spot another dog or a cat across a busy street. If you are momentarily distracted, the dog can dart off and tragedy can quickly result. Even if you are lucky enough to have local woods where your dog can run freely, take a lead with you. If you meet children who are not used to dogs, or people on horseback, or if your dog is likely to disappear in search of a rabbit, you may want to keep it under close control until the moment of temptation has passed.

• It is worth keeping doggy treats in your pocket whenever you are going to let your dog off the lead. Make sure it knows you have them by giving it one before letting it loose. Then reward it with another when it comes back in response to your call.

• Teach your dog to respect other animals. Most dogs will chase livestock unless they are taught not to do so. Farmers in Britain are within their rights to shoot a dog found worrying sheep. If the dog is not shot, the owner can be liable for heavy penalties.

• Most dogs enjoy car rides but it is not advisable to feed a dog just before a journey. Neither should you allow it to put its head out of a window of a moving car. This can irritate and damage the eyes, and in some circumstances can be a hazard to other drivers.

• If you have to leave a dog alone in a car, make sure it has plenty of ventilation. Do not leave a lead on it and the window open—it could jump out and strangle itself if the lead catches on the door handle. If the weather is warm, take a flask of cold water and a bowl so that the dog may have a drink. If possible, park the car in the shade. In really hot weather leave the dog at home. Never keep a dog in the car with the windows closed, no matter what the weather.

• Unnecessary barking is a nuisance both to the owner of a dog and to others. While you should praise the dog for warning you of the approach of strangers to your house, particularly if you live in an isolated area, an urban dog who barks every time somebody passes the front window will drive you mad. And wherever you live, you should not tolerate barking just for the sake of it.

• A fully and properly trained guard dog must be able to "switch off" when it is not on duty. Owners of dogs used for guarding must see that they are kept under proper control. If they are used to patrol specific areas and left loose at night, the area must be fully and securely fenced so that there can be no likelihood of children wandering into the area and being attacked. Guard dogs should be treated with respect for their training at all times.

• Every dog-owner should acquaint him or herself with the laws relating to dogs and see that these are kept. Although dog

licenses are no longer required in the UK, identification—in the form of a collar with name tag or a permanent microchip under the skin—is compulsory. Third party insurance is also a sensible precaution: the owner of a dog that causes an accident or serious damage is liable under the law. You may also choose to insure against the death or loss of your pet, or to cover veterinary fees in case of accident or illness. The breeder may already have insured your puppy for a short time, and when that policy expires the insurance company will contact you to see if you wish to renew it. For simplicity, you can arrange for the same policy to cover third party and healthcare.

• If you have not already done so, join your local breed club. The Kennel Club will be able to tell you where the nearest one is. As well as social activities with people who share an interest in your chosen breed of dog, these clubs provide opportunities for the exchange of information on training and breeding—they will know all the shortcomings as well as the advantages of the breed, and will be a source of information should you want to acquire another dog, choose a stud

dog with whom to mate your bitch, or even find a new home for your dog if for some reason you are unable to keep it. If there is no convenient breed club, there is likely to be a general dog club or canine society which will serve many of the same purposes.

Above: Dog ownership is a family matter. Make sure everyone is involved, taking a share both of the responsibility and of the pleasure.

Below: A microchip is inserted under the skin at the back of the neck, to provide permanent identification—a legal requirement in the UK.

FEEDING YOUR DOG

HEALTHY DOGS ARE NOT difficult to feed if they have been sensibly reared. Possibly because of their long association with humans, dogs thrive on food similar to ours. They need a little more protein and do not require fruit or green vegetables because they can make vitamin C in their own bodies. Nearly all foods of animal origin, cereals, root vegetables, and fats are easy for them to digest, but some may need to be cooked. Water is, of course, essential to all life and therefore plays an important part in the feeding of your dog. He should be supplied with a constant supply of clean, fresh, cool water.

The secret of correct feeding is to give a balanced diet which supplies all essential nutrients in adequate amounts and in the proper proportions to one another for the purpose intended—work, breeding, growth, or healthy adulthood.

The essential nutrients are: a source of energy (protein of high quality), fat as a source of essential fatty acids, about 20 mineral elements, and a dozen vitamins. Energy is supplied by the digestion of fat, protein, and carbohydrate. Carbohydrate in the form of cooked cereal starch or sugar can supply up to 70 per cent by weight of a dog's food (after deducting any water present) or about two-thirds of the calories. Biscuits, bread, and cooked potatoes are three useful energy foods for dogs.

Protein varies greatly in its usefulness to the animal. Plant protein is generally inferior to animal protein, though a mixture is satisfactory. The dry matter of a dog's diet should contain at least 15 per cent protein, of which at least half should come from animal foods (meat, fish, poultry, offal, and dairy products) or from high-quality vegetable protein such as soya. Fat adds to palatability, but otherwise is needed only as a source of essential fatty acids, sometimes referred to as polyunsaturates.

The most important minerals are calcium, phosphorus, and sodium chloride (common salt). Combined calcium and phosphorus make up most of the mineral matter of bone and should be supplied at the rate of about 3 per cent calcium phosphate in the dry diet. A small amount, 0.5 per cent, of iodized table salt in the diet is sufficient. Further minerals occur naturally in meat, cereals, and other ingredients of the balanced diet. Vitamin B_1 is supplied by cereals, while meat, fish, and dairy products provide other B vitamins. Liver is the most readily available source of all vitamins, including A, D, and E. Alternatively, vitamins can be provided

Bones are not only good for a dog's teeth but they also include minerals, such as calcium, which are not present in meat.

	Protein	Energy value	
	%	kcal/lb.	kcal/kg
Traditional food			
Minced beef	20	1250	2750
Ox liver	21	750	1650
Ox lung (lights)	18	500	1100
Ox spleen (melts)	17	500	1100
Ox tripe	15	450	990
Shank bone	10	250	550
Whole egg	12	650	1430
Whole milk	3.5	300	660
Potato	2	100	220
Wholemeal bread	9	1000	2200
Manufactured food			
Biscuits/meals	11	1600	3520
Canned, jelly type	11	400	880
Canned, cereal type	8	500	1100
Expanded meal	24	1500	3300
Intermediate moisture	25	1400	3080

It is natural for dogs to squabble over food. Giving each puppy its own bowl helps to reduce competition at mealtimes.

as a concentrate or in specially supplemented manufactured foods.

Traditionally, dogs have been fed on meat mixed with household scraps such as stale bread, trimmings, and so on. This can be satisfactory if the proportion of scraps is restricted to a quarter. All types of fresh meat and offals are suitable, as are fish and dairy products. Liver is rather laxative but highly nutritious; 5 per cent is an appropriate amount. Fresh meats should be lightly cooked for reasons of hygiene. Large bones such as pieces of ox shank-bone provide the calcium and phosphorus lacking in meat. Gnawing bones also keeps the teeth clean. Small dogs in particular are prone to teeth problems and can also benefit from being encouraged to eat raw carrot. Bones of chicken, fish, and rabbit should not be given as they may lodge in the throat or puncture the intestines. Excessive gnawing of bones may cause a block of mineral matter in the bowels.

If you wish to feed your dog manufactured dog food—and this is often the most convenient way of ensuring it receives all the nutrients detailed above—you can choose between four main types:

• *Biscuits and meals* are based on wheaten flour and prepared as either whole biscuits or broken meal. Most are supplemented with vitamins and minerals. Fat and protein meals may be added to improve palatability.
• *Canned foods* are based on meat, offal, poultry, or fish and supplemented with vitamins and minerals. Some use minced meats and contain cereals; in others the meats are diced and set in gravy or jelly.

• *Complete dry meals* are a mixture of cereals, protein meals, and other ingredients to make a balanced diet. They are made as loose mixtures (usually with pre-cooked cereals), compressed pellets or "expanded" meals—pellets of open texture that have been coated with fat to improve palatability.
• *Intermediate moisture foods* consist of cooked meats mixed with sugar and other preservatives plus other ingredients to make a balanced diet.

The amount of food needed depends mostly on a dog's size but is also affected by its activeness, its individual nature, and the temperature of its surroundings. Be careful not to overfeed. Given the chance, many dogs will overeat until they become obese and this will have serious effects on their health and life expectancy. Young dogs and those being worked may need a great deal more food (calories) than the average dog, whereas an inactive, old dog will require less. If possible, weigh a dog regularly and watch its condition.

Using the nutrition information supplied in the panel above, it should be possible to devise many satisfactory diets.

The following are some useful examples:

15 lb. (7 kg) Shetland Sheepdog: ¼ lb. (113 g) minced beef, ¼ lb. (113 g) wholemeal bread, one saucer of milk a day.
25 lb. (11 kg) Cocker Spaniel: ½ lb. (225 g) tripe, 6 oz. (170 g) biscuits a day.
65 lb. (25.5 kg) Labrador Retriever: 1 can cereal dog meat, 11 oz. (312 g) biscuit meal a day.
100 lb. (45 kg) Bloodhound: 1½ lb. (680 g) expanded meal a day.

Healthy adult dogs need only one meal a day, because they are adapted to take in large meals of concentrated food. Very small dogs and breeds prone to digestive problems may be fed two or three times a day. Working dogs are normally fed in the evening after the day's work but may also be given a light morning meal. A common pattern with pet dogs is to give the main meal in the morning and a few biscuits in the evening. Variety in either the food or the dietary regime should be avoided. Dogs do not become bored with a consistent diet of palatable, wholesome food, and their digestions benefit from the regularity. They should not be given snacks between meals.

GROOMING

ALL DOGS NEED GROOMING, some more so than others; it depends on their coat. A Shih Tzu, Afghan, or Old English Sheepdog will take a lot of time to keep attractive, but Dobermans, Boxers, and other smooth-coated breeds require a minimum of grooming. Poodles and many terriers need professional attention at least twice a year if they are to look their best. The glamour of a long coat without hours of tedious grooming is combined in such breeds as the Japanese Chin, Saluki, or Cavalier King Charles Spaniel. Do not buy a breed that needs a lot of grooming if you are not prepared to put in the work. The dog will not only look untidy, it will be uncomfortable, and the dead hair can cause irritation and eczema. It is close to sacrilege to clip a long-haired dog's coat short because you cannot be bothered to look after it, or because it sheds its hair all over the carpet.

The ability to keep still while being groomed is an important lesson your dog must learn. It should be placed on a sturdy table; if it has to go to the veteri-

Opposite and right: Grooming is best done on a solid table. Put one hand around your dog's chest and shoulders to steady it. Start with the back of the neck and brush down the back and sides, then between the hindlegs and under the body. Brush the legs and finally the head. Be gentle with the head, talking comfortingly to the dog and praising it if it does not make a fuss.

narian for treatment it will then know how to behave on a table and have no fears. If you try to groom a dog on the floor, which is normally a play area, you cannot expect it to realize that this is not a game too.

To groom a smooth-coated dog, you need two pieces of cotton wool, one dampened with warm water and one dry. You will also need a hound glove, an old towel, and a dry, soft chamois leather or piece of velvet. First wipe over the eyes with the moist cotton wool and then the dry. Lift up the flaps of the ears to see

that the ear is not red, inflamed, or dirty inside. If it is and you see the dog scratching, take it to a veterinarian for a thorough examination.

Brush the dog well with the hound glove. This removes any loose or dead hairs. About 100 strokes from nose to tail (not forgetting chest and sides) is a good rule. Repeat with the towel and chamois or velvet.

Terrier breeds should be groomed daily with a brush and wire glove in a similar manner to the smooth-coated dog. Their legs and whiskers should be

combed daily with a steel comb. They should also be stripped at least twice a year. Brush thoroughly first to remove all traces of dirt and loose, dead hair, then remove any excess hair either by hand plucking or by using a stripping knife. If you do not feel very confident about performing this task yourself, have a professional at your local grooming parlor or boarding kennels to do it for you. With breeds such as the Soft-coated Wheaten, which have long fringes or beards, regular trimming is required in order to keep them looking neat.

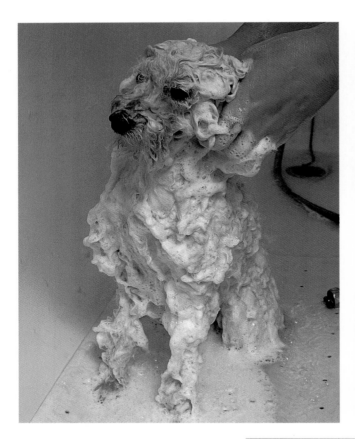

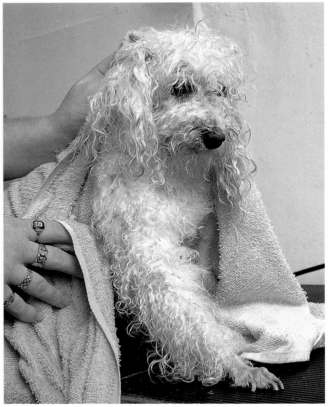

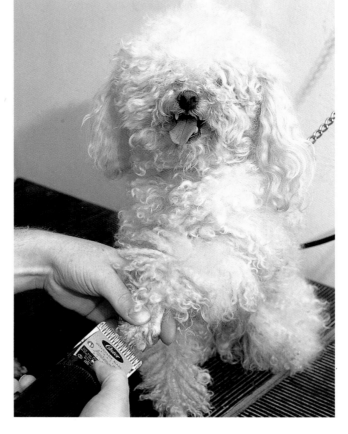

Long-coated breeds do not need to be brushed down to the skin every day. Once or twice a week will be sufficient and it is best to use a pure-bristle brush for this. If you do find any "knots"—which tend to form behind the ears, under the front legs, and in the "armpits"—sprinkle them liberally with talcum powder and ease them out with your fingers, finishing off with the brush. If you have a long-coated dog, you should especially examine the hind end to see that there are no epatches of excreta sticking to the hair.

A "slicker" is the best type of brush to use for thick, harsh-coated dogs. It is an oblong wire-pin brush on a handle, and effectively removes dead hair. A stiff brush and comb should be used once the dog has dried off after being out in mud.

Spaniels and other dogs with plenty of hair between their toes should be checked regularly for matted hair. Grooming is also a good opportunity to check long-eared dogs for any sign of infection—smelly or red, inflamed ears should be seen by a vet.

Above left and right: You can bath a small dog in a sink; larger breeds need the bathtub, with a nonslip mat. Use a dog shampoo or baby shampoo, never detergent. Use a shower attachment or cups of water to rinse the dog thoroughly, and dry it carefully so that it does not get chilled.

Left: Walking a dog on hard pavements will keep its nails reasonably short, but even so they will need to be clipped occasionally.

Clipping a poodle in preparation for showing is an art best left to the professionals. Long-coated or curly-coated dogs, as well as terriers such as Airedales whose coats require stripping, will also benefit from expert attention.

Always dry your dog thoroughly if it gets wet in rain or snow. For smooth-coated breeds a chamois and a towel are ideal. Use a towel with a squeezing motion rather than rubbing long-coated breeds, as rubbing tends to matt the coats. Terriers enjoy a good rub with a rough towel. Low-slung dogs such as Corgis and Dachshunds are susceptible to chills if their tummies get cold—so make sure you that dry them properly even if they have only been out on the lawn on a dewy morning.

Most dogs do not require frequent bathing; once every few months is plenty unless they have been rolling in something disgusting. Small breeds will fit in a sink and can be showered down with a detachable spray. Larger dogs will need to be put in the bath, with a rubber mat to prevent slipping. Use a shampoo formulated specifically for dogs. A baby shampoo can be used for small long-coated dogs; in this case finish off with a cream rinse. Never wash your dog in any form of detergent. Be sure to rinse thoroughly, working backward from the head, and dry your dog well as soon as you have finished. Many dogs soon get used to a hand-held hair-drier, as long as it is not too hot.

Trimming your dog's nails is a task you can learn to do for yourself if you have steady hands and a reasonably docile pet. Again, put the dog on a solid table. Use clippers that will give a clean cut. Hold the foot gently but firmly and cut above the quick. If you cut into the quick, it will bleed and hurt the dog. The quick is usually visible in clear nails, but dark nails are more difficult. If you don't feel able to do this yourself, ask your vet or grooming parlor to do it for you.

At certain times of the year, mainly in the summer, your dog can pick up a flea or tick from grass (see Common Ailments, pages 146–153). Look out for these when grooming. Your veterinarian will be able to advise you of a good spray, powder, or special shampoo to use, depending on the severity of the problem. If your dog does pick up any parasites, it is important to treat the bedding as well as the dog.

GOING ON VACATION

Kennel owners do not normally allow you to go down to the kennels when you leave your dog, but may let you go down to collect it on your return.

YOU MUST MAKE SUITABLE arrangements for the care of your dog at holiday time. If you are camping or going in an RV, it may not be too difficult to take the dog with you. Check with the camping or caravan site well in advance to make sure that this is allowed.

If you are going somewhere where you cannot take a dog, make sure that you book your pet into a reputable boarding kennel at the same time as you book your own holiday. It is important to know that your dog is being well looked after while you are away. It is fair neither to your pet nor to your neighbors to leave it in their care. Ask the breeder, your veterinary surgeon, or other dog-owners whose standards are likely to match your own, to recommend a good kennel. Word of mouth is the best way to find a reliable establishment. In many countries boarding kennels have to be licensed and inspected by local government authorities at regular intervals, so this gives you an assurance of basic standards of hygiene and safety.

When you are considering holiday accommodation for your dog, it is quite in order for you to telephone the kennels and ask about the facilities they offer and if the dogs are housed singly in sleeping compartments with adjacent runs. Ask if you can make an appointment to view the kennels before making a booking. If they say no, take your business elsewhere. On the other hand, once you have made the appointment, keep to the time. Particularly in holiday periods, kennel staff are busy people who stick to a fairly strict routine; they do not want visitors turning up unannounced at feeding time or when they are trying to settle the dogs down for the night. When you go to see them, ask if you can take the dog to meet

the staff, but do not expect to be allowed to take it down to inspect the kennels. It is better to leave children at home when you go on this exploratory visit.

Make your reservation at the kennels in plenty of time. Let them know the day and time you will bring your dog in and the day and time you will collect it. Ask what the boarding fees include. Many kennels charge a small weekly fee for insurance in case of the need for veterinary attention, and this is likely to be over and above the daily rate. Many also have a "checking out" time, so that if you collect your dog after, say, 1 p.m., you will be charged for an extra day. Make sure you understand all this to avoid any risk of unpleasantness later.

Most kennels will ask for a deposit to confirm the booking. They will also insist on seeing a current vaccination certificate. Usually they will ask you what you have been feeding the dog to avoid any upsets that may be caused by changing the food, and may invite you to bring the dog's bed or blanket, or a favorite toy. This is so that the dog will have something familiar with it and settle down

more quickly in the strange surroundings. Do not take your dog's feeding dishes unless you are asked to do so.

When you take your dog for its stay in the kennels you will usually leave it at the reception area and collect it from the same place. This is because other dogs already in the kennels would be disturbed and excited by a stream of strangers; it is the kennel owner's responsibility to keep the dogs as quiet and content as possible during their stay. Also, if your dog has guarding tendencies, as many breeds do, it may think that you have asked it to guard the kennel until you return—causing considerable difficulties for the kennel staff.

If your dog has recently received any veterinary treatment or is in season, let the receptionist know. It is always advisable, before you leave your dog, to give the name, address, and telephone number of a friend or relative who can be contacted in case of an emergency. You should also leave the name of your vet, in case your pet needs treatment—it is unethical for a vet to treat an animal registered with another practice.

Above: Reliable kennels will maintain good levels of hygiene and safety and your dog will be well looked after.

Right: Luxury weekend breaks for dogs are available at a price. Don't expect every kennel to provide this sort of service!

SHIPPING AND QUARANTINE

TRANSPORTING DOGS ABROAD is a specialized business. Anyone moving overseas should contact a kennel or agency that specializes in shipping. Countries have different requirements and a dog may need to have vaccinations and blood tests as much as 28 days before departure. Documentation also varies from country to country. It is important that this is carried out correctly, otherwise the dog may be refused admission upon arrival at its destination. Getting the right documentation together can take several weeks, especially where import permits are needed from the country to which the dog is being consigned. It is thus necessary to start making arrangements for your dog well in advance of the date of departure in order to be sure that everything is completed in good time.

Let the experts carry out the shipping itself. They can provide a traveling crate of the correct size for the comfort of the dog and one that will be in accordance with the relevant regulations.

Most dogs adapt well to air travel and arrive in excellent condition. It is wise to get the dog accustomed to its traveling crate for a week or so before the journey. This can be done by locking it in the container for short periods, initially for feeding, and gradually increasing the length of time until it willingly stays there all night. If this is done the dog will not find its confinement strange, or be frightened, when the time for the journey finally comes.

Dogs are carried on passenger ships, and kennels are usually provided, often staffed by kennel maids on long voyages on some vessels owned by the large shipping lines. Container ships plying between Britain and Australia also carry dogs, and an attendant is employed to look after them. This is not necessarily a trained person but rather someone who is working his or her passage. However,

If your dog is going on a long journey by air or sea, it is a good idea to accustom it to its traveling cage in advance. Shut it in for a short while at first, gradually increasing the length of time until it is happy to stay there for several hours.

In quarantine kennels, each dog is kept in isolation from all others for a period of months.

a dog may find a long sea journey stressful; temperature changes and a lack of proper exercise and care can mean that the animal may arrive in poor condition.

Several countries apart from Britain have quarantine regulations. The reason for this is simple. Any warm-blooded animal can contract rabies and this disease, nearly always fatal, can be transmitted to humans (see page 152). Vaccination of animals against rabies is still not 100 percent effective, so the laws of some countries require animals to undergo a period of quarantine on entry. Up until 1999, every dog brought into Britain from abroad, even if it was from a rabies-free country, had to spend six months in a government-approved quarantine kennel. During this entire period it would not be allowed to come into contact with any other animal. If during quarantine the dog did not develop the symptoms of rabies, it would be released to its owners.

Starting January 2000, however, a pilot scheme was introduced that allows dogs and cats to avoid quarantine. Under the scheme, the animal has a microchip inserted under its skin as a permanent means of identification (see page 125). It is then given a rabies vaccination followed 30 days later by a blood test and, provided it is rabies-free, is issued with a passport permitting it to travel abroad to any one of 22 "approved" countries, mostly in Western Europe.

Vaccinated animals must wait six months after the blood test before re-entering Britain, to ensure that there is no risk that rabies has been incubating. Once this initial waiting period is over, however, the vaccination can be kept effective by an annual booster. The only proviso is that a vet must examine the animal and declare it free of worms and ticks within 24–48 hours before it returns to Britain. It is thought that the total cost of vaccinations and fares for pets is likely to be appreciably less than the cost of six months in quarantine.

At the time of writing, this scheme is in its infancy, with animals permitted to travel only via Heathrow Airport, the Channel Tunnel, and ferries from Dover or Portsmouth. Critics have predicted chaos because of a long waiting-list for blood tests, and objected to the introduction of the "ticks and worms" check, which did not exist under the old laws. If you do want to take your dog with you on holiday abroad, consult your vet about vaccinations and blood tests well in advance to avoid disappointment.

Other countries, including Australia and New Zealand, still impose six months' quarantine on all new arrivals. Smuggling an animal into countries that have quarantine regulations quite properly carries severe penalties. These range from very large fines to a period of imprisonment. In addition the animal may be destroyed.

BREEDING YOUR DOG

I F YOU OWN A FEMALE DOG, you may decide that you want to breed from her. In order to do so, you need to know something about the reproductive system of the dog, and a lot about the extra care and attention that a mother and puppies will need. In no circumstances should you consider breeding from a bitch who is less than a year old, or older than eight. Choose a male dog that you know is from sound stock.

The owners of stud dogs advertise in the dog papers, but the best way to find a suitable mate for your bitch is by word of mouth. Ask around at your local breed club, and make sure that the dog is sound in temperament as well as physical appearance. It is usual to take the bitch to the dog, rather than vice versa. Since he takes the dominant role, he "performs" better in his own territory. It is normal for the pair to mate twice, two days apart, to ensure that you catch the bitch at her most fertile time. If you are breeding pedigree dogs, you will have to pay a stud fee to the owner of the male. This will be a lot of money if you want to breed from a champion, but you can find many good-quality studs for reasonable sums.

Most bitches reach puberty between the ages of six and 14 months, the time being determined by such considerations as type of breed, feeding, health, and

Above: A mating pair investigate each other by sniffing until the bitch decides she is ready.

Above right: She then stands steadily with her tail out to one side to allow the dog to mount her.

environmental factors. Thereafter, most will come into season or heat twice a year, although some breeds (for example the Basenji) do so only once a year. A season lasts about 21 days and may be divided into two periods of roughly equal length. The first period is when the vulva becomes enlarged and discharges a fluid that is opaque at first but later becomes stained with blood. This occurs when the walls of the uterus prepare to receive

fertilized eggs. After 10 to 14 days the discharge loses its color. From then until the end of heat, a bitch is most likely to be receptive to mating. This is the period when the eggs produced by the ovaries are liberated and flow into the Fallopian tubes to await fertilization and eventual implantation. A bitch is not receptive to mating at any other time in her six-monthly cycle.

The male dog, on the other hand, is always ready for mating once he is sexually mature. He will normally be sexually indifferent to a bitch who is not in season, but will be attracted to her when her body releases the chemicals known as pheromones, indicating a change in her sexual condition. This happens a few days before she becomes sexually receptive, which explains why male dogs are

so excited by bitches who are not yet ready to receive their advances—and who may repulse them fiercely.

Dogs go through a courtship ritual before mating. It includes sniffing each other and play fighting. Finally the bitch will adopt a characteristic standing posture with tail held to one side, signifying acceptance of the male. He then mounts her from the rear, holds her flanks with his forelegs and inserts his penis into her vagina. The vagina closes firmly around the penis, forming what is known as the copulatory tie or lock. Although it is not essential to mating, the tie does help prevent the sperm-bearing fluid from escaping. The animals may hold the tie for up to 30 minutes or even longer. They should not be forcibly separated, as this will cause them pain. Let them uncouple

The pair often remain "tied" for half an hour or more. In the wild, this behavior would have ensured that the male's sperm fertilized the eggs and passed on his genes, before other dogs had the opportunity to mate with a fertile female.

when they are ready to do so. Assuming fertilization takes place and all goes well with the pregnancy, puppies will be born about 63 days later.

The mating process takes longer for an inexperienced pair, and dogs of either sex that have had little contact with other dogs may have difficulties. The breeder of the stud dog is likely to be experienced in these matters and can help if necessary. Noise or disturbance can often distract a pair while mating. There is evidence of individual preferences, especially with the bitch, which may refuse some males.

PREGNANCY AND WHELPING

THE BEHAVIOR OF THE BITCH undergoes considerable change in the course of pregnancy and lactation. Near the end of pregnancy, she will frequently become restless and may roam around the house. This probably indicates her search for a nest site. She may also make digging movements, even at a solid floor, or may tear up paper or other material. She may also cease obeying commands. Her appetite will also fluctuate (see page 140).

When whelping time is near, you should help your bitch by preparing a whelping site for her, in a place where she can be quiet and undisturbed—a spare bedroom is ideal. You can buy whelping boxes from pet shops, or make one yourself from pieces of hardboard and planks of wood. Cover the floor with washable synthetic fleece and make sure the room

is warmer than it would usually be. If you are able to install an infrared light above the whelping box, this will keep the puppies warm without roasting the rest of the house.

Talk to your vet before your bitch is due to give birth and discuss whether you need professional help to deliver the puppies. Most bitches have relatively few problems at whelping and instinctively perform the necessary tasks. A bitch will lie on her side during labor and pups will be born at irregular intervals with either head or breech presentation, generally about 20 to 60 minutes apart. Disturbance may interrupt the normal process of labor. After the birth of a pup, the bitch removes the sac enclosing it and then vigorously licks it. She then bites through the umbilical cord and eats the afterbirth. She may even continue to lick

stillborn pups until they get cold. Although puppies may be stillborn because of some defect that has prevented them from developing healthily, the risk of a healthy pup dying in the womb is greatly increased if the bitch becomes overtired. Hormone injections can stimulate the contractions of labor, so if there is any sign of the bitch beginning to struggle, call the vet at once.

After the birth of the pups, most mothers stay in the nest with them, leaving only for brief intervals such as to feed. By the time the puppies are two weeks old, she may leave the nest area for periods of two or three hours. Lactation usually declines at about four to five weeks. At this time an unusual form of behavior may be seen as the mother regurgitates food in the nest for her young. Such action is inherited from the

If all goes well, a bitch can deliver her puppies by herself, clean them, and nudge them into a suckling position. If, however, any of the puppies is very weak, or if the bitch gets overtired giving birth to a large litter, calm assistance will be very welcome.

Left: At three days old, puppies are interested in little more than eating and sleeping. When their eyes open, they take interest in other things.

Below: Weigh each puppy daily for the first two weeks, then at least twice a week until they are too big for the scales.

dog's wild ancestors, when the mother used this method to bring back food she had caught away from the nest.

Before the age of four weeks the newborn pup shows only the most basic of behaviors. These have to do with feeding, keeping warm, and sleeping, the last taking up about 90 per cent of its time. While awake the pup either searches for a teat, using swimming-like movements of its front legs to pull itself along on its stomach, or else it is busy suckling. Young pups will make a mewing call if in distress for any reason such as cold. Surprisingly, if the mother can hear but not see a mewing pup she will not usually respond to the call. She will, however, retrieve a pup if she sees it moving around some way from her nest. Once the puppies are old enough to move out of the nest or whelping box, make sure the surrounding area is covered with several layers of newspaper. You will need to change this several times a day as it will rapidly become soiled.

Most bitches are naturally good mothers, assiduous in keeping their puppies clean and treading very carefully over the tiny wriggling bodies as they go in and out. However, a few take less easily to motherhood and you may need to help in the cleaning or feeding process if the mother is neglectful.

Be careful when handling young puppies—as is the case with human babies, their muscles are still developing and they need support. Put one hand under the puppy's chest and the other under its rump. Never lift a puppy up by its elbows or you risk straining its back.

If you have bred pedigree dogs, you should register the puppies with the Kennel Club, using forms which they will provide. You should also ensure that they have the vaccinations required by law— these vary from country to country and may change from time to time, but the first ones are usually due when the puppies are four weeks old. Ask your vet what the latest requirements are. You should have the puppies dosed for worms at the same time.

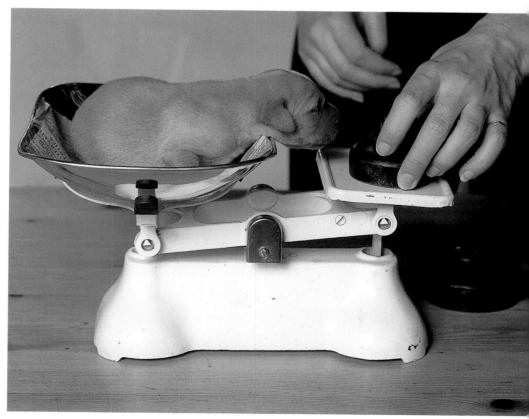

BREEDING AND FOOD

IF DOGS ARE FED A BALANCED diet of adequate quality and maintained in lean, hard condition, there is no need to adjust the diet before mating or during the first four weeks of pregnancy. In the fifth week a bitch's appetite should grow. Increase her food gradually and divide the total amount about equally between two meals. By the ninth week a medium-sized bitch carrying an average litter of five or six should be eating about two-thirds more food than she would ordinarily need for daily maintenance. A small bitch may need twice as much food. The extra food may be mostly meat, although this is not essential with a balanced diet. Shortly before whelping, a bitch will lose her appetite and may vomit her last meal. During whelping, provide only water or a little milk at intervals.

Within a day of a normal whelping, the bitch should regain her appetite as the puppies begin to suckle. During lactation, assuming a litter of average number, she will need about three times as much food as usual, divided between three meals. The third meal should be rich in protein, vitamins, and minerals. Calcium is particularly important, to protect her from eclampsia or milk tetany. This dangerous condition is caused by a lowering of the blood calcium level brought about by the bitch's production of milk. Cows' milk is a useful supplementary food during lactation, but is laxative if given too freely.

Weigh each puppy every day for the first two weeks. Puppies of small breeds should gain about 1 oz. (28 g) a day, those of medium-size breeds 2 oz. (56 g), and of large breeds about 4 oz. (112 g). Continue to weigh at least twice a week. The bitch is "dried off" during the next two or three weeks as the litter is weaned.

Gradually decrease her food, first by reducing and then eliminating the third meal, and then by bringing the other meals back to their normal level. When weaning is complete, the bitch should be at her normal weight and in healthy condition. If she appears thin, give her a little extra meaty food until her condition is restored; if she is overweight, cut down her carbohydrate intake.

Unless a bitch has a very large litter, she will supply all her puppies' needs until weaning begins. Even in an average-sized litter, however, there may well be one or more puppies appreciably smaller than the rest who are elbowed out of the way on their mother's teats and are in danger of being undernourished. Watch out for this and whenever the litter is suckling, place a small puppy firmly on a teat, making sure that it stays there until it is satisfied. With a large litter it may be necessary to wait until the stronger puppies have finished.

With very large litters, some supplementary feeding will probably be necessary. More rarely, a bitch dies during whelping or for some reason fails to nurse her litter. The puppies must then be reared entirely by hand. Orphan puppies should be given a little glucose solution (1 oz. to 1 pint, 28 g to 0.5 liter, of boiled water) via a dropper or a premature baby's feeding bottle. Keep newborn puppies warm and massage them to promote excretion. After one or two glucose feeds, begin milk feeds at two-hourly intervals (day and night), lengthening to three-hourly after a day or two, and then to six a day by the end of the first week. Four feeds a day should be sufficient from then to weaning.

Fortify cows' milk with extra protein and calories. Evaporated or condensed milk tends to be too laxative. Instead, blend casein (milk protein) and vegetable oil into high-fat, creamy milk at the rates of 1 oz. and ½ oz. respectively per pint (28 g and 14 g per 0.5 liters). Use a kitchen homogenizer for efficient dispersion and warm the mixture to blood heat before use. Give as much as the puppy wants at each feed. This preparation is also suitable for supplementary feeding of backward puppies. Begin weaning orphan puppies as soon as they can stand to lap, or will take solid food from your fingers.

Changing a puppy's diet from its mother's milk to the more solid diet of adult dogs can usually start at about three weeks of age. In nature the mother starts to regurgitate her own partly digested food as her milk begins to dry up. Breeders attempt to simulate this diet either by scraping meat to a fine paste or by soaking pre-cooked cereals in cows' milk. The second method is, on the

Left: Supplementary bottle-feeding may be necessary if the mother dies or rejects the puppies, or if a puppy is failing to thrive.

Right: As the puppies grow, their mother may begin to get bored with feeding them, so they will have to struggle to suckle while her attention is attracted elsewhere.

whole, less trouble and means that the dog will not become reliant on an expensive meat diet. You can also buy complete puppy diets that contain all the necessary nutrients, but check that the product is designed for the correct age of puppy.

Begin by teaching the puppies to lap warm milk from a saucer. If necessary wet your finger in the milk, or dampen their muzzles with it to encourage them. Offer a fresh saucer of milk three times a day, in the early morning, around noon and in the early evening. As the puppies begin to lap, start to reduce the mother's food and keep her away from the litter for periods of two or three hours. Continue to weigh each puppy at least twice a week, or even daily, in order to check on their progress.

When the puppies are lapping freely, introduce solid food. Soak a little baby cereal or specially prepared puppy meal in an equal volume of hot milk and allow the mixture to cool to blood heat. Offer this food two or three times a day at what you intend to be regular mealtimes. At first the pups will attempt to suck out the milk but in about a week they should be eating the solid food. The texture should not be sticky but consist of separate, soft, moist pieces. Continue to reduce the bitch's food. Remove her from the pups except at night, and for one or two brief periods during the day.

After five to six weeks the puppies should be fully weaned and the bitch separated. If she is in discomfort, consult a veterinary surgeon. It is now important to increase the quantity of the puppies' food rapidly to keep pace with growth. Keep the midday meal small while increasing the quantity of solid food, but not of milk, at the morning and evening meals. Water must now be freely

available. You might also like to offer a little warm milk in the late evening. The total amount of milk each day should range from about ½ cup (0.15 liter) for very small breeds to 2 cups (0.5 liter) for giants. It is wise to feed puppies from individual bowls, since this will ensure that each gets its share.

As soon as the pups are satisfactorily weaned, gradually introduce meat if you have not already done so. Nearly all types, including tinned foods, are suitable but at this stage give liver in very small amounts only. All meat should be cooked and minced. Start by mixing the meat with the milk and cereal feeds morning and evening. If neither meat nor cereal contains added vitamins and minerals, provide a reputable proprietary supplement. Increase the two main meals to meet the demands of the puppies' appetites. From the age of about ten weeks a puppy eats more than it will

when fully grown. Give milk separately, as a dry mixture is beneficial for the puppy's teeth. From the age of three months, if not before, omit the midday small feed and optional late milk.

Variation in size and the rate of growth makes it impossible to prescribe precise quantities of food. Continue to weigh the dog regularly and chart the results. When it is clear that growth is slowing down, stop the milk and begin to reduce one of the two meals. With miniature breeds this may be as early as five months; giant breeds continue to grow rapidly to at least eight months. It is wiser to underfeed slightly rather than to risk producing an obese young dog, but with experience it is possible to adjust feeding so that the dog remains in prime condition. From the age of about nine months feed as for an adult dog, but observe your pet's condition carefully and adjust the food intake if necessary.

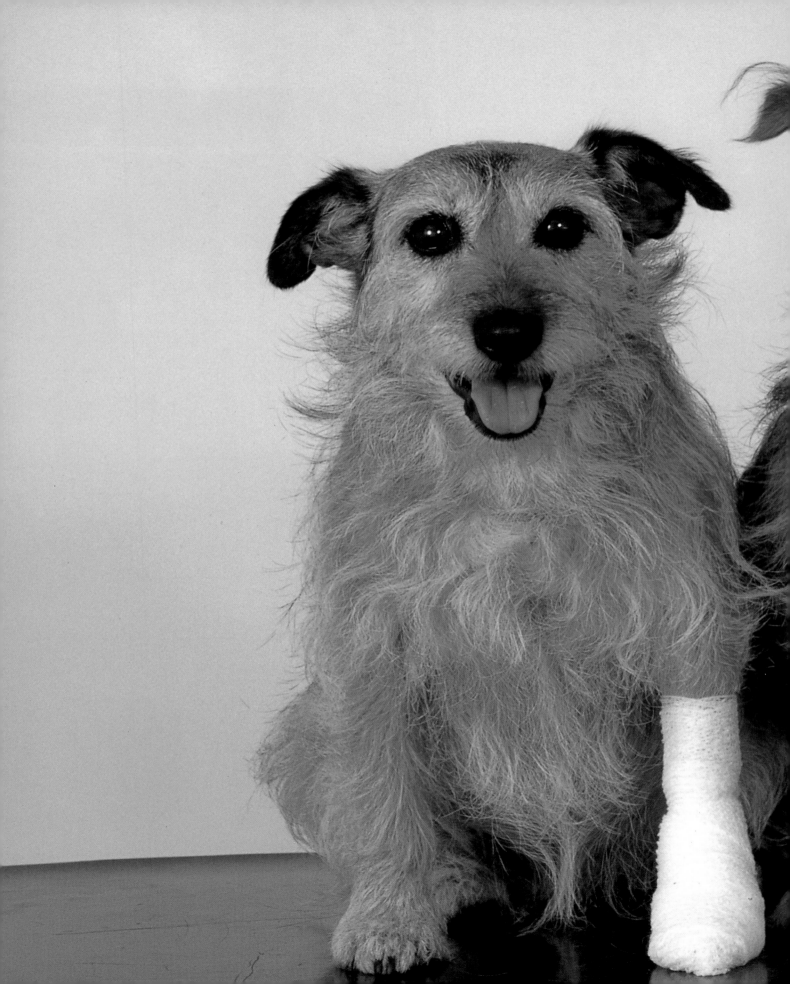

Part Five

Sickness and Medical Care

If your dog is out of sorts, there are a number of basic treatments you can carry out yourself, just as you would with a sick child; but you should also learn to recognize when something is seriously amiss and call the vet without delay.

DETECTING ILLNESS

Left and right: In the wild, dogs do not communicate by touch, so being handled does not come naturally to them. Get your dog used to the sort of handling it might expect at the vet's by routinely checking inside its ears, wiping around its eyes, and lifting its lips to look at its teeth. These are also useful routine checks that will help you to spot early signs of a problem.

MANY OWNERS HAVE an almost instinctive awareness of something being not quite right with their dogs, but not every sick dog is recognized quickly enough. The ability to decide whether a dog is healthy or sick comes from a combination of experience and observation, both of which should be consciously developed by the concerned owner. Normal behavior is an important indicator of a healthy animal and should be carefully noted. All dogs sleep a great deal, but should be alert and lively when they are awake. Sluggishness may result from a variety of causes, from old age or obesity, to such serious diseases as acute anemia.

Disease may be acute or chronic; the former develops rapidly, accompanied by signs of obvious illness, while the latter is insidious and consequently often unnoticed until it is far advanced. Appetite and bodily conditions are helpful guides in both forms of disease. Healthy dogs usually have a good appetite, but that of a sick dog may be reduced or vary from normal. Excessive thirst is often an important sign of certain diseases—sometimes, indeed, the only obvious sign. Acute disease may be accompanied by a complete refusal to eat, but equally important is the slight, not necessarily obvious, loss of appetite which may accompany chronic disease. Prolonged, gradual weight loss should never be neglected; normal weight for its age is an essential sign of a healthy animal.

Chance observation is the usual way of noticing something amiss with a dog, but a straightforward methodical check over the animal's body will often help confirm the suspicion that it is not well, and can be a considerable help to the veterinarian.

Starting from the head:
• Do the eyes appear normal? They should be bright with no sores or ulcers, the whites of the eyes clear, with no signs of being affected by swollen veins, but not excessively pale.
• Is there any discharge from the eyes or nose, and is the nose free from encrusted material?
• Is the mouth a healthy, pink color and do the teeth look normal and white, without any marked discoloration? Look into the dog's opened mouth. Pieces of wood or bone can be wedged between the upper teeth for months without being recognized.
• Are the ears clean, free from waxy deposits, or do they smell? Healthy ears have a clean, pink look. There should not be matted hair in the ears (often a problem with poodles), as this can lead to more serious ear infection.
• The head, limbs, and trunk of a healthy dog's body will have no unusual swellings and the skin no wounds, other than perhaps minor scratches, and no sign of hair loss or sore, inflamed patches. Standing or moving, the dog should appear comfortable; a "hunched" stance or lameness always indicates that something is wrong.
• Location of a lameness may be extremely difficult (or blindingly obvious), but if you imagine the effect of a stone in your own shoe, it will remind you how a lameness affects movement. The dog's head or rump drops when the sound limb has weight on it, and lifts by comparison when the lame leg is on the ground. After that, it becomes a matter of gentle but firm pressure with the hand to discover where the pain is located, but once again this is often easier to do when the dog is relaxed at home, instead of tense at the vet's office.
• The skin should be elastic, and spring back into place rapidly after it is lifted away from the animal's body. This varies from breed to breed. For example, a Labrador puppy's skin always seems several sizes too large, but it still feels elastic and somehow "healthy."

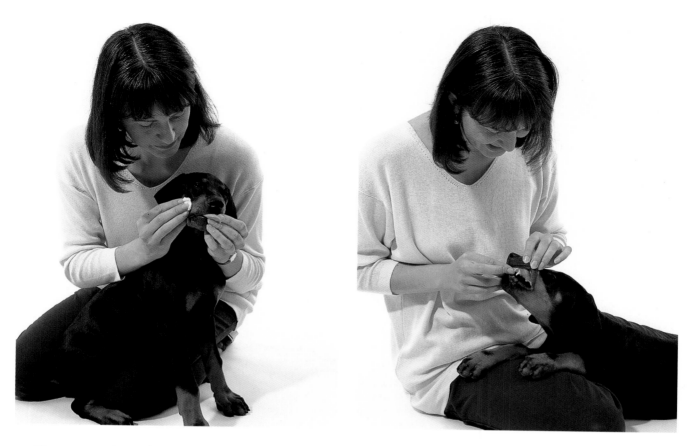

The most popular guide in determining health is the dog's temperature, which is normally between 100.4° and 102.2°F (38–39°C). In good health it is unlikely to fall much below 100.4° except just before whelping, when it is usual to record rectal temperatures as low as 98.6°F (37°C). Excited or nervous healthy dogs may go as high as 103.1°F (39.5°C) for short periods. There is no reason why a careful dog-owner should not take a dog's temperature. Use a snub-nosed clinical thermometer and grease the end. Make certain it is shaken down to well below the 100°F mark. Insert and hold it into the dog's rectum for approximately half the thermometer's length, applying slight sideways pressure to hold the bulb against the wall of the rectum. Nearly all thermometers are "30 second" tested, but it is usual to keep it in place for a full minute to make sure. Wipe the thermometer before reading and wash it afterward in cold water with disinfectant.

Pulse and respiration rate are probably not worth recording in most circumstances, but difficult or heavy breathing and unusual sounds should be noted. Vomiting and diarrhea, alterations in the pattern or type of urination and vaginal discharges should never be ignored.

Owners rarely have difficulty in deciding that a particular problem in their dog is serious. Most are inclined to over-emphasize the urgency of need for attention, and this is understandable when the well-being of a beloved pet is in question. It is more difficult to decide what first-aid measures to take. The question to ask yourself is: should you do anything? Most people feel that they should do something, but, although they rarely do harm with first aid, they often do little good at some hazard to themselves. A dog having a fit is a case in point. Forget about it swallowing its tongue and choking—it won't. But if you try to put a gag in its mouth in the traditional way you will probably get your fingers bitten, so just leave it alone, and move breakable objects out of its way. Similarly with a dog in collapse, forget heart massage and just get it to the vet.

On the other hand, animals which are bleeding badly do need rapid first aid, preferably not by tourniquet but with a pressure bandage applied tightly to the wound. A dog's life can be saved by a sensible owner using, say, a scarf in this way. Open wounds that are not bleeding badly, but that look large enough to need stitching, should simply be kept clean; old cotton sheets are probably ideal for the purpose. Don't cover such wounds in antiseptic ointment or wound dressing powder—it only means a longer cleaning job for the nurse before the vet can see what he or she is meant to be sewing up.

Leg injuries and possible broken bones should be disturbed as little as is compatible with reasonably rapid transportation to a vet. Better to take the slight risk of further injury through movement than to leave the animal in an exposed place. All dogs involved in a road accident, however trivial, should be checked by a vet because of the risk of shock or internal injury.

COMMON AILMENTS

Bad breath

An offensive smell from a dog's mouth may result from infection in the mouth itself or be associated with a generalized disease such as chronic nephritis (inflammation of the kidneys). But the most common cause is a buildup of plaque on the teeth. Plaque occurs when, over a period of time, a mixture of saliva products and bacteria mineralize to form a cement-like substance on the teeth. If not removed, this plaque inflames and causes retraction of the gums, as well as allowing food products to accumulate round the teeth; these eventually decay and produce foul smells. In time, a neglected buildup of plaque will cause gum retraction, leading eventually to loose teeth or abscesses on the roots of the teeth, which make the smell worse.

The best way of preventing bad breath is to brush the dog's teeth regularly. If you are unable to do this, providing abrasive chews can help. Once plaque has mineralized, the only way to remove it is to have the teeth scaled under general anesthetic. Most dogs need to have this done at some stage in their lives. Changes in diet are unlikely to affect the smell of your dog's breath.

Cannibalism

Bitches at whelping, even normally placid ones, may become sufficiently psychologically disturbed to attack, kill, and even occasionally eat their offspring. There is no treatment, but it is essential to have as undisturbed and peaceful a situation as possible at whelping time, and to allow the bitch to whelp in surroundings with which she has become familiar, preferably over weeks rather than days. Quiet vigilance is needed rather than over-anxious "help."

Carsickness

Some dogs have this trouble and others do not. Depending on the puppy's size, up to half an anti-travel sickness tablet, administered about an hour before the journey, may be effective. Some dogs are not actually sick in the car but exhibit inappropriate behavior such as urinating, defecating, or persistent barking. To prevent this, it is important to familiarize a young puppy with car travel as soon as possible. Since most social and behavioral conditioning occurs before the age of 12 weeks, start with short journeys well before this age and gradually increase their length. Once your puppy has had all its vaccinations and is allowed to go out, take it somewhere nice—for a walk or to visit people who will be pleased to see it—so that it does not associate car journeys solely with going to the vet's or being left in the car park.

In extreme cases your vet may prescribe tranquilizers, but their effect is often unpredictable and they should be avoided if at all possible.

Constipation

Simple constipation occurs fairly often as a result of eating bones or indigestible matter. It may also arise from the dog's refusal to defecate because of pain from infected anal glands, or even matted hair around the anus. There are other, more fundamental causes, and chronic constipation, particularly if it is associated with alternating bouts of diarrhea, needs veterinary attention and may be treated by an enema. Constipation is accompanied by frequent attempts to defecate. A dog which makes no attempt to pass feces for several days is not necessarily constipated. The best first aid for this problem is probably liquid paraffin by mouth, about a dessertspoonful for small dogs, and four or five times that amount for larger dogs. This should be administered two to three times daily, and it is often necessary to dose for up to three days or until liquid paraffin is seen coming from the dog's rear.

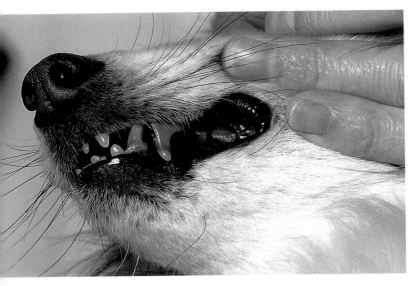

Examining and cleaning your dog's teeth at regular intervals, and giving it bones or chews, should prevent this sort of decay, and certainly mean that it will be noticed and dealt with promptly.

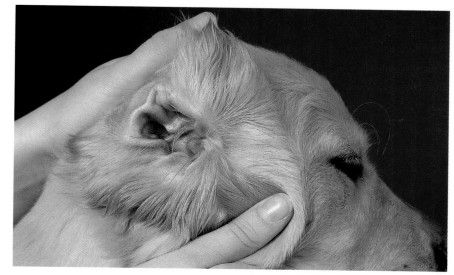

The inside of a dog's ears should be pink, healthy-looking, and free of unpleasant smells. Check regularly, and consult your vet if you notice anything amiss.

Coprophagy

This is the term for eating feces. It is almost invariably simply a bad habit which is likely to have arisen out of boredom and close confinement, although it can occur for no discernible reason. There is no deficiency or disease condition which makes a dog eat feces, and it will not be cured by providing additional vitamins or other supplements. The habit has to be cured by discouragement, and avoidance of the situation by removing feces quickly. Some dogs will eat horse manure if they get the chance. Coprophagy is so common that it has come to be regarded as normal behavior, but it should be firmly discouraged.

Cough

Coughing is simply a sign of irritation in the dog's throat or bronchial tubes. It must be considered with other symptoms in determining the cause. Only rarely is a foreign body such as a bone involved, but an apparent attempt to clear the throat of something is often a sign of tonsillitis or kennel cough, a highly infectious although usually not serious disease. There is now a vaccination against kennel cough, and this is strongly recommended before your dog goes into kennels. A moist cough may also be a symptom of heart disease. Any type of persistent cough requires veterinary attention. If the cough is accompanied by distress, or by refusal of food, the attention should be prompt.

Deafness

This is not common in dogs, but it can occur as a congenital condition and can be noticed by an observant owner while puppies are still in the nest. A simple hand-clap will usually show whether or not the puppy is reacting to noise, but hearing which is simply less acute than normal may be extremely difficult to determine. The onset of deafness frequently accompanies old age. There is usually no treatment available. Cleansing the ears of wax is unlikely to be of more than of marginal benefit.

Degenerative Joint Disease (DJD)

Strictly speaking, dogs rarely suffer from arthritis, which is defined as inflammation of the joint. But joint problems due to natural wear and tear resulting from the aging process or as a result of injury are common, particularly in the heavier breeds. Other joint problems such as hip dysplasia (see below) and Legge-Perthe's disease (a disorder of the hip bone) may occur in young dogs. Obesity tends to aggravate the condition. Signs are usually insidious, with slowly developing pain and lameness, often noticeable as stiffness in the morning which wears off with exercise. Diagnosis may require X-ray examination. Treatment is palliative, but weight reduction of obese dogs should be attempted, and the dog's bed should be kept warm and dry.

Diarrhea see Enteritis and Diarrhea

Distemper and Hard pad

Both terms refer to a disease that is caused by a single virus that may show some variation in symptoms. The first sign of either form of the disease is a high body temperature, about 102°F (39°C). The dog refuses food and may have a cough or diarrhea; the whites of the eyes are usually inflamed. If infection progresses, it will eventually affect the nervous system, leading to intractable fits. The hard pad symptom occurs when the virus affects the horny layers of the pads, causing enlargement and a leathery feel to the feet. Luckily, effective vaccination means that distemper is now rarely seen.

Ear diseases

Head shaking, ear scratching, and an unpleasant smell are usually the first signs of ear disease, and when this is noticed the ears should be examined. Healthy ears are pale pink inside, shiny, and free from discharge or wax. If the ear looks sore, the dog needs veterinary attention. If the ears are simply dirty or contain a little clean-looking wax, use a proprietary product available from your vet to break down the wax. It is not safe to push wads of cotton wool into the ear unless you know there is nothing further down causing trouble. Acute inflammation, particularly in spaniels, is often caused by a grass seed. More chronic infections frequently start off with ear mite infestations. Veterinary treatment depends on the cause, and in some cases may even require surgery to expose the inflamed area.

This neglected mongrel has developed a sore skin condition, possibly mange, and requires immediate treatment.

Eczema

Many skin problems in the dog have a considerable element of self-infliction, and a dog can turn an itchy spot into a large patch of severe moist eczema in less than an hour. But eczema is frequently caused by an allergy or nervous reaction, and the vet's first step would be to try to isolate the cause in order to treat the condition appropriately and prevent a recurrence. As part of the treatment he or she would try to prevent the animal making matters worse by scratching or biting itself. Itching without symptoms of eczema is likely to be caused by parasites, probably fleas. There are effective powders available both to prevent and to treat this problem.

Enteritis and Diarrhea

Although most attacks of simple diarrhea probably have a nutritional cause, specific diagnosis and treatment are necessary if an attack persists for longer than 48 hours. Parvovirus Enteritis, closely related to Feline Enteritis, is a highly infectious and frequently fatal viral disease. First signs are likely to be serious vomiting and often blood-stained diarrhea. Veterinary help should be sought immediately. First-aid treatment for simple diarrhea consists of removing all sources of food and drink for 24 hours, giving the dog frequent small amounts of glucose and water to avoid dehydration. Then give a bland diet for three to four days, before gradually weaning the dog back on to his normal food.

Eye troubles

Eye infections are common in the dog, usually in the form of conjunctivitis, and prompt treatment with antibiotics usually effects a cure. Ulcerated corneas may be more serious, and any indication of blueing, or damage to the surface of the eye, should be attended to without delay.

Old dogs do sometimes go blind, like this Bouvier des Flandres, but they can continue to live a contented, if rather restricted, life.

An acute eye problem is usually signalled by watering of the eye and closing, partially or completely, of the eyelids. Gentle examination may reveal the cause. If it is a foreign body, such as a piece of grass, and you can remove it using your fingers or the corner of a handkerchief, do so. But greater interference than this should not be attempted.

False pregnancy

This phenomenon, which mimics the symptoms of pregnancy, is not uncommon even in bitches that have not been mated. It usually occurs about the time that physical and behavioral changes would be expected in the pregnant animal—that is, abut 6–8 weeks after mating. It is thought that as many as 75 percent of bitches develop false pregnancies at some time—a reflection of behavior in the wild when only the dominant female gives birth, but other lactating females in the pack help to nurse the puppies. Signs of a false pregnancy include increased appe-tite, loss of interest in exercise, increase in weight, particularly in the abdomen, and increase in affectionateness to the point of "clinginess." The bitch may even try to find a suitable place to give birth and exhibit signs of "nesting" behavior. Until recently hormone treatment was unsatisfactory because it did not act directly on the hormone prolactin which causes the changes. An effective prolactin inhibitor is now available, but is relatively expensive. Before resorting to veterinary treatment, owners should try discouraging the behavior, keeping the bitch out of her chosen nest area, encouraging her to take exercise and feeding her less. These remedies are usually sufficient to eliminate the problem.

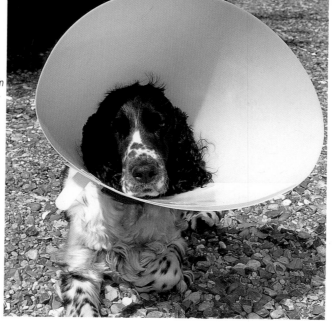

Collars like these are useful for a dog suffering from a skin complaint such as eczema, or after an operation. They prevent the dog from licking the sore or wound, or from tearing at stitches.

Fits

Epilepsy is a common cause of repeated fits in dogs of any age. Idiopathic epilepsy (that for which there is no known cause) often starts when the dog is between one and three years old. In older dogs, it may develop as a result of another disease, such as liver or kidney failure, or as the result of pressure on the brain due to a tumour or lesion. Remove any object that might injure the dog and do not put anything into his mouth "to stop him choking." This won't help and you may get bitten. Take him to the vet.

Dogs with heart conditions may occasionally collapse when exercising, due to insufficient oxygen being supplied to the tissues by the blood. In these circumstances the dog does not show any of the classic signs of a fit and will usually recover within a couple of minutes. Again, veterinary attention should be sought.

Fleas see Parasites

Fractures

Suspected broken bones can be confirmed and treated only at a vet's office or animal hospital. Despite a widespread belief to the contrary, sensible movement of the dog is unlikely to make the injury worse. The animal should be carried, if necessary on a blanket, and taken for treatment as soon as possible.

Gastric distension

Bloat, gastric torsion, or gastric distension is a well-recognized problem in larger breeds of dog. Two to four hours after feeding the dog may show signs of obvious distress and pain. The abdomen will be distended and hard. This is a surgical emergency and must be treated immediately by a veterinarian.

Gastritis

Vomiting is the most likely indication that a dog has an inflamed stomach, or gastritis, but grass-eating without vomiting may occasionally be a sign. Gastritis is also often associated with simple diarrhea. Severe diarrhea and vomiting may also be symptoms of the more serious disease of gastro-enteritis. Both of these may have mechanical origins, possibly a swallowed rubber band or undigested bone, or be caused by bacterial or viral infection. See also Enteritis and Diarrhea.

Grass-eating

This may be of no significance, or it may indicate irritation in the stomach (see Gastritis). It is believed that a dog instinctively takes grass to induce vomiting. Grass wraps itself around jagged foreign bodies in the stomach, so helping to prevent damage to the bowel.

Hemorrhage

Heavy bleeding is obvious if the hemorrhage is external. Pad the wound with cotton wool and bandage firmly. Severe hemorrhage is an emergency needing instant action. Surgery is the sole means of checking internal bleeding. Obvious signs are blanching of the membranes of the mouth and eyes, and collapse of the dog. It may be necessary to muzzle a severely injured dog, since it may panic and bite even its owner. Wrap a strip of fabric gently around the dog's muzzle.

Hair loss

Shedding of hair in a seasonal pattern is normal in most breeds, other than those with a Poodle-like coat, but central heating seems to have interfered with the pattern in many dogs. Hair loss occurs after whelping or at the same time in an unbred bitch's cycle. No regular treatment can reduce or prevent this; but regular grooming is essential at these times to avoid matting and itchiness from the dead coat. Excessive hair loss may be the result of the dog scratching itself because of an itch caused by allergy or a skin complaint. In such a case, the underlying cause may require veterinary treatment.

Hard pad see Distemper and Hard pad

Heart disease

This is almost as common in dogs as in humans, and often has similar causes. Acquired heart disease takes two forms—valvular disease, which generally occurs in small breeds such as Yorkshire Terriers, and myocardial disease, which is more frequent in larger breeds such as Dobermans. Most casess are treated by drugs rather than surgery. Proper management of cardiac patients is important. Weight loss is frequently required and moderate exercise often desirable. Many dogs will indicate their own exercise tolerance limits. The canine "blue baby" syndrome can be treated by surgery.

As with humans, swollen glands may be a sign of infection. A vet will feel the glands as part of a routine investigation if your dog is feeling out of sorts.

Hepatitis

Viral hepatitis is infectious among dogs. Adult animals may develop fever, with temperatures of up to 105°F (41°C), lose appetite, and show blood-stained diarrhea and vomit. Intensive veterinary care is required, but death can result. Vaccination as a preventive measure is 99 percent effective.

Hernia

xternally noticeable hernias in the dog are almost always congenital, and may occur at the umbilical or in the scrotal or inguinal areas. Small hernias are not significant and are composed of fat trapped in a sac of tissue. If the bulge varies in size, veterinary attention is necessary to advise on possible surgery. The rare, serious sequel to a hernia is "strangulation," when intestines or some other vital organs become trapped in the sac. Prompt surgical treatment is required.

Hip dysplasia

This is a deformity of the hip joint caused when the joint is too shallow and the head of the femur is malformed. It occurs more often than usual in certain larger breeds, such as St. Bernards, German Shepherds, and Retrievers. It manifests itself by pain in the area of the hip, and by a swinging gait and "hopping" run. X-ray is needed for accurate diagnosis, although there is no cure. Pain can be alleviated by drugs or through surgery. This deformity is generally considered to be hereditary, although the extent of this is unknown; in any case, no dysplastic dog should be allowed to breed.

Jaundice

Obvious jaundice with yellowing of the skin and membranes is comparatively uncommon in dogs, but the underlying causes—blood breakdown or liver disease—are regularly seen. The jaundice itself is a minor symptom but should never be ignored. Leptospirosis (see right) and virus hepatitis may both cause jaundicing of the tissues. These diseases are extremely serious. Effective vaccines are available for both and are usually included in the routine vaccinations administered to puppies.

Kidney diseases

Kidney diseases may be divided into two categories, acute or chronic. Acute renal failure may be caused by: infections causing nephritis (inflammation of the kidneys); toxins, shock, and dehydration; or urinary tract obstructions. Acute renal failure is reversible if the cause is identified and corrected; otherwise permanent damage occurs, leading to chronic renal failure. Treatment for this can only be symptomatic, providing a low-fat, low-phosphorus diet.

Lameness

The precise source of a problem can be difficult to pinpoint; it is sometimes even hard to tell which leg is affected. It is useful to remember that the dog nods its head downward as the sound leg touches the ground; similarly its rump will drop as the sound hind leg is put to the ground. It will help diagnosis at the veterinarian's if you notice whether, for example, the lameness is worse first thing in the morning, or if it is intermittent. Careful observation will help. Pain on slight pressure, indicated by tensing of muscles and withdrawal of the leg, may guide you to the site of the lameness. Any lameness that is not obviously improving in 24 hours needs veterinary attention; but young puppies may be crippled with lameness at one moment and virtually sound in half an hour.

Leptospirosis

This serious bacterial infection used to be common, but owing to effective vaccination is now quite rare. Although one type of the infection can be caused by contact with rats, the most frequent transmission is by the urine of carrier dogs. For this reason the infection is considered to be more common in male dogs, which are more prone to lamp-post sniffing than bitches and consequently more likely to be contaminated by infected urine. In country districts carrier foxes may transmit the disease. Leptospirosis causes fever, marked depression, sometimes diarrhea with yellow feces, and often bright yellow urine. Visible jaundice is rarer, but both liver and kidneys are affected. Treatment is by antibiotics and effective nursing care. The disease can be prevented by annual re-vaccination.

Lice see Parasites

Mites see Parasites

Nephritis see Kidney diseases

Paralysis

This is usually caused by injury to the spinal cord and may occur at any point from the neck downward. Many breeds of dog may be affected by various causes

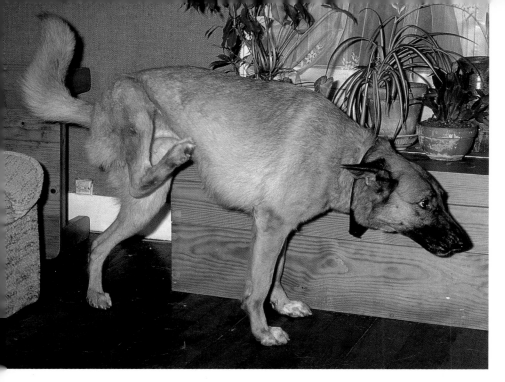

Determined application over weeks or months may be necessary to eliminate them altogether.

"*Fly Strike*" occurs in untreated wounds of dogs. Certain flies lay their eggs in the dog's coat, attracted by the decaying flesh, and small white larvae hatch in a day or two. Treatment of the wound and insecticidal attack on the larvae are essential. Fly egg deposits in fecal matter caught around the anus of hairy breeds such as Old English Sheepdogs can also be a serious problem.

Internal parasites include the common intestinal worms. *Roundworms* infest almost all young puppies and are passed on from the mother. The worms are responsible for the extremely rare condition in humans, *visceral larva migrans*. Because of this and their adverse affect on puppies, all litters should be dosed from about three weeks of age and every three weeks thereafter until they are six months old. Residual worms in the adult are activated during pregnancy; the bitch should be dosed before she gives birth.

of injury, which include infectious, anatomical, and traumatic factors. Long-backed breeds such as Dachshunds are particularly affected by protrusion of the intervertebral disc. This can cause a range of symptoms from loss of sensation to complete loss of use of the limbs. Mild attacks can be controlled by anti-inflammatory drugs, but many cases require expensive surgical intervention.

Parasites

Common external parasites include *fleas*, which are light or dark brown, very mobile, and readily visible when numerous. They are often passed back and forth between dogs and cats. *Lice* tend to be present in large numbers. They or their egg cases are quite firmly attached, often around the ears; they are white and may be mistaken for skin scales or dandruff if not examined closely.

Sarcoptic mange is very serious and is caused by a smaller parasite that lives in the superficial layers of the skin. It causes intense itching and skin sores. Diagnosis can be confirmed only by taking skin scrapings and examining them under a microscope.

Harvest mites are parasitic only in their larval form. The larvae are often found around the head, ears, and flank of the animal and may be recognized by their bright orange color. They are not mobile, and cause intense local irritation.

Ticks are rarely important in Europe, although they are carriers of serious diseases in Africa and parts of the United States. The sheep tick, *Ixodes*, is the common one to affect dogs in temperate climates. It looks like a small gray bladder when mature and is very firmly attached. It can be dealt with by killing it with insecticidal spray, then removing it from the skin by rotating while applying gentle traction. The sheep tick has long mouthparts that are difficult to remove from the skin and cause localized infection if left in place. Tropical ticks are easily removed, but may carry the blood parasite *Babesia*, which causes tick fever.

All these parasites may be controlled by baths, powder, or spray insecticides.

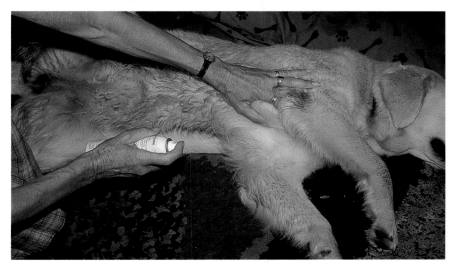

If necessary, use a blanket to transport an injured dog.

Tapeworms are common. All have a life cycle that includes a secondary host. The commonest dog tapeworm is one that has the dog flea as its secondary host. Other tapeworms have a life cycle involving sheep and are a great nuisance in sheep-farming countries. For example, New Zealand, has a compulsory treatment program for dogs.

Hookworms and *whipworms* are less common, but they both cause intermittent diarrhea and other symptoms.

Different drugs are effective individually against each of these worms. Some newer ones are able to combat most worms. It is worth discussing a routine with your veterinarian.

Peritonitis

Acute peritonitis is relatively uncommon in dogs, despite the great variety of apparently dangerous objects many of them swallow. Signs include high temperature and a tense, painful abdomen. More chronic inflammation can occur with remarkably few symptoms. Take your dog to a veterinarian if you suspect peritonitis.

Pneumonia

Although pneumonia is caused by viruses, a number of opportunistic bacteria may invade and produce secondary infections, making the clinical picture even worse. Symptoms include difficult or distressed breathing and general malaise of the dog. General nursing care is needed while the animal's own immune system fights the virus; antibiotics are also administered to treat the secondary bacterial infections.

Other causes of pneumonia include fluid or food inhalation, and hemorrhaging within the lung fields.

Poisons

Poisoning in dogs is uncommon. Signs fall into two general groups: nervous involvement, with either heightened reactions ranging from muscular twitching to convulsions, or reduced reactions leading to coma; and the "enteric" group, causing acute symptoms of gastro-enteritis, with vomiting and diarrhea. Modern insecticides are prominent in the poisons involving the nervous system. Caustic poisons result in an inflamed, ulcerated mouth and tongue, and the Warfarin (Coumarin) type of rat poison may cause severe blood disorders in dogs.

In cases of suspected poisoning, do not treat the dog without reference to a veterinarian. Take any suspected container or material with you when the dog goes for treatment.

Prolapse

Rectal prolapse can sometimes occur through straining during defecation, more especially in old dogs with weak muscles. Vaginal prolapse is an even less common sequel to whelping, but prolapse of vaginal polyps, giving the appearance at first sight of vaginal tissue itself, is more often encountered. The prolapsed tissue should be kept as clean as possible and the dog prevented from licking or biting the lesion. Veterinary attention should be sought.

Rabies

Rabies is one of the most feared of all animal diseases. It can be transmitted to man and other mammals, has horrible consequences, and invariably kills. An infected dog may suffer convulsions, snap and bite any object, and refuse to drink. Dehydration later sets in, then total paralysis, and death. But first signs are unlikely to be specific. The most commonly reported symptom is a complete change in the dog's nature, often involving apparent fear of its owner. Quarantine regulations are aimed at preventing the disease entering a country. If rabies is suspected, a veterinarian must be told without delay and the dog kept in total isolation.

Rickets

Rickets is a disease of growing animals, caused by an imbalance of Vitamin D, calcium, or phosphorus. There may be lameness, but the most obvious signs are enlarged limb joints, even enlarged

It is less dangerous to carry an injured dog gently to the car and drive to the vet's than to leave it without medical attention.

bone–cartilage junctions down the length of the ribs. Giant breeds are particularly prone to the disease. A well-balanced diet is the best means of prevention.

Road accidents

The place to treat a dog injured in a road accident is at the animal hospital. Telephone first to make sure a surgeon is available, and transport the dog on a blanket or something similar, moving it as little as possible. The possibility of further injury through transportation is slight compared with the risk of complications caused by delay. If the dog is attempting to bite because it is in pain, tie a cord or belt around its muzzle and behind its neck.

Sex play

Male or female puppies will mount each other, or humans, in apparent sex play. In the young this is considered more as "dominance play" than as an act of overt sexual implication and should be regarded in that light. The sometimes aggressive sexual behavior of mature male dogs toward their owner may have the same origins, but it becomes actively sexual and antisocial if not curbed. It can sometimes be cured only by castration.

Shock

The symptoms of shock are pale mucous membranes, cold extremities, a subdued, nonresponsive animal, and increased heart rate. This is a medical emergency and needs to be treated promptly or the condition may become life-threatening.

Shyness

This term tends to be used to cover any untoward behavior of a dog, from disinclination to leap joyfully into a stranger's lap, to attacking everyone it sees on sight. The first step toward overcoming it is to decide what the problem really is. If the dog is genuinely shy, give it a chance to meet new people on its own terms. If it is vicious, acknowledge the fact and decide whether you can handle the problem. It may be that the animal is hopelessly antisocial, in which case it should be rehoused or, in extreme situations, even put down. There is an undoubted inherited tendency to shyness and similar behavioral problems, but many of them can be overcome with patience and advice on training.

Ticks see Parasites

Vomiting

The usual cause of vomiting is some degree of gastritis, but other causes include digestive upsets, bacterial infection, systemic diseases such as hepatitis or nephritis (inflammation of the liver or kidneys), and the presence of foreign bodies or indigestible bones. Vomiting is a symptom, not an illness in itself. Dogs can voluntarily vomit. If this happens more than a few times in a short period, if blood is present, or if the dog appears to be in pain, seek veterinary help. See also Gastritis.

Warts

Older dogs of most breeds suffer from warts, but they are particularly common in Spaniels and Poodles. Surgical removal may be necessary, particularly if, as often happens, the warts become infected. A vaccine may be effective in preventing their re-appearance. Young puppies occasionally suffer from a crop of warts, but treatment to prevent soreness until they disappear is usually all that is necessary.

Worms see Parasites

VISITING THE VET

MOST VETERINARIANS prefer to treat dogs at their office; some even refuse to make house calls in any but the most exceptional circumstances. The reasons for this are primarily medical. Proper examination demands suitable facilities and these are rarely to be found in domestic surroundings. When a receptionist tries to persuade a client to bring the patient into the office, it is not because the vet "cannot be bothered" to call, but because experience has shown that in nine cases out of ten attention at the office is likely to be more satisfactory.

It is important that pet-owners know the consulting hours of the veterinarian, and are aware whether such times are given over to consultations by appointment or are run as "open" clinics on a first come, first dealt-with basis. You should also know whether the office's telephone number is the same as the out-of-hours emergency number, and, if not, make sure you know the emergency number too. Anyone with a pet who does not already have this information should obtain it without delay as a precaution against future need. Even though it may not be necessary for your dog to be seen by the vet at the moment, it is

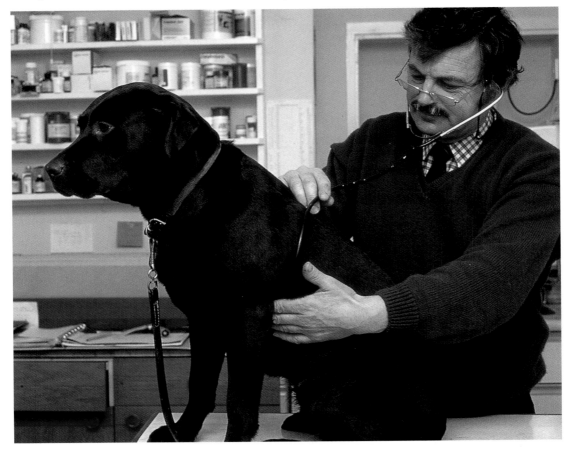

Heart disease is most common in elderly or overweight dogs, but some breeds are particularly prone to it. Here, a vet checks a patient's heart function.

Left: Veterinary clinics and animal hospitals have reception areas where you can make appointments, pay bills, and ask for advice. Many also sell collars and leads, flea powder, and other items.

Right: A veterinary nurse assists the vet by restraining a patient as a drip is put into its leg.

sensible to call in on the receptionist during business hours and register your intention to use the practice should the need arise.

If the practice holds open surgeries only, prior arrangements for attendance are not necessary and for most purposes you simply go along and wait your turn. But a phonecall beforehand is appreciated if you intend to present anything out of the ordinary, such as a case which may take longer than normal to deal with, or a dog that may be suspected of suffering from an infectious disease which could affect other animals.

Practices which run an appointment system require you to telephone beforehand. The receptionist answering the phone will routinely ask about the problem in order to make the most suitable placement on the list. She will not need the case history, just your name and address, the dog's name, and briefly the reason for the desired visit.

All services that have to deal with emergencies recognize that a routine procedure is the quickest way to handle problems and that short cuts rarely work. If veterinary staff do not seem to respond adequately to your demand for emergency attention, it is because they are viewing the situation dispassionately but efficiently. If an accident occurs either at home or in the road, and an emergency arises, telephone first. Few veterinary practices can guarantee to have professional staff on the premises at all times, although all will have a veterinarian "on call" at short notice. An advance telephone call will often be the quickest way to obtain attention.

In an emergency, most veterinary practices will advise you to bring the dog into the office as quickly as possible (although practices with an equipped ambulance may prefer to send it out). Common sense in careful handling of an injured animal is a safe guide in almost all circumstances. If a leg is hanging uselessly, support it. If the dog is unable to move, carry it, if necessary in a blanket. Remember—if you cannot get close enough to it to restrain it, neither can the veterinarian. Dogs which are not able to run away because of injury, but are nevertheless defending themselves by biting at all comers, can usually be restrained by throwing a blanket over them; they won't suffocate. Injured animals are often very frightened and need calm and quiet handling, but it is sometimes necessary to be firm yet careful in order to restrain them without risking being severely bitten.

VETERINARY TREATMENT

Right: Administering eye drops. Some treatments will be carried out by the nursing staff under the supervision of the vet.

Below: Scaling a dog's teeth or other complex dental work is routinely performed under a general anesthetic. If your dog has chronic bad breath, consult your vet about possible dental problems.

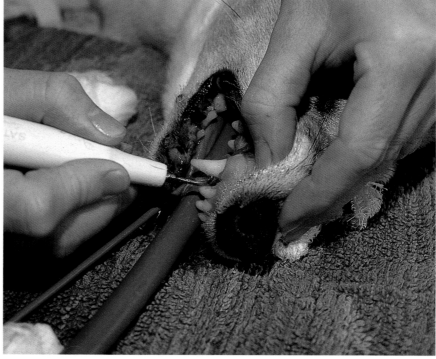

MOST PEOPLE ARE probably more familiar with their medical GP's office than with veterinary surgeries. There are obvious similarities, but many essential differences, and the first may strike you as you go through the door. It is a basic difference: all floors in veterinary surgeries have to be impervious to liquids and easily cleaned. Occasional accidents occur in doctors' waiting rooms, but they are everyday occurrences in veterinary reception areas.

Reception and waiting rooms may be separate or combined. On the one hand, there may be the consideration that a client wants to discuss something confidentially with the receptionist—an arrangement about an account perhaps; on the other hand, the veterinarian may feel that a receptionist working in the waiting room is more welcoming and can help to put clients, and perhaps patients, at ease.

Most veterinary surgeries will have one or more examination rooms, the equivalent of the doctor's consulting room, which will probably have only minimal equipment for clinical examination of the patient. The two essential items are good lighting and a firm examination table. Once again the system may vary. Immediate treatment following diagnosis may be carried out in the examination room, an injection perhaps or irrigation of an ear, or this may be passed on to a side room where a nurse may carry out straightforward procedures on the veterinarian's instructions. A particular difference between medical and veterinary practice in Britain is that a prescription for treatment of an animal will almost certainly be dealt with on the premises, usually immediately by a nurse or assistant, whereas the majority of

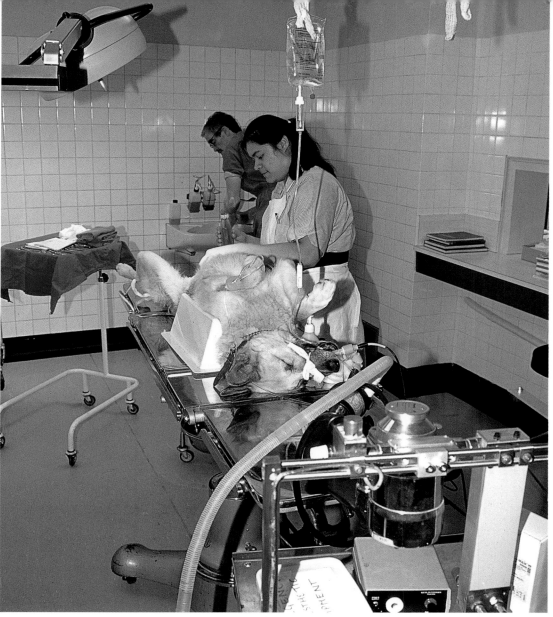

Your vet is basically a general practitioner and surgeon. Sometimes it may be appropriate to refer your dog to a specialist hospital for treatment.

doctors write a prescription to be filled by the local pharmacist.

Another matter for some measure of choice is whether the owner or a nurse holds the dog for examination. Many dogs are less disturbed if their owner holds them, and this method is often preferred if it is apparent that no harm is likely to occur to anyone. If the owner cannot safely restrain the dog, the veterinary assistant takes over. Quite often a calmer firmness is all that is needed, although every owner must understand that considerably firmer handling, including a nose bandage to muzzle the dog, may be required occasionally. For prolonged examination or treatment, sedation is probably more widely used in veterinary than in human medicine.

There are very few practicing veterinarians who will not carry out surgical techniques more complicated than injections or lancing an abscess (although these are close to the limits of the modern-day medical GP). To many veterinarians, much of the interest in practice lies in the development of their surgical skills. The tradition of general veterinary medical and surgical treatment being carried out by the same person has led to a low degree of specialization in veterinary surgery, and one vet's morning may well consist of seeing a series of patients with the usual, or perhaps some unusual, diseases, followed by a spaying and a spell of orthopedics. Both types of operations will be done as competently as in a human operating room.

The majority of veterinarians are equipped to exercise their surgical skill to reasonable limits, which will vary from person to person. Most vets are aware of their own limits. If a particular operation seems desirable but is beyond a certain veterinarian's technique, the owner will be referred to a colleague who is better qualified and equipped to perform the task.

If your dog's problem is an unusual one, or one requiring more specialist treatment than the average veterinarian can provide—for example, delicate eye surgery—it may be referred to a specialist hospital. Just as with humans, blood tests or urine analysis will also be carried out off the premises, in a specialized laboratory.

HOSPITALIZATION

ONE OF THE INTERESTING contrasts between human and veterinary medicine is in the use of hospitals. In Britain the extensive state hospital service is one of the largest employers in the country. Many hospitals have become massive and impersonal centers for the administration and treatment of ill health rather than pursuing their traditional role of the provision of nursing care.

The lack of tax-payers' money has forced the British veterinary profession to move slowly into hospitalization of its patients, and given its members the opportunity to evaluate the use of a hospital system of treatment in terms of their patients and their clients rather than by considerations of "efficiency." It has become noticeable that in both the United States and Europe, the growth of veterinary hospitals has slowed considerably, being displaced by smaller units offering necessary hospitalization facilities but with treatment based on out-patient attendance.

The decision to hospitalize a dog for treatment is primarily one for the veterinarian, but it will be influenced strongly by the owner's attitude and circumstances. After much routine surgery and in the management of many diseases, the main ingredient is still "tender loving

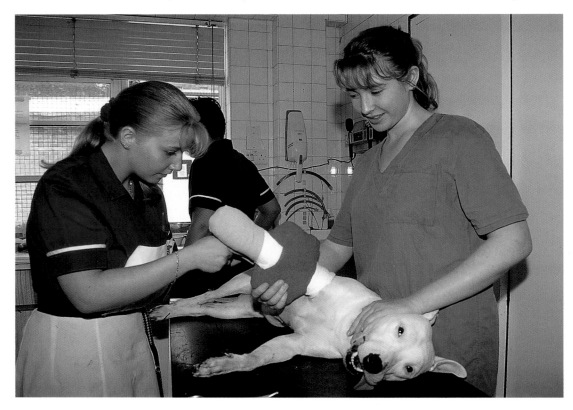

Bandaging may make the injury look more serious than it is, but it is important that the dog does not do itself further damage by licking or scratching a wound, or by biting out stitches.

care" and in most cases this is best given at home by the owner. The point at which care becomes special nursing is not easily defined. There may, rarely, be reasons why a dog which has not fully recovered from an anesthetic may be allowed home into the care of an owner who is experienced, competent, and in whom the veterinarian has considerable trust. For many owners, however, a dog which is only slightly depressed after an anesthetic for minor surgery still poses problems that are outside their experience or ability to cope, and anaesthetic recovery cases probably occupy more hospital space in the average veterinary clinic than all others combined.

Apart from this routine use of hospitalization, in-patient care is mostly concerned with special attention which cannot be given by the owner. This is usually determined by the nature of the treatment and the use of particular equipment, or by the need for frequent observation and assessment. The use of an intravenous drip is a good example. The equipment has to be set up by trained hands and then continuously monitored and adjusted. Most critically, however, it requires efficient restraint of the patient. Most drips are given when the dog is in no condition to move about, but every veterinary nurse has had to cope with dogs that suddenly decide they feel much better and try to get up.

Some hospital care facilities must be available for dogs with "owner problems," and it is important that owners discuss the question of care with the vet. If an owner is out at work all day, for example, difficulties in home care could arise that may well delay the dog's recovery. Take, for instance, the routine operation of spaying a bitch. Most such cases

are sent home the same day or the day after, on the assumption that the owner will keep an eye on them. Most bitches will lick the operation wound, but only very rarely will one attempt to bite the stitches out. If this happens, however, and the chances of it happening are increased if the bitch is on her own at home and is bored, veterinary attention is needed urgently.

In this situation, no nursing ability is required on the part of the owner, but observation can be critically important. If the owner is forced to be away from

home, it is worth considering hospitalization for two or three days.

Hospitalization should also be considered where, for emotional or other reasons, home treatment is not acceptable to the owner. Perhaps an owner cannot bear the sight of an unpleasant sore on a dog's body, or is unable to administer the prescribed tablets (and it can be extremely difficult). But if for any reason care or treatment of a sick dog cannot be carried out at home alternative arrangements must be made by talking matters over with the veterinarian.

Part Six

Shows and Trials

Each year thousands of shows and trials around the world test a wide range of dogs' physical attributes and abilities, from their obedience to their conformity to standards.

SHOWING YOUR DOG

Small local shows may have a less formal atmosphere than the Championship shows, but the style of judging and the criteria of what makes a champion are the same as at major national events.

BRITAIN LEADS THE WORLD in the size of show events, in part because the distances that have to be traveled by entrants are relatively short. Ten thousand dogs are regularly entered in six or seven British shows each year. The total number of events and the total number of entrants are much greater in the United States, although the numbers attending each event are smaller. In the United States and Australia 3,000 to 4,000 entrants is a figure often attained, as it is in European countries such as Sweden and Belgium.

Every country has separate classes for dogs and bitches. Additionally, the classes for each sex are subdivided to make competition more equal. Britain has by far the largest number of these divisions, which also serve to prevent classes becoming unwieldy through growth in the number of entries. Classes for puppies are based on age: Minor Puppy, for dogs of 6–9 months; Puppy, up to 12 months; and Junior, up to 18 months. There may also be a class for Veterans, for dogs at least seven years old. Eligibility for all other classes depends on whether a dog has already won a specified number or level of certificates or prizes. A list of the classes available at any show, and an explanation of which dogs are eligible for them, are always included in the Schedule you receive with your entry form.

There are also various different types of show, eligibility for which is clearly defined. A Championship Show is one which is open to all exhibitors (unless the Kennel Club has approved a qualification for entry) and at which Kennel Club Challenge Certificates are offered; an Open Show is open to all exhibitors. There are also Limited Shows, Sanction Shows, Primary Shows, Matches, and Exemption Shows.

The Commonwealth system follows this pattern quite closely, although classes are fewer. The American system is much simpler and is usually restricted to Puppy (often subdivided into 6-9 months and 9-12 months), 12-18 Months, Novice, Bred-by-exhibitor, American-bred, Open, and Champion classes. There are only three types of show—Speciality (restricted to a particular breed), Group (restricted to all the breeds

For many, the highlight of a show is the choosing of overall best dog. First the individual class winners parade before the judge. The best of all the males of a breed is chosen, and then the best female. This dog and bitch then meet and one is adjudged Best of Breed; the Best of Breeds are then all judged in their relevant groups (Hound, Gundog, Terrier, Utility, Working, Pastoral, and Toy). One will be chosen as Best of Group. The seven group winners file back into the ring and the judge makes his or her choice for the Best in Show. It is always an exciting moment.

in a particular group, such as Hound or Terrier), or All-breed. At shows organized under FCI rules, the subdivisions usually comprise Puppy, Junior, Open, Working, and Champion.

Even if you have bought a pedigree dog primarily as a pet, there may come a time when you decide to try your hand at showing it. If you know from the start that you might be interested in this, talk to the breeder at the time you buy the puppy. He or she will be able to advise you on how to start. Even before the puppy is allowed to go out to training classes, you can begin teaching it how to stand for a judge.

The next step is to join a ringcraft class. You should be able to find one through your veterinary surgery, dog or breed club, or the local library. Your dog club may run ringcraft classes alongside basic puppy training and more advanced obedience classes.

The rudiments of showing vary from breed to breed. For example, small dogs are always judged standing on a table, so they need to become accustomed to this. Setters are shown with one of the handler's hands under the dog's chin and the other holding the tail out behind. Some breeds, such as Clumber Spaniels and Chows, stand four-square with their legs straight down under them; others, such as Airedales and Soft-Coated Wheatens, stand with their back legs stretched out behind them. It is all a matter of convention and you need to know what is expected of your particular breed.

When you feel confident at ringcraft, you should enter a few Exemption Shows. Your dog club may run them, or you can find them advertised in the pages of dog papers such as the weekly *Our Dogs*. For an Exemption Show you simply turn up on the day, pay a small fee and put what you have learned into practice. In addition to the usual classes mentioned above, exemption shows may have "novelty" classes such as "Dog with the waggiest tail" or "Dog that looks most like its owner." This is a good way for both you and your dog to try out your skills in a competitive but not too serious environment.

Open and Championship Shows are also advertised in the dog papers, but you need to apply in advance. Write to the Secretary of the club organizing the show and you will be sent an application form and a Schedule of Classes. This is your first serious step along the road to owning a champion.

SHOW JUDGING

THE PRINCIPLES OF JUDGING a breed are easily understood, though their interpretation can differ widely in practice. When showing first began, the societies of particular breeds drew up breed standards. These are, in effect, word pictures of a breed. Enthusiasts knew what the dog was required for, they knew what its historical characteristics were, and they did not want them to alter substantially in the future. The breed standards became the "blueprints" for both breeders and judges, and they remain so today.

All good judges have fixed in their minds a picture of the ideal dog for the breed. They examine the individuals presented to them and compare them with their conception of this ideal configuration. But why should dogs have to conform to a certain shape, and why should humans lay down what this shape should be? The answer is found in history. Most domestic dogs were originally working dogs, and individual breeds evolved in different ways because they were required to perform different tasks. Their descendants still have in their make-up the breed characteristics that fit them for their work.

The Cocker Spaniel, for example, is bred for rough shooting and the recovery of small game. Although small enough to go into close cover, where space is limited, this dog must have sufficient strength to force its way through dense undergrowth. Hence the thick, short body. A Cocker should have well-laid-back shoulders, otherwise a day's activity would tax it beyond endurance. Its head must be held high, because it carries game which can be quite heavy. This also means that the neck should be fairly long and elegant. The foreface needs strength

for the same reason. So we have a general picture of a Cocker Spaniel that is well suited to perform its traditional role, and even if an individual is never used as a gundog, in order to be a true Cocker Spaniel it must conform to this standard.

If every effort had not been made down the years to make individual animals within a breed conform to a uniform style and shape, it would now be almost impossible to distinguish a Cocker Spaniel from a Labrador Retriever, or even from a Welsh Terrier. The breeds would have become inextricably mixed, and few people would think that desirable. Part of the attraction of any animal is the variety of breeds or species, and no dog-lover would forgo that delight.

Judging dogs involves comparing the entries with the ideal for each breed. Let

us imagine that you are observing a class of Samoyeds that has only two entries. One of the dogs is openly affectionate to its owner and has the cheerful, smiling expression that the standard specifies. Its neck is proudly arched, its back broad and muscular, its well-feathered tail carried jauntily over its back. You can see at a glance that this is a fine example of the breed. On the other hand, the second animal looks hang-dog and nervous, its body is rather thin, and the feathering on its tail meager. It clearly does not measure up to your interpretation of the standard for an ideal Samoyed. You have no hesitation in awarding the prize to the first dog.

As you chose between these hypothetical two, so it is possible for a skilled judge to rank 20 dogs in order. The winner will be the animal that most closely

Left: Small breeds stand on a bench or table while the judge "goes over" them. Learning to stand quietly during this process is a basic part of a dog's ringcraft technique.

approximates to his or her idea of the ideal for that breed.

While judges do their best to be absolutely objective, it is inevitable that personal preferences surface occasionally. Different interpretations of the standard may also come in and out of fashion. For example, the standard for the Golden Retriever specifies a neck of good length, clean and muscular. In recent years, a number of breeders and judges have chosen to interpret this as allowing a longer, more arched neck than was usual before. This means that in order for the dog to remain in proportion, it must be longer in the body. A judge who, in private life, prefers this style of Golden is going to have to be very self-disciplined indeed to acknowledge that the older type, which to his or her eyes appears short-coupled and too square, has equal merit. This is one of the features that makes judging a lonely and thankless task. The judge, like the referee in sports, is often thought by losers to have made a bad choice, but his decision cannot be disputed.

Above: Showing a dog requires knowledge of what is expected. The angle of the head and tail, and position of the feet, are important.

Below: The owners encourage their dogs to show themselves to best advantage while the judge takes a final look around the ring.

PRODUCING A CHAMPION

THE AIM OF EVERY SERIOUS breeder or shower of pedigree dogs is to produce a champion. Different countries have different systems by which a champion is decided. In Britain and those Commonwealth countries which follow the British system, it is very difficult for certain breeds to win this coveted title. In others, including a number of European countries, it is possible for a dog to become a champion without ever being assessed against another dog of the same breed. Some countries have very few dogs of certain breeds, while competition is always toughest in the more popular breeds. There are various procedures for awarding the title of champion for dog shows throughout the world.

A judge at a British Championship Show may award what is called a Challenge Certificate to the best of each sex in a breed. This is not automatic—if the judge does not consider the animal in question to be worthy of the title of champion, even though it is the best of its breed present, he or she will withhold the award. When three Challenge Certificates have been awarded to one dog by three different judges (one must be gained after the animal is 12 months old), that dog gains the permanent title of champion. This is a much-prized acco-

Above: A little last-minute grooming for a Toy Poodle at a Championship show. The owner is naturally eager for the dog to look its best.

Left: Judy Averis with Crufts 1998 Best in Show, champion Saredon Forever Young, a two-year-old Welsh Terrier. Mel, as he is known at home, had been Best Terrier in 1997.

The Yorkshire Terrier Ozmilion Mystification—known to his friends as Justin—was Crufts best in Show for 1997. He had beaten some 20,000 other dogs to achieve the title.

lade because so few Challenge Certificates are awarded—there is an annual limit of 30 for the numerically strongest breeds. For breeds with smaller numbers of entries the most that can be given in a year may be as few as six. It is more difficult to achieve champion status under the British system than under any other.

A points system is used in the United States. Points are awarded to the Best of Breed and Best Opposite Sex for each breed at each show, the number of points increasing with the number of dogs competing. The number of competitors required to earn a certain number of points varies with the breed, sex, and geographical location of the show, but the minimum is one and the maximum five. Shows where a dog can earn at least three points are called majors, and to become a champion a dog must accumulate 15 points, awarded by three different judges and including at least two majors, each under a different judge. Less popular breeds can have difficulty meeting this requirement, because it is often hard to find a show with sufficient entries to enable the entry to merit "major" status.

The Canadian Kennel Club operates a similar arrangement to the American one, except that at least ten points must be awarded by not fewer than three different judges.

Australia also operates a points system in which the number of points awarded to the winner is based on the number of dogs in each class. The total required before a dog can apply to become a champion is 100, from at least four shows under four different judges. This may seem like a lot of points, but the winner of Best in Group is normally awarded 25, so points are easier to accumulate than they are in North America.

All Scandinavian and Western European Kennel Clubs, plus some in South America and Eastern Europe, operate under the auspices of the Fédération Cynologique Internationale, the International Canine Federation (FCI). This body was founded in 1911 by the French, German, Belgian, Dutch, and Austrian Kennel Clubs to control and organize dog shows. The FCI creates champions by awarding what are cumbersomely known as Certificates of Aptitude, Championship International, Beauty (CACIB). Four of these must be won in at least three different countries under three different judges for a dog to attain champion status. CACIBs are given in all breeds at international shows regardless of the number of dogs competing. It is therefore possible for a dog to win a CACIB without meeting another member of the same breed.

The routine of judging, although varied slightly by different practitioners, is broadly similar. It involves looking, feeling, and studying a dog's movement. When the entrants come into the ring the judge will glance at each of them and then proceed to go through a detailed physical examination, one dog at a time. He or she will use their hands quite a lot. This may appear to be "theater" but it is not; the combination of eye and hand tells a good judge all he or she needs to know about a dog.

Then comes movement, sometimes the most searching assessment of all. It is possible for a skilled handler to pose a dog in such a way that its blemishes will be minimized, or even entirely hidden from view. Toes with a tendency to turn out can be placed in the correct position; and a dog with hind legs tucked underneath can be trained to stand with them placed well out behind. Loose elbows, a badly carried head, cow hocks—all these and many other faults may not be detected when the dog is stationary. But, when the animal moves, everything is plain to see. The dog's gait can be assessed, as can the carriage of the tail and the way in which the head is held—all features which combine together to produce the ideal specimen of a breed.

FIELD TRIALS

FIELD TRIALS ARE competitions for working gundogs, and in some countries for hounds, in which judges assess the ability of the dogs to carry out the purpose for which they have been bred and trained. Dogs have worked with humans for centuries in the pursuit of game, originally for the sole purpose of providing food but in more recent times as an adjunct to field sports.

The traditional style of shooting in Britain has been dictated by the type of country in which game is to be found; this requires the dog-handler and gun-bearer to be on foot. Gundogs have been developed for specialist purposes, and thus the majority of field trials are for the specialist breeds. Four categories of field trial are licensed by the Kennel Club. The most popular are those for Retrievers and Spaniels, with Irish Water Spaniels included in the Retriever group. A number of trials are held for Pointers and Setters, breeds which although of different origin perform the same function, and a smaller but increasing number of trials are organized for what are classified as the breeds which hunt, point, and retrieve. These are the dual-purpose breeds first developed in Europe to fulfil all roles expected of a gundog.

At a field trial, dogs compete against each other and the individual competitions are designated "stakes." Generally two stakes are held at each trial—an Open or All-aged stake, which as the names suggest are open for entry by dogs of any age or experience; and either a Novice stake, which is open to any dog which has not previously won a specified award, or a Puppy stake, for dogs born on or after January 1st of the previous year. The number of dogs which may compete on any one day is limited. In

Retriever stakes lasting one day, no more than 12 dogs are allowed to run, while two-day stakes are confined to a maximum of 24 dogs. Twelve a day is the limit for the hunting, pointing and retrieving breeds; 18 a day for Spaniels. For Pointers and Setters, the maximum is 40 or 45 depending on the type of stake.

As nearly as possible, field trials mirror an ordinary day's shooting and the planting of game to be found or retrieved is positively discouraged. The object of the trial is to test dogs on live game and it is not unknown for trials to be declared null and void owing to a shortage of the necessary prey.

Retriever trials are most frequently run on fields of sugar beet, kale, or turnips and are held between October and February. The growing tendency is for one-day trials, consisting of one stake for each of the two age groups. Stakes may either be confined to one breed or include all breeds of Retriever. The most common breeds are the Labrador and the Golden Retriever, although the Flat-coated is also popular.

A draw is made before the trial to determine the order in which dogs will come under the judges. In the field, the usual procedure is for the judges, handlers and dogs, guns and beaters to walk the ground in line abreast, four or six

dogs being in the line at any one time. There are normally three or four judges; if there are three they judge individually, if four they judge in pairs. When a bird is flushed and shot, the judges decide which dog shall be sent to retrieve it. Dogs are assessed for their steadiness when being shot over, ability to mark the fall of game, drive and style while retrieving, and nose work. Note is also taken of their quickness in gathering game, the degree of control required by the handler, and the way in which game is retrieved and delivered back to the handler. Unless a dog disqualifies itself on the first round, each competitor is run twice and on the second occasion must be assessed by a different judge. The most common reasons for disqualification are being out of control or failing to retrieve a bird which is then found by another dog.

The annual Retriever Championship is organized by the International Gundog League (Retriever Society), entry for which is earned by gaining points in certain Open or All-aged stakes. In addition, the first-prize winner in these specified stakes is awarded a Field Trial Certificate. Two such certificates qualify a dog for the title of Field Trial Champion.

The two most common breeds of working spaniel used in Britain are

Basset Hounds assemble at a 1998 Game Fair. Originally bred to hunt hares, Bassets have great stamina and can wear their prey down by pursuing at a slow but unrelenting pace.

English Springers and Cockers, the former being predominant. Stakes at trials may be scheduled for one breed only or may be open to any variety of spaniel. They are run under two judges. Each dog is run in turn under the judges, odd numbers under one judge and even numbers under the other. In the second round, this sequence is reversed so that both judges see all dogs. A third run for the best dogs may also be held.

The ground for spaniel trials must contain plenty of cover for game as the dogs are assessed for their questing and quartering, game finding and flushing skills, in addition to their ability to retrieve and deliver.

Pointer and Setter trials are traditionally run in the spring and early summer, when no game is actually shot, or at the beginning of the grouse season in August and September. Breeds which take part are Pointers, English Setters, Irish Setters, and Gordon Setters. The ground must be open with plenty of space for the dogs to quarter, yet contain enough depth of cover to prevent the game from being flushed too early. The dogs are run in pairs under two judges.

Judges assess the pace and control of dogs while quartering, their game-finding ability, and their style on point when they have scented game. Credit points are given for natural backing, that is to say recognizing that the other dog in the pair is on point and turning to stand and face toward it. At trials where game is not shot, dogs are expected to drop to a shot fired into the air as the pointed game is flushed. Normally each dog will have two runs under the judges, with a third or even fourth run to decide the final order of the best dogs.

Trials for breeds which hunt, point, and retrieve may include German Pointers, Weimaraners, Hungarian Vizslas and other general-purpose gundog breeds, usually of European origin. The dogs are run singly under two judges and are required to: quarter ground in search of game; to point game; to be steady to flush, shot, and fall; and to retrieve on command. Great emphasis is placed on the work of these dogs in water and their inclination to enter it.

In hunting dog trials, the trial grounds for spaniels must contain plenty of cover, in order that the dog's ability to find and flush game is properly tested, along with its ability to retrieve.

The title of Field Trial Champion is awarded to those Retrievers, Spaniels, Pointers, and Setters who win the championships of their respective categories, or gain two first prizes in Open or All-aged stakes which qualify for the championships. There is no championship stake for the breeds which hunt, point, and retrieve; for them the title of Field Trial Champion is earned by winning two open stakes.

More than 1,000 field trials are held in the United States each year. They are divided into four categories—those for pointing dogs, retrieving dogs, flushing dogs, and trailing hounds—and into three types. A Member Field Trial is one at which championship points may be awarded, and it is held by a club or an

Right: Cocker Spaniels are among the most popular and successful of working gundogs because they are eager to please and so to train.

Below: Trial grounds for spaniels contain plenty of cover, so that the dogs' ability to find and flush game is tested along with their ability to retrieve.

association which is a member of the AKC. A Licensed Field Trial is given by a club or association which is not a member of the AKC but which has been specially licensed to hold the trial.

Championship points may be awarded at such a trial. Informal events at which championship points are not awarded can also be held by clubs whether or not they are members of the AKC. These informal events are termed Sanctioned Field Trials, for which AKC approval must be obtained.

Judges in the United States are not licensed for field trials in the same way as they are for show. Any reputable person who is in good standing with the American Kennel Club may be approved to judge a field trial. Nevertheless, all dogs which are to run in Licensed or Member Field Trials must be registered with the AKC.

The AKC licenses almost 400 Pointing Breed Trials in any given year. They are organized by speciality clubs, and the following breeds are recognized for entry in these trials: Brittanys, Pointers, German Short-haired Pointers, German Wire-haired Pointers, English Setters, Gordon Setters, Irish Setters, Vizslas, Weimaraners, and Wire-haired Pointing Griffons. Trials may contain Puppy stakes (for dogs of 6–15 months), Derby stakes (6–24 months), Open or All-aged stakes (for dogs of any age over

A gundog points toward the game, and is ready to retrieve the moment its master has fired a successful shot.

6 months), and Limited stakes (confined to non-winners of any age over 6 months). In addition, some stakes may be entered only by dogs which are owned and handled by *bona fide* amateurs.

The qualities required of dogs of the pointing breeds in the United States are similar to those sought in Britain, but the larger tracts of land available mean that the dogs quarter more widely and range further, with judges and frequently handlers on horseback. Bird fields may be designated, in which game placed previously is available for the dogs to seek and point. Dogs may also have to retrieve fallen game.

Championship points are gained by the dogs placed first, the number of points to a maximum of five being determined by the number of starters in the trial. A dog which wins ten points in at least three trials is recorded as a Field Champion, with the reservation that in some breeds points must also have been gained in certain specified stakes. The title of Amateur Field Champion can be gained by winning ten points in Amateur stakes. Parent breed clubs—there is one

for each breed—also run one National Championship stake per year for which dogs must qualify for entry.

Hound Trials are popular in the United States, Beagle Trials running second in number to those of the pointing breeds. The hounds are run in pairs (known as braces) or as packs of seven on rabbit, or as larger packs on hare. Dogs are entered in classes according to their height and are run in series of packs as decided by the organizers. They gain points toward the title of Field Champion depending on their placing, the points being multiples of the number of starters. Hound trials are held for Basset Hounds and to a lesser degree for Dachshunds.

As in Britain, Retriever Trials mirror an ordinary day's shooting as closely as possible. They are open to the various breeds of Retriever and/or Irish Water Spaniels. Only amateurs may judge Licensed or Member Retriever Trials. Procedures are generally similar to those in Britain, described above.

Interest in Spaniel Trials is relatively small in the United States, but the AKC does set out regulations for them. The

specialized ability of the spaniel in hunting has apparently not been generally needed, hence the breeds are not as popular for work as they are in Britain. At present, only English and American Cockers and English Springers compete in field trials.

In Continental Europe, general regulations are set out by the FCI for the various types of field trials for gundogs, hounds and the terrier breeds, but hunting customs and laws concerning the protection of animals differ from one member country to another, making it impossible for compulsory regulations to be laid down to cover all countries. There is considerable interest in the work of dogs in the field, and the species of game available vary a great deal.

Fewer trials are held in Australia than in the United States and Western Europe. There are, of course, fewer clubs and organizations and the wildlife pattern varies considerably throughout the country. Nevertheless, the interest in working the sporting breeds exists and continues to be encouraged.

WORKING AND OBEDIENCE TRIALS

REGARDLESS OF ITS BEAUTY, conformation, or purpose, it is necessary that a dog should be an acceptable member of the society in which it lives, and this in turn means that it must be trained and must be obedient. A considerable amount of ringcraft training has always been essential for the show dog, and a high degree of specialized training is vital for field trial competition. The encouragement of obedience training generally, however, and the setting up of formalized competition in obedience since the 1920s has been enthusiastically received in all parts of the world. It has led to the establishment of qualifications which can be gained by achieving set standards rather than purely by winning over other dogs. It is not necessary for a dog to be better than others for it to gain a recognized title, but simply for it to demonstrate that it has reached the necessary standard of training and has a degree of agility. At the same time, the competitive element has been maintained by the awarding of prizes and titles.

Standards are graded, the initial emphasis being on the basically obedient dog which will walk at heel and sit as instructed—in effect, the companion dog. At more advanced levels, the exercises become increasingly difficult, and at the highest level the natural abilities of the dog are also tested in scent discrimination and tracking exercises.

In all obedience training and forms of competition the aim is for the dog to work in a happy, natural manner. Although the performance of both dog and handler is judged in relation to closely defined criteria, great emphasis is placed on the dog's willingness and enjoyment of its work and on the smoothness and naturalness of the control by its handler.

The judging of obedience is based on the performance of the team of dog and handler. Sloppy work can be seen and noted by all observers, and a movement

Agility tests are now a popular feature of many shows, and a variety of breeds do well.

An agility course includes jumps of various types and heights.

of just a few centimetres by a dog can make all the difference between success and failure.

In Britain more than 500 dog training clubs are registered with the Kennel Club. In addition, a large number of specialist breed societies, principally in the working breeds, take great interest in obedience training. Hundreds of shows that are licensed by the Kennel Club are held annually.

The Kennel Club licenses working trials and obedience classes separately. It is not necessary for a dog to be pure-bred for it to take part in these events. A special register for cross-bred dogs, known as the Obedience and Working Trials Register, is maintained. Although working trials and obedience classes are closely allied, the actual events have an entirely different ambience. Working trials are held on open land; obedience classes are conducted within the precincts of a show venue.

The first working trial was held in 1924 and was confined to German Shepherd Dogs. There are now four trial categories: Championship, at which Kennel Club Working Trial Certificates are offered; Open, which are open to all dogs but which may limit the number of competitors; and Members Working Trials and Matches, which are restricted to dogs owned by members of the club promoting the trials.

Five types of stake may be scheduled. The lowest grade is the Companion Dog (CD) stake, which includes control exercises such as: heel on leash, heel free and sending the dog away; stay exercises; agility tests including clear jump, long jump, and scaling a vertical wooden wall; retrieving a dumb-bell; and an elementary search test. The Utility Dog (UD) stake comprises many of the foregoing and includes search and tracking exercises and a test for steadiness to gunshot. Working Dog (WD) and Tracking Dog (TD) stakes include similar tests requiring greater application. The fifth type of stake, in addition to control, nose work, and agility, requires the style of work normally associated with police and other security operations, including the pursuit and detection of a "criminal," and the search and escort of a suspected person. This is the Patrol Dog (PD) stake.

In championship working trials, the winners of PD and TD stakes are awarded Working Trial Certificates, two of which, if awarded by different judges, qualify a dog for the title of Working Trial Champion. In all stakes certification is given to those dogs which obtain 70 per cent in each group of exercises. The letters CD, UD, etc may then be added after the dog's name. An overall total of 80 per cent of marks available permits the accolade of Excellent to be added— CDX, UDX, and so on. A rather complicated system of qualification enables dogs to progress through the grades of stake at working trials.

Obedience trials were developed from working trials. In Britain they do not involve tests of agility or other aspects of physical dog work. They are concerned almost entirely with the dog's response to the command of its handler. Only in the scent-discrimination test and the temperament test is the dog not under direct instruction. Classes are graded as Pre-beginners, Beginners, Novice, A, B and C. Dogs graduate through the classes by virtue of wins in the lower grades.

Obedience shows are classified as Championship, Open, Limited, or Sanction in the same way as beauty shows. Limited and Sanction shows are confined to members of the organizing club, as are Matches. Open shows have no such restriction. There are also Exemption Shows, which are open to pure-bred and cross-bred dogs alike. All classes may be included in any show, dogs and bitches being scheduled separately, but the qualification for entry in Championship Class C is very stringent. It is in this class that the first-prize winner is awarded an Obedience Certificate. Some 40 sets of Obedience Certificate (dog and bitch) are allocated by the Kennel Club each year, and a dog which gains three Obedience Certificates under three different judges is entitled to be described as Obedience Champion.

Each year at Crufts dog show, the Kennel Club schedules the Obedience Championships, open to all dogs which in the previous year have won Obedience Certificates. This is an event which holds nationwide interest, and the winner in each sex is automatically elevated to the title of Obedience Champion.

American arrangements for the testing of dogs in obedience differ from those in Britain but the tests themselves are very similar. There are no working trials as such but almost all the exercises involved are grouped in obedience trials. Tracking tests, the equivalent of the tracking element in British working trials, are conducted separately.

Obedience competition began to develop in the United States in the late 1920s and early 1930s. It was felt that man-work—involving dogs being trained to attack even a protected man—was not appropriate, and to this day no AKC obedience title requires this activity. The AKC encourages not only clubs formed for the express purpose of obedience training, but also many speciality clubs which are members of the AKC.

Whereas in Britain obedience competition is largely confined to Border Collies, German Shepherd Dogs, and working sheepdogs (crossbreeds normally with a predominance of collie ancestry), in the United States only purebred registered dogs are permitted to compete in obedience trials, tracking tests, or sanctioned matches. Some relaxation is allowed in that spayed bitches and neutered dogs may be entered in obedience competition, as may dogs which might be disqualified from the show ring for noncompliance with the breed standard. As in Britain, bitches in season are not permitted to compete in obedience trials.

The regulations for obedience trials provide for three main classes or standards—Novice, Open, and Utility. Within each level, classes are divided into A and B: A classes are for handlers whose dogs have never won a title; B classes are for more experienced handlers.

Novice classes are for dogs which are not less than six months of age and have not won the title CD. Simple exercises are involved: heel on leash, stand for examination, heel free, recall, long sit, and long down. A qualifying score is obtained by gaining 170 points out of a possible 200, provided that more than half marks are obtained in each separate exercise. Three qualifying scores in Novice classes earn the title CD, and a Companion Dog certificate is issued by the AKC. The test of standing for examination by the judge is a crucial one, since it is easy for a dog to lose all points by showing shyness or resentment.

The second grade is Open class. Dogs which have won CD may be entered in Open A. The title CDX is granted after a dog has gained 170 points at three different trials in Open class under three

This is the scrambling test, another essential part of the agility course.

different judges when the total entry in each class was at least six. Open B class is for dogs which have won CD or CDX, and dogs may continue in this class even after they have won the next grade of UD.

The exercises in Open class are more demanding and include a retrieve on the flat and over a high jump. The height of the jump demanded varies, one-and-a-half times the height of the dog being the standard. Heavier breeds such as Mastiffs and St. Bernards and some of the smaller breeds such as Dachshunds, Skye Terriers, and Bulldogs are given a dispensation that requires them to jump only their actual height. The maximum height for the high jump in any event is 36 in. (91.4 cm), the minimum 8 in. (20.3 cm).

Utility class is the next and highest grade, Utility A being for those dogs which have won the title CDX. The UD title is won in the same way as other titles, with the stipulation that there must have been at least three dogs competing in each qualifying class. Utility B class is confined to dogs which have won the UD title. Tests in Utility class include control by signal, scent discrimination, and directed retrieve and jumping.

First- or second-prize wins in Open B or Utility classes earn a dog points which count toward the title Obedience Trial Champion. The number of points gained on each occasion is related to the number of competing dogs. A set number of first-prize wins is also mandatory before the title is awarded.

The AKC also licenses tracking dog tests which enable dogs to gain a separate series of titles culminating in Champion Tracker (CT). Herding tests and trials leading to the award of Herding Champion are available for dogs of any

registered breed in the Herding group, plus Rottweilers and Samoyeds. There is a variety of other competitions, including Lure Coursing, for sighthounds such as Afghans, Greyhounds, Borzoi, and Rhodesian Ridgebacks; Earthdogs tests, for Dachshunds and the smaller terriers which were originally bred to chase their quarry in burrows or dens; Coonhound events and Agility trials.

The FCI encourages obedience training in member countries, the emphasis lying on working and herding breeds. The tests are similar to those for working trials in Britain. It is recognized that the

working dog should be useful as well as good-looking and in order to obtain the title of FCI International Beauty Champion, working dogs must qualify in a working trial in addition to gaining the requisite show awards.

There is great and growing interest in obedience competition in Australia, where the American system of grading has been adopted. As in some other countries, it is common to find "encouragement classes" scheduled at obedience trials, these being very simple tests intended to introduce the newcomer to competitive obedience.

Part Seven

The Dog at Work

Although they are often thought of simply as objects of pleasure, dogs are still highly valued for the special services they perform in town and country. They may be found on the farm, aiding the police, hauling loads, guiding the blind, and bringing comfort to the lonely.

PASTORAL WORK

ONE OF THE OLDEST functions of a dog is herding. Dogs that herd show great variation of type, which is only to be expected, for herding animals are found the world over, working with different animals in very different climatic conditions.

Training demands individual attention. Formal sheepdog training usually starts at about six months with normal heel and sit commands. The young sheepdog will be taught to get used to sheep before actually working with them. Over a period of time, commands—mostly by whistle—will reinforce the dog's understanding of what is required.

The collies are now the most commonly used shepherding dogs, and the Border Collie is probably the best for the job. This highly intelligent breed has also proved popular for obedience tasks and does exceptionally well in both sheepdog and obedience trials.

Before the growth in popularity of the Border Collie (which was recognized by the Kennel Club only in the late 1970s), the Rough Collie was extremely popular. For millions of people the "Lassie" films immortalized the Rough Collie as an intelligent and affectionate animal, hero of many desperate situations. The Rough's close cousin, the Smooth Collie, is also a working dog, but the fourth type of collie is very different and today is mostly a show dog. This is the Bearded, which looks more like a miniature Old English Sheepdog than the other collies.

Also of the collie type, but not actually known as a collie, is the Shetland Sheepdog or Sheltie. This dog, as its name suggests, originated in the Shetland Isles, where it was developed by crofters for the tough conditions that prevail there.

Other popular herding dogs are the two types of Welsh Corgi. These are more likely to be found as pets, particularly the tailless Pembroke Corgi, as opposed to the rarer Cardigan, which has a long brush-like tail. Although the Corgi has, for very many years, been used for herding cattle and then sheep, and driving them to the markets of England, the breed achieved little recognition until the 1920s. The popularity of the Pembroke Corgi has grown tremendously since the breed became a favorite with the British Royal Family.

Closely resembling the Welsh Corgi is the Swedish Vallhund. This breed was not officially recognized in its native land until the early 1940s, although it is a cattle and sheep dog of many years' standing. In appearance, it is extremely similar to the Corgi.

Almost every country where cattle or sheep are reared has its own particular type of herding dog, and the majority have been adapted to suit local conditions. Most European breeds are bigger than those found in Britain. This is because, until quite recently, they were called on to act not only as herding animals but also as guard dogs, protecting the flocks from wild animals, especially wolves. Dogs of this category

In Australia, the Kelpie is a working dog, essential for mustering sheep on the large farms.

Rounding up sheep and lambs in the Snowdonia National Park in north Wales. The working relationship between a shepherd and his dogs relies on good training and understanding.

include the Appenzell and Entlebuch Mountain Dogs of Switzerland. They are used for herding and droving, and are well known in their native land as extremely alert watch dogs.

In neighbouring Italy, the best-known of that country's breeds is the Maremma, a large white dog not dissimilar to the Pyrenean Mountain Dog at first glance. It makes an excellent guard, especially of flocks of sheep. The origin of the breed goes back to the Kuvasz from Hungary, the watch dog of the ancient Magyars with a history of being a first-rate herding dog. Again in Italy there is the Bergamasco which, although not so well-known as the Maremma, is widely used in Lombardy.

The Bergamasco has affinities with the Komondor, which succeeded the Kuvasz. The Kuvasz is also renowned as a guard dog of exceptional ferocity. Until recently these breeds were little known outside their country of origin, but the Maremma, the Kuvasz, and the Komondor are all now recognized by the Kennel Club and are beginning to make an impact on the British show-ring. The Maremma and the Kuvasz are both beautiful dogs with eye-catching soft, white coats; the Komondor resembles its Hungarian cousin the Puli in having an extraordinary long corded coat, although the Komondor's is white while the Puli's is rusty black. These coats evolved to kept out the harsh weather in the dogs' original working environment.

The Komondor and Puli may share a common ancestry with the Briard, France's best-known shepherd dog. Again the Briard is versatile, being used as both a pack dog and a general army dog, displaying the ability of many working dogs to do more than one job. Across the border are the various types of Belgian Shepherd Dog which also double as guard dogs and herding animals.

In Holland, there are three varieties of the Dutch Herder, which has both Giant Schnauzer and German Shepherd Dog in its make-up. Among other pastoral dogs are the Russian Owtcharka, a herder and guard dog; the Estrela or Portuguese Sheepdog, another heavily built and valuable protector of flocks that has hauled carts; and the Pyrenean Mountain Dog, originally a herder but now more a fashionable pet than a worker, having handed over its duties to the smaller Pyrenean Sheepdog.

Butchers in southern Germany used the Rottweiler, named after the town where it originated, as a droving dog to take cattle to market. It was nearly extinct in 1900 but has increased in number since then.

The best-known of all sheepdogs is the German Shepherd or Alsatian, though nowadays it is rarely used for herding. Other functions have taken over and it is much more often found working with the armed services, the police, and as a security guard. It is also used as a guide dog for the blind and is justifiably popular with those who specialize in obedience. It can also be a spectacular show animal. However, it demands careful training. GSDs can be used only if they genuinely wish to please their handler. Anything less than total dedication to the task may result in a dog uncertain in temperament and unpredictable in action. Unfortunately, many GSDs are incorrectly trained, and often not trained at all. They can therefore become a public nuisance if their natural instincts are not properly harnessed.

Australia has banned the import of German Shepherd Dogs, but has produced some spectacular dogs of its own. The best-known is the Kelpie, which is probably the world's most energetic working dog. It is well equipped to cope with cattle and sheep in an often harsh and difficult environment.

Another tough Australian is the Australian Cattle Dog, which is particularly popular in New South Wales and Victoria. It owes its ancestry in part to the old blue merle type of collie that was introduced into Australia by Scottish immigrants. Both these breeds are gaining in popularity in other parts of the world, although they remain better suited to hard work than to the easier lifestyle of companion or show dogs.

HAULING

DOGS THAT DRAW CARTS or sleds may be divided into two main categories: those found in countries with cold climates, which are mainly of the Spitz variety; and those of warmer countries, which are generally of the mastiff type. Many dogs have been active as draught animals for centuries, but the advent of motorized transport has reduced the number now used for this purpose. Spitz are still used for such tasks as pulling sleds over snow and ice during winter and carrying packs in the warmer weather. The mastiff types have been associated with hauling dairy or bakery carts in provincial towns in Europe for very many years.

Not all Spitz are employed as sled dogs, but it is to this family that the husky belongs. There are many types of husky, of which probably the most famous is the Alaskan Malamute. It was originally found throughout Alaska, but since the Gold Rush days of the 19th century it has deteriorated as other breeds have been introduced to the strain. The Alaskan Malamute is no longer confined to cold areas, and has acclimatized successfully to temperate and warm climates in North America and elsewhere. The Siberian Husky is a smaller sled dog, also used for racing. Both are now recognized throughout the world as show dogs and as affectionate pets for those who can cope with their strength and occasional over-exuberance.

Versatile is probably the most appropriate description of the Samoyed, one of the show-ring's most popular, glamorous competitors, but originally a general-purpose working dog found in northern Siberia. For centuries the breed was used for herding as well as for hauling sleds, but today it works almost exclusively as a sled dog. It has been trained for hunting animals for their pelts and supplying its owners with fur, wool, and hide.

The native peoples of North America who still follow their traditional lifestyle rely heavily on their sled dogs, as indeed do trappers, police, and traders in the frozen north. A true sled dog is easily recognized by its sharp, pointed muzzle and broad skull, sharp and pointed ears, a powerful body, and a coat of rough hair standing out from the body.

Mastiff haulage dogs generally have rounded heads, deep muzzles with a pronounced stop, and mostly pointed ears. They have powerful bodies and the tail is usually low-set. Two such are the Large Swiss Mountain Dog and the Bernese. Coming from the canton of Berne, the latter was widely used for hauling carts to market.

Another type is the Newfoundland. In the fishing season, these dogs haul the fishermen's carts loaded with cod, and in the winter they haul fuel for fires. The Newfoundland is also prodigious swimmer, and as a result is extremely useful as a sea and river rescue dog.

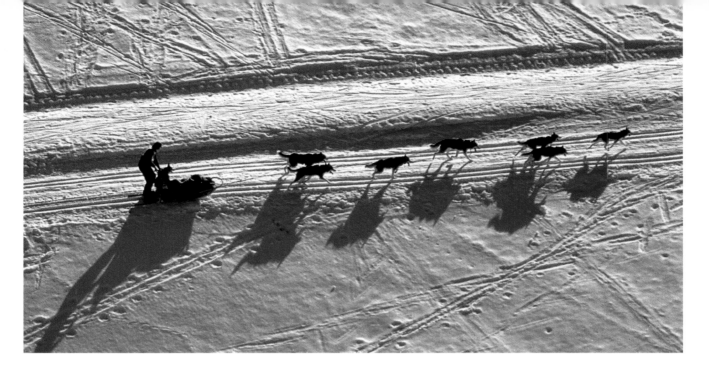

The famous St. Bernard is, unfortunately, no longer a true working dog, and its rescue work is now negligible. For some 300 years, however, these animals were used by the monks of the Hospice of the Great St. Bernard Pass in their native Switzerland, when travelers became lost in the snowy uplands. It is estimated that they rescued some 2,000 people. Today, however, the greatest achievement of the St Bernard is attained in the show-ring.

Above: An aerial view of a dog team, covering the ground easily in a vast white Alaskan wilderness.

Below: An Eskimo dogsled traveling over sea ice in the North West Territories of Canada.

UTILITY

THROUGHOUT THE WORLD the Bloodhound has been used for hunting criminals and escaped convicts, and in the days of slavery in the United States it was used to track down runaways. The scenting ability of the breed is of the highest order. The Bloodhound is tenacious in following a trail: one such event involved a total of 104 hours of tracking. A feature of this animal's appearance is the abundance of skin that wrinkles over its forehead, which gives it a rather superior look. The head is large, but the long ears reduce the impression.

The Doberman has also proved itself as a first-class police dog, guard dog, and cattle dog. Its greatest impact is probably as a patrol dog in police or armed service, or as a guard keeping intruders out of a

Customs officials use dogs to inspect incoming vessels. With their superior sense of smell and ability to work their way into awkward corners, dogs can carry out this task more quickly and efficiently than humans.

variety of premises. With the advent of motorized transport, the Dalmatian has outlived its usefulness as a working animal. Its duty used to be to run alongside the carriages of wealthy folk and, if a stop was made by the roadside, to protect the travellers and their belongings. The black-spotted white coat enabled the dog to merge with the shadows at night, which often meant that it could not be seen by highwaymen and other criminals.

No amount of technological innovation has displaced the role of dogs as working members of the armed forces throughout the world. They are especially useful as patrol animals, particularly on airfields where much open ground has to be covered. They run faster than humans, attack efficiently, and command great respect from anyone who has to face them. They are agile enough to squeeze into places where people cannot, and their powers of scent and hearing are superior to ours. Correctly trained, a dog can be invaluable to police, prison officers, service personnel, and all who have to protect human beings and property, or enforce the law and control crowds.

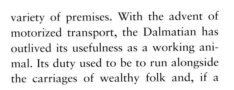

A police dog is trained to apprehend a suspect, holding on firmly without causing injury.

Left: This agility test is a basic part of a police dog's training. It must combine great fitness and stamina with instant obedience to a number of commands.

Below: A dog's sense of smell can be used for detecting survivors in a building damaged by an earthquake.

German Shepherds can be trained to track, guard, attack, and "arrest." In addition, Dobermans, Weimaraners, the Belgian Shepherd Dogs, Schnauzers, and even Airedales and Labradors are all regularly used in service. For scenting and tracking, the German Shepherd may be useful and the Bloodhound incomparable, but the Labrador Retriever has proved ideal for sniffing out drugs and secret caches of arms and ammunition. It is widely used around docks, where there is much work involved in checking passengers, vehicles, and freight.

Dogs have also served as messengers. Work of this nature was regularly performed for the French army during the First World War and has been continued since, though on a diminished scale. Today, of course, much messenger work has been taken over by radio and motorized transport. Another little-recognized duty is the scenting out of wounded people. Red Cross dogs are among those trained specifically to find injured soldiers and civilians. The usual practice is that when a dog has located an injured person it will return to its handler and guide him or her to the place where the person was found.

DOGS FOR THE DISABLED

Guide dogs are trained to accompany their owner anywhere and to remain calm in situations that would disturb other dogs, such as crowded and noisy streets.

O F ALL SOCIAL WORK done by the dog, the one that most readily comes to mind is that of guide dog for the blind. This was, strangely, a role that developed from the First World War. At the end of hostilities blinded German soldiers were each given a trained guide dog to help them return to normal civilian life. The success of the venture soon encouraged other European countries to adopt the scheme. In the United States the Master Eye Institute was formed in 1926, and the British equivalent, the Guide Dog for the Blind Association, in the 1930s.

Training a guide dog takes at least six months. During part of that time the dog lives in the home of a sighted person whose role is to take the dog to shops, on buses and trains, and so on to accustom it to the busy places in which it will eventually have to accompany its blind owner. The British association uses mainly Labrador Retrievers, both black and yellow, plus quite a number of Golden Retrievers and German Shepherd Dogs. Crosses of these breeds are also accepted. About 70 percent of dogs used are bitches, being neither so dominant nor so easily distracted as the male. All guide dogs are either spayed or castrated before starting their training.

No dog is kept in the training program unless it clearly enjoys the tasks it is taught. The average working life of a guide dog is eight to nine years, during which time it is the friend, companion, and the "eyes" of its owner. All dogs are given regular medical checks throughout their period of service.

The charity called Hearing Dogs for the Deaf, founded in 1982, trains carefully chosen unwanted dogs to alert their owners to certain important sounds—the

telephone, the kettle, the baby alarm, or the alarm clock. The dog touches the deaf or hearing-impaired person with a paw, then leads him or her to the source of the sound. If a smoke alarm goes off, the dog alerts the owner, then lies on the floor to signal danger.

Hearing Dogs for the Deaf also provide companion dogs for the elderly— perhaps dogs that have failed the full "hearing dog" test or been considered to be too old to undertake the training. The charity's view is that many elderly people deprive themselves of the company of a dog because they are concerned about what will happen to it when they die. Hearing Dogs for the Deaf remove that particular anxiety by taking the dog back when this eventuality occurs.

A similar service is available through the Cinnamon Trust. This is a charity that helps with the day-to-day care of animals belonging to the elderly or terminally ill, fostering pets if the owner is taken into hospital and, if requested to do so, finding it another home after the owner's death.

Support Dogs are to the disabled what Hearing Dogs are to the deaf. All sorts of breeds and crossbreeds may be trained to open and close doors, fetch the

telephone, retrieve dropped articles, help the disabled person get out of bed and get dressed, load and unload the washing machine, and a variety of other tasks. It is said that if there is sufficient rapport between the person and the dog, the dog may even be able to give warning of the approach of an epileptic fit.

Another charity providing help for the elderly, and for people of all ages in residential homes, hospitals, and hospices who cannot keep pets of their own is Pets As Therapy, incorporating PAT Dogs. Dogs of a particularly reliable and friendly temperament go, with their owners, to any such institution where the residents may benefit from contact with a dog. Patting and cuddling a dog has been proved to be soothing to lonely, withdrawn people and to those suffering from stress or emotional disturbance.

GLOSSARY

AKC American Kennel Club.
ANKC Australian National Kennel Council.
Arched Of loins cut high at the hip.

Barrel chest One that is rounded in cross-section.
Bat ear One that is erect, broad at the base, rounded at the tip, with the opening facing forward, normally rather trim.
Blaze White stripe on the center of the face, between the eyes and running down the nose.
Blue merle Blue and gray mixed with black.
Breed Group of pure-bred dogs with the same appearance, identified by the same standard; in North America the term is also used to refer to the act of mating.
Brindle Fine, even mixture of black hairs with others of lighter color.
Brisket Forepart of the body below the chest and between the forelegs.
Brush tail One that is heavily haired and bushy.

CACIB Certificate of Aptitude Championship International, Beauty; awarded by FCI.
Canidae Family of animals that includes dogs, wolves, foxes, and jackals.
Castration Operation to sterilize a male dog by removal of the testicles.
CD Certificate Companion Dog Certificate;. awarded to competent dogs in AKC Obedience Trials, Novice Class.
CDX Companion Dog Excellent Certificate;. awarded to competent dogs in AKC Obedience Trials, Open Class.
Challenge Certificate May be awarded at the judge's discretion to the best dog of its sex in a breed at a Championship Show and certifies that the dog is of sufficient merit to be worthy of the title of Champion.
Chiseled Of the head, clean-cut, particularly under the eyes.
Clip Style of trimming of the coat, as for Poodles.

Close-coupled Short in the body from the last rib to the hip. Also short-coupled.
Collar Marking around the neck, usually white.
Cropped ear One with leather cut so that the ear stands erect.
Crossbreed A dog produced by mating two different breeds or varieties.
Culotte Longer hair on the back of the thighs.
Cut-up Highly arched under the belly.

Dam Female parent.
Dew-claw Rudimentary fifth digit, borne on the inside of the leg, usually on the forelimbs only but some breeds produce them on the hind limbs also.
Dewlap Loose hanging skin under the throat.
Docked Of the tail, shortened by surgery.
Dog show Competitive event at which prizes are awarded to the best examples of each breed or variety.
Drop ear One with the ends folded or drooping forward.

FCI Fédération Cynologique Internationale (International Canine Federation), the governing body of kennel clubs and dog shows in Western Europe, Scandinavia, and some other parts of the world.
Feathering Fringe of longer hairs on the ears, legs, tail, or body.
Field trial Outdoors event at which gundogs and hounds are judged on their working abilities.
Field Trial Certificate Awarded to the winner of a Field Trial Stake.
Field Trial Champion Winner of two Field Trial Certificates.
Flews Pendulous upper lips, particularly at the corners.
Foreface Front of the head between the eyes; upper part of the muzzle.
Frill Longer hair on the chest and sides of the neck.

Furnishings Longer hair.

Gait Manner in which a dog walks or runs.
Gazehound (See Sighthound.)
Grizzle Bluish-gray color.

Half-prick ear One that is erect, but for tips which fall forward.
Harlequin Having small splashes of color, usually black on white and usually confined to Great Danes.
Hound glove Grooming brush with short bristles made in the form of a mitten or glove.

In-breeding Mating of dogs with a recent common ancestor.
International Beauty Champion Award made to working dogs by FCI.

KC Kennel Club (of Great Britain).

Leather Flap of the ear.
Line-breeding Mating of a dog to a member of its own family, e.g. a dog to its grand-dam.
Linty Of the coat, soft and close.
Liver Deep, reddish brown color.
Loin Side of the body between the last rib and the hindquarters.
Looped tail, a tail carried over the back in an arch.

Mane Long hair on the top and sides of the neck.
Mask Dark shading on the foreface.
Muzzle The part of the head in front of the eyes; the upper and lower jaws.

Obedience Certificate Awarded in various classes of Obedience Trials.
Obedience Trial Event at which dogs are judged on their ability to follow commands
Obedience Trial Champion The highest award in AKC Obedience Trials.
Occiput Upper, central ridge of the skull.

Otter tail One that is thick at the root, flat in section and tapering, with hair parted on the underside.

Pack hound Hound which hunts as one of a group.

Parent breed club In USA, national club, one for each breed.

Particolored Having patches of two or more colors.

Pendent ear One that hangs down the side of the head, also called pendulous.

Pepper and salt Evenly distributed mixture of white or light hairs with brown.

Pied Having large patches of two or more colors.

Plume Long fringe of hair on the tail.

Points The ears, face, legs, and tail of a contrasting color, usually white, black, or tan; also refers more generally to any desirable characteristics, as in "breed points."

Prick ear One that is erect, usually with pointed tip; bat ear if it is erect and rounded.

Puppy In showing terms, a dog that is less than 12 months old.

Purebred A dog whose parents are known, of the same breed as each other and themselves of unmixed descent.

Ring tail One that curves up and around almost in a circle.

Roached Having the back curving convexly above the loin.

Roan Unevenly distributed, fine mixture of colored and white hairs.

Rose ear A small drop ear folded over and back, revealing inside of ear.

Ruff Longer thick hair around the neck.

Sable Having a lacing of black hairs over a lighter ground color.

Scissors bite One where the outer side of the lower incisors bears on the inner side of the upper incisors.

Screw tail Tail short and twisted in a spiral.

Selective breeding Successive mating of selected animals to produce offspring having desired characteristics.

Self color Of one color.

Semi-erect ear (See Half-prick ear.)

Short-coupled (See Close-coupled.)

Sight hound One that hunts by sight as opposed to by scent. Also Gazehound.

Sire Male parent.

Spaying Operation to sterilize a bitch by removal of the ovaries.

Spitz Dog, usually of Arctic origin, with a pointed face, prick ears, and bushy, usually curled tail.

Stake Individual competition at a Field Trial.

Stifle True knee joint, between the femur and the tibia and fibula.

Stop Step up in profile from the muzzle to the top of the skull at the eyes.

Stud Male used for breeding.

TD Tracking Dog Certificate—awarded to competent dogs in AKC Tracking Tests.

Throatiness Excess of loose skin beneath the throat.

Topknot Tuft of long, usually soft hair on the top of the head.

Topline Profile of the spine.

Toy Small or miniature dog.

Tracking Tests Events in USA at which dogs are judged on tracking ability; equivalent to similar parts of British Working Trials.

Tricolor Having three colors: black, white, and tan.

Tucked-up Where depth of body is markedly shallow at the loin; small waisted (see Cut-up).

Type Characteristic qualities that distinguish a breed or family group.

UD Utility Dog Certificate, awarded to competent dogs in AKC Obedience Trials, Utility Class.

Undercoat Fine coat closest to the skin.

Undershot Where the lower incisors lie in front of the upper ones when the jaw is closed.

Wheaten Pale yellow or fawn color, like wheat.

Whole color Of one color only.

Wiry Of the coat, hard and wire-like.

Withers Highest point of the shoulders.

Working Certificate Awarded in various classes at Working Trials and elsewhere.

Working Trial Event in which dogs are tested on agility, nose work, and ability to follow commands. In USA this is incorporated in Obedience Trials.

INDEX

Page numbers in *italics* refer to picture captions; **bold** numbers refer to main entry for each breed

ACKNOWLEDGMENTS

Ardea, London: 16–17, 99 Bottom, /John Daniels Back Endpaper, 26, 28, 35 Bottom, 38 Bottom, 39, 41 Top, 51, 60 Bottom, 82, 100 Left, 111, 117, 134, 136, 137, 138, 139 Top, 160–161, 167, 176–177, /Jean-Paul Ferrero 178;
Bridgeman Art Library, London: Christie's Images London, ALJ Van Den Tempel *Portrait of a Young Lady in Blue Dress with Lapdog* 15 Top, /Private Collection /Wingfield Sporting Gallery London, HW Standing *Driving the Tandem Cart* 1905 14;
British Museum: *Le Livre de Chasse* 13 Bottom;
Bruce Coleman Ltd: Adriano Bacchella 1, 66–67, /Hans Reinhard 100–101, /Jane Burton 140, /Nicholas Devore 180–181, /Tore Hagman 121 Bottom;
Corbis: /Jim Richardson Front Cover;
The Kennel Club Picture Library: 165, 166 Bottom;
Frank Lane Picture Agency: David Dalton 30–31, 37, 42 Bottom, 73 Bottom, /David Hosking 105, 150, 159, /Foto Natura 2–3, 10, 56–57, 99 Top, 126 Bottom, 173, 182 Bottom, 185 Top, J Van Arkel 174, J&P Wegner 76, /Gerard Lacz 18 Top, 32, 34, 60 Top, 68, 69 Top, 88, 106 Top, 151 Top, 156 Top, 183 Bottom, /Jurgen and Christine Sohns 8–9, /Martin Withers 156 Bottom, /R Wilmshurst 162, /Roger Tidman 98, /Roger Williams 151 Bottom, /Silvestris 73 Top;
Giraudon, Paris: 13 Top;
Octopus Publishing Group Ltd: Front Endpaper, 6–7, 29, 41 Bottom, 42 Top, 46, 47, 48, 52 Bottom, 55 Top, 62, 65, 70, 71, 74–75, 79 Top, 90, 91, 92, 107 Top, 108–109, 112, 115 Top, 130, 131, 133 Top, 166 Top, 169 Bottom, 183 Top, /Clive Sawyer 139 Bottom, /David Wodfall 179, /John Moss 184, /Peter Loughran 182 Top; /
Ray Moller 18 Bottom, 19 Bottom, 22, 23 Bottom, 25, 27, 33, 35 Top, 36, 40, 43, 49, 50, 52 Top, 53, 54, 58, 59, 61, 63, 64, 69 Bottom, 72, 77, 78, 79 Bottom, 80, 81, 83, 86, 87, 89, 93, 96, 101 Bottom, /Robert Estall 170, /Rosie Hyde 19 Top, 102, 103 Top, 104, 106 left, 106–107, 114, 115 Bottom, 116, 118–119, 120, 122–123, 125 Top, 128–129, 141, 144–145, 175;
Marc Henrie: 55 Bottom;
Image Bank: Alain Ernoult 181 Top, /Dag Sundberg 24, /Deborah Gilbert 126–127, /Lisa J Goodman 171;
NHPA: Bill Coster 84–85, /Joe Blossom 185 Bottom, /Peter Pickford 11, /Yves Lanceau 20–21, 44–45;
Oxford Scientific Films: Alan and Sandy Carey 135;
Philadelphia Museum of Art: Edward S Curtis 15 Bottom;
Rex Features: 133 Bottom, Erik Pendzich 163 Top, /Nils Jorgensen 164;
RSPCA Photo Library: Angela Hampton 103 Bottom, 124, 142–143, 154 Bottom, 155, /Cheryl A Ertelt 148 Bottom, 152, 153, /Colin Seddon 110, 113 Bottom, 148 Top, /David Featherstone 121 Top, 163 Bottom, /E A Janes 149, 168–169, /Geoff Du Feu 94–95, /Ken McKay 157, 158, 172, /Liz Cook 113 Top, /Marina Imperi 154 Top, /Paul Herrmann 23 Top, 125 Bottom, /Tim Sambrook 132;
Solitaire Photographic: 38 Top, 146, 147;
Tony Stone Images: 4–5; /Patrick Doyle Back Cover;
Werner Forman Archive: /British Museum, London 12.